# Scuba Diving Tourism

This volume offers new insight into an important and largely under-examined area of marine leisure and tourism: scuba diving tourism. Knowledge of scuba diving has long been hidden among broad discussions of water-based sports and activities and this focused book aims to shed further understanding and knowledge on this popular international activity.

The book examines the current issues central to research into and management of scuba diving tourism from multidisciplinary perspectives, such as health and safety, climate change, policy and regulation, and the recreation/leisure context. It further reveals critical management issues of economic, environmental and socio-cultural impacts related to scuba diving tourism which extends to the influence of climate change on the industry's operations and future.

This significant volume which conceptualizes the issues surrounding scuba diving tourism, now and in the future, is written by leading experts in this field and will be valuable reading for all those interested in marine leisure and tourism.

**Ghazali Musa** is Professor in the Faculty of Business and Accountancy at the University of Malaya, Malaysia.

**Kay Dimmock** is Lecturer in the School of Tourism and Hospitality Management at Southern Cross University, Australia.

## Contemporary Geographies of Leisure, Tourism and Mobility

*Series Editor: C. Michael Hall, Professor at the Department of Management, College of Business and Economics, University of Canterbury, Christchurch, New Zealand*

The aim of this series is to explore and communicate the intersections and relationships between leisure, tourism and human mobility within the social sciences.

It incorporates both traditional and new perspectives on leisure and tourism from contemporary geography – such as notions of identity, representation and culture – while also providing for perspectives from cognate areas such as anthropology, cultural studies, gastronomy and food studies, marketing, policy studies and political economy, regional and urban planning, and sociology, within the development of an integrated field of leisure and tourism studies.

Increasingly, tourism and leisure are regarded as steps in a continuum of human mobility. Inclusion of mobility in the series offers the prospect to examine the relationship between tourism and migration, the sojourner, educational travel, and second home and retirement travel phenomena.

The series comprises two strands:

**Contemporary Geographies of Leisure, Tourism and Mobility** aims to address the needs of students and academics, and the titles will be published in hardback and paperback. Titles include:

1. **The Moralisation of Tourism**
   Sun, sand . . . and saving the world?
   *Jim Butcher*

2. **The Ethics of Tourism Development**
   *Mick Smith and Rosaleen Duffy*

3. **Tourism in the Caribbean**
   Trends, development, prospects
   *Edited by David Timothy Duval*

4. **Qualitative Research in Tourism**
   Ontologies, epistemologies and methodologies
   *Edited by Jenny Phillimore and Lisa Goodson*

5. **The Media and the Tourist Imagination**
   Converging cultures
   *Edited by David Crouch, Rhona Jackson and Felix Thompson*

6. **Tourism and Global Environmental Change**
   Ecological, social, economic and political interrelationships
   *Edited by Stefan Gössling and C. Michael Hall*

7. **Cultural Heritage of Tourism in the Developing World**
   *Edited by Dallen J. Timothy and Gyan Nyaupane*

8. **Understanding and Managing Tourism Impacts**
   An integrated approach
   *C. Michael Hall and Alan Lew*

9. **An Introduction to Visual Research Methods in Tourism**
   *Edited by Tijana Rakic and Donna Chambers*

10. **Tourism and Climate Change**
    Impacts, adaptation and mitigation
    *C. Michael Hall, Stefan Gössling and Daniel Scott*

**Routledge Studies in Contemporary Geographies of Leisure, Tourism and Mobility** is a forum for innovative new research intended for research students and academics, and the titles will be available in hardback only. Titles include:

1. **Living with Tourism**
   Negotiating identities in a Turkish village
   *Hazel Tucker*

2. **Tourism, Diasporas and Space**
   *Edited by Tim Coles and Dallen J. Timothy*

3. **Tourism and Postcolonialism**
   Contested discourses, identities and representations
   *Edited by C. Michael Hall and Hazel Tucker*

4. **Tourism, Religion and Spiritual Journeys**
   *Edited by Dallen J. Timothy and Daniel H. Olsen*

5. **China's Outbound Tourism**
   *Wolfgang Georg Arlt*

6. **Tourism, Power and Space**
   *Edited by Andrew Church and Tim Coles*

**Research Volunteer Tourism**
Volunteer voices
*Angela Benson*

**Travel, Tourism and Green Growth**
*Min Jiang, Terry DeLacy and Geoffrey Lipman*

# Scuba Diving Tourism

**Edited by Ghazali Musa and
Kay Dimmock**

Routledge
Taylor & Francis Group

LONDON AND NEW YORK

First published 2013 by Routledge
2 Park Square, Milton Park, Abingdon, Oxon OX14 4RN

Simultaneously published in the USA and Canada
by Routledge
711 Third Avenue, New York, NY 10017

*Routledge is an imprint of the Taylor & Francis Group, an informa business*

*British Library Cataloguing in Publication Data*
A catalogue record for this book is available from the British Library

*Library of Congress Cataloging in Publication Data*
Scuba diving tourism / edited by Ghazali Musa and Kay Dimmock.
   pages, cm
1. Sports and tourism.   2. Scuba diving.   I. Musa, Ghazali.
G156.5.S66S28 2013
338.4'7797234–dc23

                                                          2012047419


ISBN: 978-0-415-52344-8 (hbk)
ISBN: 978-0-203-12101-6 (ebk)

Typeset in Times New Roman
by RefineCatch Limited, Bungay, Suffolk

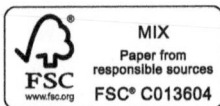

FSC MIX Paper from responsible sources FSC® C013604 www.fsc.org

Printed and bound by CPI Group (UK) Ltd, Croydon, CR0 4YY

# Contents

# Figures

# Tables

# Contributors

**Terry Cummins**, scuba industry professional, 'Yellow Mountain', Condoblin, New South Wales, Australia.

**Kay Dimmock**, School of Tourism and Hospitality Management, Southern Cross University, Lismore, New South Wales, Australia.

**Joanne Edney**, School of Environmental Sciences, Charles Sturt University, Albury, New South Wales, Australia.

**C. Michael Hall**, Department of Management, College of Business and Economics, University of Canterbury, Christchurch, New Zealand.

**Amran Hamzah**, Centre for Innovative Planning and Development Tourism Planning Research Group Faculty of Built Environment, Universiti Teknologi Malaysia, Johor Bahru, Malaysia.

**Jonathon Howard**, School of Environmental Sciences, Charles Sturt University, Albury, New South Wales, Australia.

**Kelsey Johansen**, School of Outdoor Recreation, Parks and Tourism, Lakehead University, Ontario, Canada.

**Peter Jonas**, Director Certification, Austrian Standards plus GmbH, Vienna, Austria.

**Balvinder Kler**, School of Business and Economics, Universiti Malaysia Sabah, Malaysia.

**Selina Khoo**, Sport Centre, University of Malaya, Kuala Lumpur, Malaysia.

**Alan A. Lew**, Department of Geography, Planning and Recreation, Northern Arizona University, US.

**Emily Moskwa**, Centre for Regional Engagement, University of South Australia, Whyalla Norrie, Australia.

**Ghazali Musa**, Department of Management and Business Policy, Faculty of Business and Accountancy, University of Malaya, Kuala Lumpur, Malaysia.

**Tah Fatt Ong**, Department of Sport Management, Universiti Teknologi MARA, Kuala Lumpur, Malaysia.

**Thinaranjeney Thirumoorthi**, Department of Management and Business Policy, Faculty of Business and Accountancy, University of Malaya, Kuala Lumpur, Malaysia.

**Douglas G. Walker**, independent researcher associated with DAN Asia-Pacific, founding member of South Pacific Underwater Medicine Society.

**Caroline Walsh**, Kent Business School, University of Kent, Canterbury, Kent, UK.

**Kee Mun Wong**, Department of Management and Business Policy, Faculty of Business and Accountancy, University Malaya, Kuala Lumpur, Malaysia.

# Foreword

Scuba diving is a popular holiday activity among tourists. Previously considered as a hard adventurous activity, it has now begun to be accepted as a soft adventurous activity which has an increasing appeal to the masses. Technology is largely responsible for this change, through continuous invention of more efficient and safer equipment and transport.

The overwhelming interest in experiencing nature in general – and the underwater scene in particular – has led to the development of scuba businesses and services to cater for divers. At the losing end is the environment, which struggles with the impact of over-activity and over-development in coastal areas and islands. Tourism stakeholders, including the policy makers, are yet to establish a balance of activity and business so that the sustainability of scuba diving tourism will not be jeopardised.

This book provides a review of these issues through an overall examination of the scuba diving tourism system. There are three essential elements in the industry meriting this examination: divers, environment and business. All the chapters and reviews included in the book are carefully selected to examine these and the past and current issues in scuba diving tourism. Central to the system is the continuous struggle for sustainability. The book concludes with a discussion on aspects of the future of scuba diving tourism and an attempt at a forecast of its development and suggestions for its sustainability.

Ghazali Musa and Kay Dimmock

# Acknowledgements

The editors count themselves fortunate in this endeavour, in being able to work with the generous scholars who have assisted in the planning, writing and publishing of this book. First of all, they wish to thank James Higham who made the first contribution to its list of contents, which was later reviewed by C. Michael Hall and Alan A. Lew. The editors were introduced to each other by Michael Lück. The four distinguished scholars mentioned above were the main source of the ideas which led to the development of the book.

Perhaps the greatest help we received was from Sir Dato' Dr Peter Mooney who proofread the entire contents of the book. We are also greatly indebted to Sedigheh Mogavvemi for checking all the references and making sure the manuscripts were prepared according to the requirements of the publisher.

Invaluable support and contributions were received from Alan A. Lew, Amran Hamzah, Balvinder Kler, Emily Moskwa, Kelsey Johansen, C. Michael Hall, Caroline Walsh, Douglas G. Walker, Joanne Edney, Jonathon Howard, Kee Mun Wong, Selina Khoo, Tah Fatt Ong, Peter Jonas, Terry Cummins and Thinaranjeney Thirumoorthi.

Carol Barber and Emma Travis of Routledge have been unfailingly helpful in providing us with detailed information required for the publication. Our gratitude is also due to the colleagues in our respective universities – University of Malaya and Southern Cross University – for their generous help with ideas and friendship.

We are grateful to Dave Thomas, Cognizant Communications, and to the organisations of PADI, NAUI, CMAS, BSAC and SSI for allowing us to use the images and figures in this book.

Last, but far from least, we dedicate this book to all divers out there, who really can make a difference to the future of scuba diving tourism.

# Part I
# Context

# 1 Introduction

## Scuba diving tourism

*Ghazali Musa and Kay Dimmock*

### Introduction to scuba diving tourism

Scuba diving is a relatively recent development in the field of tourism. It has grown very rapidly to attract millions of people whose interest in the sea, lakes and rivers had never before extended beyond surface activities and what could be seen underwater in the very limited time a human could spend there. With the technology which is described later in this book, this very limited time is now greater, and allows divers to view and delight in the underwater world as part of a unique and fascinating recreation. Scuba diving is a totally new experience involving two spheres of human perception. First, the force of gravity, which is a constant limitation in human life, does not control our movements underwater. Like fish and birds, we can ascend and descend; we can move freely through the three dimensions of liquid space. This unfamiliar novelty is an undiminishing joy offered by no other form of recreation. Second, there is the aesthetic delight in the perception of the infinite and immensely colourful variety of underwater scenes, complete with myriad forms of life.

Scuba diving has developed into what is now an industry and a constituent of tourism, a major contributor to the economy of many nations. It is this relatively new industry – and all its aspects, studied in depth by research scholars – which is the subject of this book.

Scuba diving is high-yield special interest tourism. The sector flourishes, with increasing interest among tourists who wish to be in contact with nature. The successful contact with nature has been greatly facilitated by ever-improving technology. Historically regarded as hostile to humans, the marine environment is now a recreational destination for scuba divers. In response to high levels of demand, the industry provides the facilities and services which enable the activity.

This introductory chapter introduces the concept of a Scuba Diving Tourism System (SDTS) as a holistic framework for better understanding. Figure 1.1 depicts SDTS in visual form. In this book, SDTS is framed by three main elements: environment, divers and scuba diving industry. Within these elements are important aspects of SDTS which will be discussed in the chapters and reviews.

As part of the first element, Environment, discussions are presented on the history (Chapter 2) and geography (Chapter 3) of scuba diving. These are two basic factors which attract individuals to scuba diving for recreation. While the

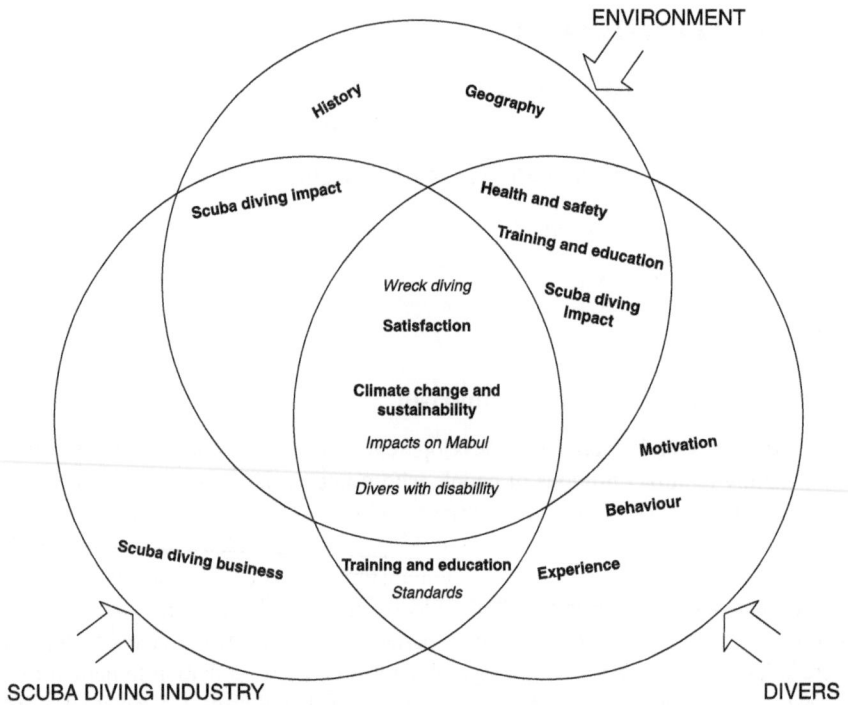

*Figure 1.1* Scuba Diving Tourism System.

geography chapter examines the current state of scuba diving landscapes, the history chapter reviews important milestones and breakthroughs which have supported the industry's evolution to the present day: technology, recreational culture and education and training.

The involvement of divers in the activity is the subject of the second element of the SDTS: divers themselves. As divers are the main focus of the activity, this element will be examined in detail under the headings of motivation (Chapter 6), behaviour (Chapter 7) and experience (Chapter 8). Each is a major determinant of scuba diving satisfaction (Chapter 9) and satisfaction is a crucial determinant in the sustainability of scuba diving businesses.

The third element of SDTS is the scuba diving industry itself. This element focuses discussion on scuba diving business (Chapter 10). Education and training (Chapter 5) is situated in the interactions of divers and the scuba diving industry and environment. The latter interaction is reflected in the knowledge and skills divers should acquire to prepare themselves for an activity in the unfamiliar marine environment. The results of this interaction are twofold. First, the hostile marine environment remains a continuing threat to the health and safety (Chapter 4) of divers. Second, divers' irresponsible behaviour could be detrimental to the environment. As a result, aspects of environmental impact and a review of social cultural impact are examined in Chapter 11.

Chapter 5 also examines the interface between divers and the scuba diving business. This interface may be explained by the need of divers and industry players to interact and understand one another's roles in service delivery, so that the result of their contact will be beneficial: a satisfactory dive for the diver and the tourist, and the continuing economic viability of the scuba diving business. One aspect uniquely derived from the interaction between divers and the scuba diving business is discussed in the review of standards (Review 3). It proposes a minimum guideline, which is increasingly being set for industry and divers world-wide, to be closely followed for a safe and satisfactory experience.

There are two main issues which will be discussed within the interface of all three elements in the SDTS. These are satisfaction (Chapter 9) and climate change and sustainability (Chapter 11). Climate change itself is the element within Environment which is influenced by both nature and human activities. However, sustainability demands the holistic management of all three elements in SDTS: environment, divers and the scuba diving business.

Three reviews – wreck diving (Review 1), divers with disability (Review 2) and international diving standards (Review 3) are situated within the three interfaces of environment, divers and scuba diving industry. The discussions within the reviews are illustrations of how divers, environment and the scuba diving business interact to facilitate a satisfactory scuba diving experience.

## Book content

### Chapter 2: history

History is a fundamental aspect to be examined within the element of Environment to provide background discussion and introduce key factors which have stimulated growth in scuba diving. One of these key factors is technology, which has played a critical role in several areas of the industry's growth, including diver safety, equipment and the generation of interest among the public through media exposure, popular culture and tourism destination development.

As an equipment intensive activity, perhaps the greatest advance in technology for scuba diving was delivered in 1943 by Jacques Yves Cousteau and Emile Gagnan, who provided a simplified, independent and reliable underwater breathing apparatus (Brown 1988). This device was complemented by the invention of the Buoyancy Control Device (BCD), through which the inflation and deflation of air within the apparatus allowed a diver to ascend and descend in the water almost effortlessly. Other scuba diving equipment includes neoprene wetsuits, pressure gauges, diver decompression tables, dive computers, Nitrox 'enriched air' and rebreather.

### Chapter 3: geography

Geography is the main pull factor among divers, causing them to embark on the activity within the SDTS. This chapter highlights the magnitude of human impact on the marine environment in terms of over-fishing and pollution of the ocean due to coastal development and human commerce. However, some researchers optimistically argue that scuba diving could result in transformative experiences which change perception and attitudes towards sea life and the conservation of ocean resources (Arin and Kramer 2002; Lück 2003; White 2008).

Despite being a global activity, most scuba diving is carried out in tropical coral reefs. Today, diving has extended to more remote locations, including less-developed regions and colder waters. Google Trends shows the word 'scuba' used less for searches in North America, the UK and Australia. The opposite is the case for searches in Malaysia, Singapore, South Africa and the Philippines. The two most common dives are cold water dives and warm water dives. Specialty dives can be experienced in the form of night diving, cave diving, wreck diving, high altitude diving, shark or predator diving, liveaboard diving, muck diving, free diving, snuba and Scuba-doo.

The majority of the world's dive sites are located in Europe, which reflects the destination origin of most divers. The chapter author analyses in detail the various reports of the current best dive regions in the world. The result shows that the Coral Triangle of insular Southeast Asia is the world's leading recreational dive destination region in terms of outstanding features and accessibility for divers. This region benefits considerably from western European and Australian dive markets, along with a growing domestic Southeast Asian dive market. Burke *et al.* (2011), however, warns that large areas of Southeast Asia's coral reefs are also endangered due to over overfishing, pollution and development, and global warming. Other important regions for scuba diving include the Red Sea and the Great Barrier Reef.

### Review 1: wreck diving

Shipwrecks have become important recreational sites, and many wrecks have wider historic, social and cultural significance. Research shows that, while wreck divers seek particular experiences, divers have the capacity to damage the places they come to visit. Wreck diving sites should be carefully managed to protect cultural heritage, through effective strategies which involve and empower all stakeholders.

### Chapter 4: scuba diving health and safety essentials

Safety and health issues are paramount in the scuba diving industry. Within the SDTS, this aspect is situated in the interaction between environment and divers. Any misadventure in this activity may cause detrimental results for the health and safety of divers. Being underwater is not where any human being should be for an extended period. Thus any attempt to be underwater longer than usual subjects the diver to physiological changes which could be harmful to health.

The chapter begins by highlighting a grim consequence of scuba activity, the mortality of divers. Health factors of significance are age, general and mental health, and personality. Divers need to be mindful of medical conditions which are considered as high risk in scuba diving activity. These are cardiovascular, respiratory and visual conditions, asthma, epilepsy, diabetes, physical disability, pregnancy and certain medications.

Environmental factors could also pose danger to divers. Examples of these factors and their consequences are water power, freshwater diving, hypothermia, visibility, drowning, pulmonary barotrauma, ear and sinuses, nitrogen narcosis, decompression sickness, altitude, flying after diving and some dangerous marine life. Both divers and dive operators should know the location of the nearest hospital and its accessibility from the dive destination. Similar information is also required for decompression chambers. Any mortality among divers will have serious repercussions for the image of operators and destinations, which may result in court proceedings. The sustainability and the viability of a scuba diving business could be severely jeopardised if such event occurs.

### *Review 2: scuba diving and persons with disability*

Chapter 4 includes a review of scuba diving and people with disabilities. The Takayama Declaration defines accessible tourism as 'tourism and travel that is accessible to all people, with disabilities or not, including those with mobility, hearing, sight, cognitive, or intellectual and psychosocial disabilities, older persons and those with temporary disabilities' (United Nations Economic and Social Commission for Asia and the Pacific 2009:5).

Diving for persons with disabilities started in the late 1970s in the United States (Walsh *et al.* 2012). It was initially introduced as part of rehabilitation. Today, divers with disability also dive for leisure. The review highlights both the benefits and the health risks among scuba divers with disability who take up the activity. The authors discuss issues related to engagement with scuba diving including constraints experienced by persons with disability. The review outlines the role of organisations supporting scuba diving for persons with disability including those involved with training and policy regulation.

### *Chapter 5: education and training*

Education and training are prerequisites for scuba diving activity. The industry comprises independent international and national scuba diving certifying agencies including the British Sub Aqua Club (BSAC), La Confédération Mondiale Des Activités Subaquatiques (CMAS) (the World Underwater Federation), the National Association of Underwater Instructors (NAUI), the Professional Association of Diving Instructors (PADI), and Scuba Schools International (SSI). The chapter considers each organisation's diving certification progression from novice to advanced levels, and continuing education as well as specialty courses. A number of organisations have grown to become international providers of the education and skill development required to access scuba diving. Their efforts help ensure diver training remains relevant. Diver education has been a key feature in the development of scuba diving tourism.

### Review 3: scuba diving standards

Within Chapter 5 (Education and training), a review of standards is included. The standards were forwarded by the European Committee which represented scuba diving stakeholders at the International Organisation for Standardisation (ISO) (www.iso.org), for publication as international standards. The two categories of standards available are (1) training system standards, and (2) service provision standards. All standards specify the required levels of experience and competency of scuba divers and instructors, as well as the safety practices and requirements for recreational scuba diving service providers appropriate to the different diving levels.

There are four main objectives of the standards. First, divers are ensured of a high level of quality and safety for an activity which demands proper training. Second, for diving professionals, the standards provide a safe benchmark for their training organisations and service providers. Third, for tour operators, the standards are a tool to select the proper partner for diving operations which could enhance their liability protection. Fourth, for governments and regulators, the standards are increasingly being used for regulatory purposes, making them a part of local licensing systems for dive centres.

### Chapter 6: scuba diving motivation

Motivation is a major aspect of consumer behaviour. Motivation is an inner state of an individual that drives and directs behaviour (Kassin 1998; Murray 1964), to satisfy both psychological and physiological needs (Berkman *et al.* 1997). Drawing on empirical knowledge in scuba diving literature, this chapter highlights the detailed methods and factors which are used to measure scuba diving motivations. The authors propose that scuba diving motivation could be examined from the perspective of extrinsic and intrinsic motivations, recreational development, recreational specialisation, destination profiles and gender.

The authors stress that understanding divers' motivations is necessary for countries or diving operators wishing to develop and promote their destinations as a divers' paradise. The knowledge can guide the provision of services and experiences which are sought after by divers. Also, effective marketing communication can then be directed to the particular market segment of divers. Additionally, knowledge of divers' motivation may delineate the potential harmful motives that drive irresponsible behaviour underwater, which could jeopardise the industry effort to achieve sustainability.

### Chapter 7: scuba diving behaviour

The behaviour of scuba divers underwater is often directly influenced by the motivation previously discussed. Divers' behaviour considerably influences the very core of SDTS, which is sustainability. The increasing popularity of scuba diving activity may pose threats to the growth and reproduction of the coral reefs (Barker and Roberts 2004), especially because of those who behave irresponsibly underwater. Perhaps the most common industry practice to control divers' behaviour is the adoption of Codes of Conduct (Garrod 2008).

Ong and Musa (2012) state that responsible diving behaviour refers to specific responsible behaviour exhibited by divers while diving underwater, regarding their own safety and health, as well as the protection of marine environment. From their empirical studies, they discovered three distinct factors of underwater responsible behaviour: 'safety diving behaviour', 'buoyancy control diving behaviour' and 'non-contact diving behaviour'. This is elaborated in Chapter 7.

## *Chapter 8: experience*

In scuba diving literature, 'experience' can mean (1) the level of skill and competency of divers, and (2) the state of mind divers have underwater. Experience can be gauged through the total number of dives made and level of diving certification (Todd 2000; Todd *et al.* 2000; Musa *et al.* 2011; Ong and Musa 2012) achieved from continuous education.

Scuba diving tourism activities are intimately tied to particular underwater settings. A sense of place is defined as the extent to which an individual values or identifies with a particular natural setting, within which experience is derived. The authors state that experiences are dynamic and emergent, not static and discrete, and focus on the understanding of personal connections through stories about the recreational experience which produce fulfilling narratives consistent with the recreationist's life.

Sense of place allows managers to access, assess, inventory and monitor socio-cultural meanings of places, and incorporate these into planning and management processes (Brandenburg and Carroll 1995; Mitchell *et al.* 1993). It also allows people to evaluate natural environments, improve the provision of optimal recreation experiences, and plan and encourage the use of public spaces. Sense of place is synonymous with place attachment, which denotes the positive attachments individuals have with places, attachments which help people form a sense of belonging or purpose (Relph 1976; Tuan 1980).

## *Chapter 9: scuba diving satisfaction*

The sustainability of the scuba diving business requires not only the minimisation of environmental impact, but also the provision of satisfying scuba diving experiences. Thus satisfaction is situated in the middle of the SDTS together with sustainability. Satisfaction measurement requires the identification of attributes or factors which contribute to satisfaction (Fuller and Matzler 2000). Earlier scuba diving satisfaction researchers primarily focused on the rating of individual scuba diving attributes (e.g. O'Reilly 1982; Tabata 1992; Davis and Tisdell 1996; Musa 2002; Graham *et al.* 2001; MacCarthy *et al.* 2006; Paterson *et al.* 2012). Lately, some attempts have been made to measure satisfaction in the form of specific factors or dimensions (e.g. O'Neill *et al.* 2000; Musa *et al.* 2006).

The authors identify three main aspects of divers' satisfaction. These are destination characteristics, dive operator service and social interaction (see Table 9.2). Destination characteristics refer to visibility, marine life, underwater scenery, water temperature, and so on. The dive operator service is concerned with the service quality provided by dive operators including boat facilities, safety, dive equipment and staff. Social interaction is concerned with the exchanges and dynamic between fellow divers and dive buddies. Of the three, the most important aspect which contributes to overall satisfaction is destination characteristics, and this clearly indicates the need to maintain the ecological balance of marine life and coral reefs.

## Chapter 10: the scuba diving business

Scuba diving business is the only chapter discussed within the element of scuba diving industry. The focus of the scuba diving tourism business is on service delivery and experience. Critical to business are successful relations with dive tourists and other sectors of the diving industry in the provision of dive training, travel, equipment and charter operations, as part of the experience.

The authors recognise a transition which has taken place in scuba diving business management from lifestyle entrepreneurs who set out to pursue a particular lifestyle to a new breed of managers entering the industry. In business there is a need to balance competing issues and values to achieve success. Scuba diving tourism managers today must work with international organisations and generate a culture of safety in the organisation (Coxon *et al.* 2008).

In scuba diving, consumers visit a dive centre and purchase goods (equipment) and services (training, charter, travel). The industry is well positioned to enhance customer experiences using electronic distribution channels for training and education. While a range of communication channels for promoting diving exist, industry surveys find that word of mouth (WOM) remains the most successful form of communication – where people tell each other about diving, whether this be via the telephone, face-to-face, or using the Internet, blogs, Facebook or Twitter.

Progress towards real sustainability within tourism, according to Lane (2009), has been slow, with discrepancy between the intent and implementation of sustainable practices in tourism (Weaver 2004). For scuba diving tourism business operations, there are distinct areas where sustainability demands attention. These are: (1) marine environment awareness and conservation management, (2) service delivery and customer satisfaction management, and (3) sustainable business management.

## Chapter 11: scuba diving: environmental change and sustainability

This chapter examines discussion of environmental change and sustainability in the scuba diving industry. It proposes that scuba diving tourism is both affected by, and contributes to, environmental change, with many of the long-term effects of such change on the scuba tourism market yet to be learned. The chapter defines the concept of global environmental change and examines the different dimensions of change including climate change and emissions, habitat loss and biotic exchange. It also examines the potential implications of marine environment change on scuba diving.

The chapter author points to the contribution of tourism to Global Environmental Change (GEC). This contribution is expected to grow with the increasing numbers of domestic and international tourist trips. The further the travel, the higher is the GEC contribution of individual tourists. The author estimates that growth in travel to more peripheral destinations for scuba diving produces higher than average per trip emissions from scuba diving tourism.

Scuba diving tourism directly affects habitat loss as a result of the construction and development of tourism infrastructure (Steinitz *et al.* 2005), as well as the direct damage to reefs (Miller *et al.* 2004) and indirect impacts of scuba diving, such as acting as vectors of disease or invasive species. Hall (2010) found a positive relationship between tourism and the number of endangered species in Pacific and Caribbean island states.

The author is optimistic that scuba diving tourism can be sustained with the development of more sustainable forms of travel, grounded in ecological economics, whereby travel is contextualised within the entire consumptive patterns of individuals and households and within the bio-physical boundaries of environmental services.

### *Review 4: Mabul Island*

Mabul Island is a microcosm of the social, economic and environmental challenges of popular dive destinations in many parts of insular Southeast Asia. Local residents are appreciative that tourism has brought job opportunities with low entry requirement for them to become boatmen, dive tank compressor boys, and front desk and housekeeping staff (Hamzah *et al.* 2012). The general lack of education on the island has restricted locals from securing the higher paying positions, such as being a dive instructor or resort manager.

The social and environmental issues affecting Mabul Island are not isolated, but are tied to controversial and sensitive national and international policies relating to international boundaries, nationality and citizenship, environmental conservation, economic development and subsistence livelihood, as well as human rights and the rights of children to an education.

## Conclusion

This introductory chapter attempts to present scuba diving tourism using an holistic framework for SDTS. SDTS is constituted by the interaction of three main elements of the framework: Environment, Divers and Scuba Diving Industry. The main issues within the three elements are explained as chapters in the book, supported by specific reviews. Our hope is that this book provides detailed and insightful knowledge pertaining to the significant and broad ranging aspects of scuba diving, all of which are crucial for the sustainability of scuba diving tourism.

# References

Arin, T. and Kramer, R. A. (2002) 'Divers' Willingness to Pay to Visit Marine Sanctuaries: An Exploratory Study', *Ocean and Coast Management*, 45:171–183.

Barker, N. H. L. and Roberts, C. M. (2004) 'Scuba Diver Behaviour and the Management of Diving Impacts on Coral Reefs', *Biological Conservation*, 120(4):481–489.

Berkman, H., Lindquist, J. and Sirgy, M. J. (1997) *Consumer Behavior: Concepts and Marketing Strategy*, Lincolnwood, IL: NTC Business Books.

Brandenburg, A. M. and Carroll, M. S. (1995) 'Your Place or Mine? The Effect of Place Creation on Environmental Values and Landscape Meaning', *Society and Natural Resources*, 8:381–398.

Brown, M. (1988) 'Brief History of Sports Diving in Australia', in T. Cummins (ed.) *Diving Accident Management in Australia*, North Ryde, Australia: PADI: 1–6.

Burke, L., Reytar, K., Spalding, M. and Perry, A. (2011) *Reefs at Risk Revisited*, Washington, DC: World Resources Institute. Online. Available HTTP: <http://www.wri.org/publication/reefs-at-risk-revisited> (accessed 30 March 2012).

Coxon, C., Dimmock, K. and Wilks, J. (2008) 'Managing Risk in Tourist Diving: A Safety-Management Approach', in B. Garrod and S. Gössling (eds.) *New Frontiers in Marine Tourism: Diving Experiences, Sustainability, Management*, Amsterdam: Elsevier: 201–220.

Davis, D. and Tisdell, C. (1996) 'Economic Management of Recreational Scuba Diving and the Environment', *Journal of Environmental Management*, 48(3):229–248.

Fuller, J. and Matzler, K. (2000) 'Customer Delight and Market Segmentation: An Application of the Three-factor Theory of Customer Satisfaction on Lifestyle Groups', *Tourism Management*, 29(1):116–126.

Garrod, B. (2008) 'Market Segments and Tourist Typologies for Diving Tourism', in B. Garrod and S. Gössling (eds.) *New Frontiers in Marine Tourism: Diving Experiences, Sustainability, Management*, Amsterdam: Elsevier: 31–49.

Graham, T., Idechong, N. and Sherwood, K. (2001) 'The Value of Dive-tourism and the Impacts of Coral Bleaching on Diving in Palau', in H. Z. Schuttenberg (ed.) *Coral Bleaching: Causes, Consequences and Responses*, selected papers presented at the 9th International Coral Reef Symposium on Coral Bleaching: Assessing and Linking Ecological and Socio-economic Impacts, Future Trends and Mitigation Planning. Coastal Management Report No. 2230, Coastal Resources Center, University of Rhode Island, Kingston, US.

Hall, C.M. (2010) 'An Island Biogeographical Approach to Island Tourism and Biodiversity: An Exploratory Study of the Caribbean and Pacific Islands', *Asia Pacific Journal of Tourism Research*, 15:383–99.

Hamzah, A., Hilmi, N. and Alias, L. J. (2012) 'Report for Preliminary Socio-cultural Survey at Pulau Mabul' (May). Long Term Research Scheme (LRGS) Vote No: 4L801, Ministry of Higher Education, Malaysia.

Kassin, S. (1998) *Psychology* (2nd edn), Upper Saddle River, NJ: Prentice Hall.

Lane, B. (2009) 'Thirty Years of Sustainable Tourism: Drivers, Progress, Problems – and the Future', in S. Gössling, C. M. Hall and D. B. Weaver (eds.) *Sustainable Tourism Futures: Perspectives on Systems*, Hoboken: Routledge: 19–32.

Lück, M. (2003) 'The "New Environmental Paradigm": Is the Scale of Dunlap and Van Liere Applicable in a Tourism Context?', *Tourism Geographies*, 5(2):228–240.

MacCarthy, M., O'Neill, M. and Williams, P. (2006) 'Customer Satisfaction and Scuba Diving: Some Insights from the Deep', *The Service Industries Journal*, 26(5): 537–555.

Miller, K. J., Mundy, C. N. and Chadderton, W. L. (2004) 'Ecological and Genetic Evidence of the Vulnerability of Shallow-water Populations of the Stylasterid Hydrocoral *Errina novaezelandiae* in New Zealand's Fiords', *Aquatic Conservation: Marine and Freshwater Ecosystems*, 14(1):75–94.

Mitchell, M. Y., Force, J., Carroll, M. S. and McLaughlin, W. J. (1993) 'Forest Places of the Heart', *Journal of Forestry*, 91(4): 32–37.

Murray, E. J. (1964) *Motivation and Emotion*, Englewood Cliffs, NJ: Prentice Hall.

Musa, G. (2002) 'Sipadan: A Scuba Diving Paradise: An Analysis of Tourism Impact, Diver Satisfaction and Tourism Management', *Tourism Geographies*, 4(2):195–209.

Musa, G., Kadir, S. L. S. A. and Lee, L. (2006) 'Layang Layang: An Empirical Study on Scuba Divers' Satisfaction', *Tourism in Marine Environments*, 2(2):89–102.

Musa, G., Wong, T. S., Thirumoorthi, T. and Abessi, M. (2011) 'The Influence of Scuba Divers' Personality, Experience, and Demographic Profile on their Underwater Behavior', *Tourism in Marine Environments*, 7(1):1–14.

Ong, T. F. and Musa, G. (2012) 'Examining the Influences of Experience, Personality and Attitude on Scuba Divers' Underwater Behaviour: A Structural Equation Model', *Tourism Management*, 33:1521–1534.

O'Reilly, M.B. (1982) 'Sport Diving in Texas: A Study of Participants, their Activity and means of Introduction', MS thesis, Texas A and M University, College Station, US.

Paterson, S., Young, S., Loomis, D. K. and Obenour, W. (2012) 'Resource Attributes that Contribute to Nonresident Diver Satisfaction in the Florida Keys, USA', *Tourism in Marine Environments*, 8(2):47–60.

Relph, F. (1976) *Place and Placedness*, London: Pion Limited.

Steinitz, C., Faris, R., Flaxman, M., Karish, K., Mellinger, A. D., Canfield, T. and Sucre, L. (2005) 'A Delicate Balance: Conservation and Development Scenarios for Panama's Coiba National Park', *Environment: Science and Policy for Sustainable Development*, 47(5):24–39.

Tabata, R. S. (1992) 'Scuba Diving Holidays', in C. M. Hall and B. Weiler (eds) *Special Interest Tourism*, Belhaven, New York: NY: 171–184.

Todd, S. (2000) *Scuba Diving in New York's Great Lakes: From Novice to Professional* (New York Sea Grant Institute Completion Report), Cortland: Department of Recreation and Leisure Studies, SUNY Cortland.

Todd, S., Cooper, T. and Graefe, A. R. (2000) 'Scuba Diving and Underwater Cultural Resources, Differences in Environmental Beliefs, Ascriptions of Responsibility, and Management Preferences Based on Level of Development', paper presented at the 2000 Northeastern Research Symposium, Radnor, PA.

Tuan, Y.F. (1980) 'Rootedness versus Sense of Place', *Landscape*, 24(1):3–8.

Walsh, C., Haddock-Fraser, J. and Hampton, M. P. (2012) 'Accessible Dive Tourism', in D. Buhalis, S. Darcy and I. Ambrose (eds) *Best Practice in Accessible Tourism: Inclusion, Disability, Ageing Population and Tourism*, Clevedon, UK: Channel View Publications: 180–190

Weaver, D.B. (2004) 'Tourism and the Elusive Paradigm of Sustainable Development', in A. Lew, C. M. Hall and A. Williams (eds.) *A Companion to Tourism*, Malden, MA: Blackwell: 510–522

White, L. (2008) 'See the Value: Quantifying the Value of Marine Life to Divers', unpublished Master's thesis, Duke University, Durham, US.

# 2   History of scuba diving tourism

*Kay Dimmock and Terry Cummins*

## Introduction

Scuba diving has become a very popular form of marine leisure pursuit in many areas of the world (Anderson and Loomis 2011; Brown and Cave 2010; Dimmock 2009). By the end of 2011, more than 22 million diving certifications had been issued globally to new and continuing divers (Anon. n.d.a). This chapter examines the evolution of scuba diving from a time when rudimentary equipment was being used and refined for personal leisure, about seven decades ago. Since then, developments and advances have contributed substantially to the scuba diving tourism sector. This chapter will discuss some historical aspects of scuba diving tourism development.

Scuba diving and tourism have a long association. Early diving pioneers travelled to coastal regions of Europe, particularly the Mediterranean, to pursue their underwater endeavours. Technology is an important theme to consider in the evolution of this form of tourism, as technological advances have been a benefit for accessibility and safety. Global interest has been generated through media exposure, popular culture and tourism destination development. These have underpinned the success and popularity of scuba diving, leading to its growth as an activity and as part of the tourism industry.

Scuba diving tourism is defined in this chapter as scuba diving undertaken on a trip away from a person's local area. Travel may be designed specifically for scuba diving, or a subsequent decision to dive may be made at the destination. Scuba diving tourism offers economic value to destinations, as dive tourists are known for high spending. The activity and its associated enterprises can generate income and employment opportunities which complement a location's environmental, social and cultural attributes (Anderson *et al.* 2011; Brown and Cave 2010; Petreas 2003).

Divers' pursuits and search for new diving destinations led to the birth of the dive tourism industry. Scuba diving tourism is assisted by the travel patterns of large numbers of people from temperate regions of the world to tropical holiday and diving destinations. For example, travellers from the UK, the Netherlands and Italy are likely to undertake scuba certification and training outside of their home countries. Garrod (2008) confirms that divers are often tourists, noting that around 30 per cent of them undertake overseas travel for the purpose of diving. Those interested in travelling to dive in remote and challenging locations are drawn to locations which include Papua New Guinea, the Solomon Islands, Palau and Vanuatu. For example, in 2011, Australians undertook diving certification courses in countries which included Honduras, the Maldives, Indonesia, the US and Vietnam. On the other hand, in the same year in Australia itself, travellers from France, Germany, the Netherlands, Japan and Sweden were among the visitors who completed diver training.

## Popular culture

The role of popular culture as a vehicle for creating interest in scuba diving should not be overlooked. Beyond those with an immediate interest in scuba diving, broader interest was generated in Europe and elsewhere with the release of books, films and television documentaries by diving luminaries Hans and Lotte Haas and Jacques Cousteau. Through this media coverage, awareness of the underwater world began to grow a public following. With a scientific interest in the marine world, Hans Haas generated public attention and began to promote a sense of wonder about life below the watery surface. Haas produced documentaries and books on diving expeditions to the Red Sea, followed by a successful TV series, *Diving to Adventure* (in 1956), which established Hans and Lotte Haas as matinee idols for the first generation of underwater tourists (Ecott 2001:147). These first underwater films brought the world something new: underwater scenery and an exotic leisure lifestyle (Ecott 2001).

A recreational interest in the underwater world was helped by the release of the first leisure publication with a diving focus in the 1950s. The US based *Skin Diver* magazine reached many who had an interest in diving and stimulated diving-related activities including underwater photography and scuba related travel (Eyles 2005). Today, more than 60 specialist scuba diving magazines are published globally, catering to the interests of the diving community.

The excitement surrounding scuba diving discoveries complemented the availability of scuba equipment, and the activity continued to increase in popularity in Australia, the US and Europe (Brown 1988). Byron (n.d.:12) recounts that in Australia 'the public had a fascination with divers, following them asking questions about life underwater'. Equipment advances at this time included the commercial release of a Buoyancy Control Device (BCD) which gave the average person access to diving. The flotation capacity of the BCD reduced the need for the prospective diver to undertake extensive and arduous swimming training, which would be similar to that of a highly accomplished military style diver.

When Jacques Cousteau's film *The Silent World* was released in the 1970s, it received international acclaim (Ecott 2001). The film helped the sport to continue to attract a public following and greater interest. Cousteau's international diving expeditions aboard the *Calypso* captured public imagination and revealed more about the wonders of the underwater world (Cousteau and Dumas 1989). Scuba diving was seen as exciting and created media personalities such as Lloyd Bridges in *Sea Hunt*, as well as enabling local heroes such as Australia's Ben Cropp and

Ron and Valerie Taylor – world renowned diving pioneers – to become scuba diving celebrities; they were later inducted in Diving's Hall of Fame for their accomplishments and contribution to the industry. In the period between the 1960s and 1970s, the number of diving certifications began to increase, with the Professional Association of Dive Instructors (PADI) recording growth from 25,000 to almost 50,000 certifications during that period (Anon. n.d.a).

From the 1960s, retail dive centres became part of the business landscape in metropolitan areas (including in the US and Australia), aiming to meet public demand for diving equipment and scuba training. They aided a burgeoning dive travel market, with local scuba clubs promoting social diving trips. Alas, the topsy-turvy nature of running a business saw many close their doors within a decade (Byron n.d.). Successful dive centres continued, with some remaining in business today.

## Scuba diving equipment

From the outset, any modification to diving equipment was intended to establish safety and survival underwater. Every adjustment made to underwater equipment used at the time made progress towards eventually achieving the independence divers needed to remain immersed for greater periods. Diole (1953:46) notes that the nineteenth century was important in the development of diving equipment because this was when a pressure regulator and an independent air tank gave divers the freedom to move about underwater unaided, even though equipment remained heavy and cumbersome. Refinements continued, including dispensing with lead shoes and adding a device that the diver held in his teeth through which he inhaled oxygen. In the 1930s, rubber paddles were added which helped divers to move underwater more efficiently.

This was not long before the 1943 success of Cousteau and Gagnan's refinement, the demand valve regulator, which allowed the development of simplified, independent and reliable underwater breathing apparatus (Brown 1988). De Latil and Rivoire wrote (1956:371) that 'Cousteau's aqualung allows a man to stay under water easily to the full extent of his physiological possibilities and no further fundamental improvement is desirable as far as underwater tourism is concerned'. The manufacture and commercial release of Cousteau and Gagnan's Aqua Lung by the US Divers Corporation from 1948 preceded scuba diving equipment additions such as neoprene wetsuits, pressure gauges, diver decompression tables and dive computers.

Bitterman *et al.* (2009) state that diving equipment remained fundamentally unchanged for some time, except for modifications in configuration and materials which reduced the weight of equipment. Importantly, reliability and design parameters helped to streamline and support diver comfort and offer simplicity in use and weight. These features encouraged new and casual divers to the sport, with ease of use an important and appealing feature (Bitterman *et al.* 2009). Not only did the design parameters influence style and weight, certain equipment additions (such as dive computers) meant that critical information on depth and air capacity was at hand underwater, which established safety as part of the fundamental scuba diving equipment (de Latil and Rivoire 1956).

## Scuba diving education and training

With a great deal of public interest and demand for diving, training organisations were formed to assist amateur participants in underwater safety, diving techniques and use of scuba diving gear. PADI emerged in the 1960s as a commercial competitor to non-profit training organisations which previously existed – such as the Confederation Mondiale Activities Sub-aquatique (or CMAS in Europe), the British Sub-Aqua Club and the National Association of Underwater Instructors (NAUI) – and led the way in the globalised approach to scuba education and training.

PADI is one international body responsible for commercialising scuba education and training for millions of divers worldwide (Davis 1996; Ecott 2001). International scuba training is also provided by Scuba Schools International (SSI) and Scuba Diving International (SDI). On completion of training, divers obtain certification to their level of completed skill development. In Australia, the minimum skills and knowledge obtained during entry-level certification conform to a national standard (AS 4005.1–1992). This certification (C-card) is an international standard (ISO) adopted by most countries and allows qualified divers access to marine environments and necessary equipment through the services of commercial scuba diving operators.

A formalised approach to scuba diving training and skill development was critical to legitimising individuals' involvement with the sport and its environment. PADI pioneered the modular approach to dive education. The training and education sector of the industry underpinned scuba diving tourism, with international recognition of diving certification cards preceding the growth of scuba diving tourism. Having an established set of diving skills was at the heart of the licence to dive internationally (Wilks 1992). It meant divers were not required to prove diving skill on arrival at a destination. Formerly, some resorts had the practice of reviewing the skills of divers to allow them access to diving facilities and charter services.

Along with the international C-card, availability of affordable underwater cameras, such as the Nemrod and Nikonos in the 1970s, offered another level of interest and appeal through photography. The importance of capturing visual imagery quickly gathered momentum, and increased awareness of the underwater world through photography became an influence on many people's motivation to dive. Photography allowed people the chance to share their underwater experiences and, in doing so, stimulated broader interest (Brown 1988).

## Dive sites as destinations

Along with skill development and equipment improvements, new diving sites added to the attraction because they opened up the range of diving possibilities.

Dive sites were promoted in the preferred diving media of the day: diving magazines. These magazines showcased new locations and marine life and had an emphasis on dive travel and photography, thus supporting the idea of travelling to scuba dive. The genesis of diving magazines reflects the evolution of scuba diving from an interest in skin diving and spear fishing to wildlife watching and photography. For example, *Skin Diving and Spearfishing Digest* became *Skin Diving in Australia* which became *Sport Diving* magazine.

The international movement towards protecting marine biodiversity by establishing marine parks, reserves and sanctuary zones has hugely benefitted scuba diving tourism. The world's first marine reserve was established in the Florida Keys in the 1960s and the first Mediterranean park in French waters in the late 1970s (Badalamenti *et al.* 2000). By the late 1980s, hundreds of marine reserves existed, with more to come (Tisdell and Broadus 1989). The establishment of early marine protected areas is said to have stemmed from the activity of scuba diving and the possibility it provided for leisure seekers (divers and snorkellers) to observe the underwater realm (Carleton Ray 1999). In the Caribbean, researchers hold that most of the assistance supporting marine conservation is derived from tourism (Williams and Polunin 2000). The location of marine parks as sites for dive tourism has continued to assist regional centres, with accommodation and service-based facilities being established to support and encourage diving visitors.

The establishment of the Great Barrier Reef Marine Park (GBR) in 1975 is a case in point. Coastal locations including Cairns and the Whitsunday Islands are among those former regional townships to be subsequently transformed into 'diver towns' and marine tourism hotspots. Early demand and growth in visitors to GBR exceeded expectations, with 1992 figures of 1 million visits per annum recorded (Hockings 1994). Income generated in regions of the Great Barrier Reef from tourist spending on accommodation, transport and other holiday expenditure was estimated at $AUD 1.7 billion (Driml 1994). The international appeal of a destination of this size (2900 individual reefs and 900 islands) for diving and related marine tourism was immense, and reef visits continued to increase the percentage of income for the region's economy (Parker 2001).

At GBR, diving extended to include remote parts of the park with the introduction of bigger, better and faster day boats which could easily reach outlying locations, as well as overnight liveaboard tourism. Wilks (1992) noted that up to 80,000 introductory scuba dives were being conducted each year, demonstrating the prominence of the GBR region and the Queensland coastline as an iconic and prolific dive tourism hub within Australia in the 1980s–1990s. Over the next 13 years, marine tourism visitors to the GBR reached 444,000 per annum, with scuba divers comprising almost 5 per cent of Australia's inbound tourism market (Anon. 2003) and introductory dives (such as PADI's Discover Scuba experience) growing to well over 170,000 in 2011 (Anon. n.d.a).

As scuba diving increased in popularity, reports from marine studies alerted readers to the impact of the activity on marine ecosystems, particularly in popular and crowded locations, with management strategies being recommended (Musa 2003; Bell *et al.* 2011). Diver impact studies have led to environmental attention being given to many sites including areas of the Red Sea (Zakai and Chadwick-Furman 2002), Caribbean (Williams and Polunin 2000), Australia (Davis and Tisdell 1995; McCook *et al.* 2010; Parker 2001) and Malaysia (Musa 2003). On the other hand, there is a view that divers are non-consumptive tourists and diving is offered as a leisure preference in areas where fishing and other consumptive marine practices occur (Wielgus *et al.* 2008). Internationally, divers have been supportive of marine conservation and management.

Research shows divers view favourably the introduction of fees to access marine reserves, including in the Philippines (Arin and Kramer 2002; Tongson and Dygico 2004), Curacao (de Groot and Bush 2010), Mexico, Thailand and Bonaire (Peters and Hawkins 2009). This strategy and economic contribution has been driven by the absence of centralised financial support for marine conservation management in many areas. Divers' contributions are seen as critical to marine conservation, with a suggestion being to offer divers (at additional cost) access to formerly unavailable areas of high conservation value (Thur 2010; Uyarra *et al.* 2010; Wielgus *et al.* 2008). These sites would benefit from divers seeking higher quality conditions in their underwater marine and wildlife sightings.

In recent years, the ongoing impact of diving on benthic systems has seen the diving industry actively encourage low impact diving, marine conservation and marine wildlife protection. The establishment of the Project AWARE Foundation is the diving industry's first registered charity focused on promoting environmental protection. With headquarters in the US, the organisation has an international focus and is independently registered as a charity in Australia, the UK and Japan. The feeling many divers have towards the ocean is reflected in the statement by the late Neville Coleman who said:

> Whether they like it or not, divers are the only group of individuals who could ever act as guardians to the World of Water. There are no other groups in the world with better access, training and opportunity. As guardians of the world's greatest resources divers must understand that they really have an important job to do, far more than most could ever imagine.
>
> Anon. n.d.b (www.projectaware.org/)

From the 1950s, advances in scuba technology had a dramatic impact on the capacity of divers to also explore shallow shipwrecks (Hutchison 1996). Shipwrecks with accessible entry became popular for recreational divers (Edney 2006; Nash 2007) with dive tourism sites including the *SS Yongala* (Australia) and the WWII wrecks of Chuuk Lagoon (Federated States of Micronesia) regularly listed among the 'must dive' locations. In addition, deliberately scuttled de-commissioned ships were set up specifically for scuba diving as artificial reefs and dive tourism attractions in Australia, the US, Thailand and Canada. Stolk *et al.* (2007) note that only a few studies have examined artificial reefs as resources for scuba diving, yet they provide an alternative underwater attraction for divers with the immersed structure itself, its size and the resident marine species attracted to the reef structure being features which interest divers.

Inland sinkholes and caves were also discovered and became alternative and popular freshwater diving sites in areas of Australia, Mexico, the US, the Bahamas and Brazil. Mount Gambier is seen as Australia's centre for cave diving. In 1973, the Cave Diving Association of Australia was formed, with governance dedicated to training and managing cave diving in Australia to protect divers, maintain environmental features of the sites and retain landowner interests (Dimmock *et al.* 2012). Growth in cave diving participation has seen dedicated accommodation lodges built in some areas as facilities to support visiting cave divers. As with other types, cave diving popularity has grown into a specialised area of scuba diving pursued by dedicated supporters with the relevant skills and interest in exploring closed and overhead environments.

The business and enterprise of scuba diving tourism had become apparent by the 1980s and 1990s. Diving certification figures from the 1980s climbed substantially from under 1 million in 1980 to more than 10 million in the 1990s (Anon. n.d.a). Several elements converged to underpin development of this tourism sector; transport and accommodation infrastructure were available, international scuba training and certification agencies were firmly established and well-known marine locations, including marine reserves, offered attractive locations.

## Components of scuba diving tourism

### *Coastal holiday activities*

Leiper (1995) makes us aware that, while tourism has grown in popularity since the 1840s, it only became a mass phenomenon after 1950 with major growth after 1974. The arrival of international air travel in the 1960s–1970s contributed dramatically, allowing many more visitors to venture afield. The rise in air travel in Europe for short and long haul trips was fuelled by package holidays and then low cost travel (Page and Connell 2009). International locations with the necessary infrastructure to complement natural appeal could attract visitors, and resort tourism became a popular choice for many coastal destinations. The coastal zone offers attractive and unique landscapes for tourism and by the 1930s 'a short annual holiday by the sea' was an anticipated element of working life (Page and Connell 2009:38). Since the 1970s, the transformation of coastal regions contributed to growth in coastal and marine tourism (Page and Connell 2009). Tourists could enjoy relaxing resort holidays and there were marine-based activities, including swimming, snorkelling and scuba diving, available to capture interest and involvement.

Providing marine-based activities as an option during one's resort holiday led to the emergence of the term 'resort diver' or 'tourist diver', particularly in coastal locations such as the Great Barrier Reef, Australia. Coxon (2006) and Wilks and Davis (2000) conducted studies into the 'tourist diver' market. The profile includes tourists who become involved with scuba diving as a holiday activity, allowing them to witness underwater environments and marine wildlife (Coxon 2006; Tschapka 2006; Wilks and Davis 2000). As noted earlier, tourist diver participation has grown, with 170,000 'resort dives' now conducted in Australia each year (Anon. n.d.a). Growth in the international backpacker market is also reflected in characteristics of the tourist diver in locations such as Thailand and Australia. In Australia, this diving backpacker market has significantly benefitted development of destinations or 'diver towns' along the Great Barrier Reef where reef visitors have been characterised as young, likely to be from North America or Europe, and have a desire to undertake scuba diving (Moscardo *et al.* 2003).

### An adventurous opportunity

The emergence of a 'curiosity' market in diving involved those looking for some form of adventure and challenge. Thus, it would seem dive tourism was able to extend the scope and interest in scuba diving through resort dives or 'Discover Scuba Diving' products for participants who might not yet be certified as scuba divers (Wilks and Davis 2000). Irrespective of the amount of time invested, involvement with adventure experiences was a feature of the activity. One report on the rate of diving dropout contended that 'people take dive courses for their enjoyment and the experience rather than any long term or regular commitment to the sport' (Anon. 2003:30). Yet, as well as those who dabbled with scuba diving as a holiday option, there was also huge demand for full certification diving courses during the period. For example, in the Cairns region of the GBR, more than 500,000 full certification divers – most of whom were tourists – were trained in the 25 year period from the mid-1980s until now (Anon. n.d.a).

The market reflects the high demand for adventurous tourism experiences among inexperienced tourists. The enthusiasm was serviced by a willing industry which provided transport, equipment, specialised clothing and skilled guides to enable safe, short and thrilling experiences (Buckley 2004). The appeal of activities incorporating positive approaches to risk in leisure and tourism was recognised. Risk can be a positive element of an experience, because of the thrill gained from opportunity to play with fear (Cater 2006). A sense of thrill is realised when one confronts the fears, risks and uncertainty possible in adventurous leisure (Cater 2006; McGillivray and Frew 2007). As an emerging feature of modern industrial society and industrial advancements, adventurous leisure paralleled pursuit of adventurous activities in natural locations (Schott 2007). Discovering adventure involves risk-taking and challenge in locations perceived as dangerous, where skill development is needed to manage perceived risks. Demand for these types of experiences (including scuba diving) has not waned. In fact, authors point to an irony in which modern society is more likely to accept risk and uncertainty in leisure, rather than other areas of life (Cater 2006; Ewert 1989; Holyfield 1999).

### Adventure travel

Travel to access diving sites has been aided by the growth of liveaboard tourism. These dive trips offered a dedicated and comfortable holiday option. From the

1970s and 1980s, cruise boats have been fitted out to accommodate and cater for overnight dive trips, with capacity to reach more remote diving locations such as Australia's Coral Sea, Papua New Guinea and areas of Southeast Asia. Liveaboard dive charters are a specialised option as they provide a fully-inclusive service dimension to dive travel.

Locations such as the Red Sea were vigorously promoted as diving destinations by the governments of Egypt, Israel and Jordan from the mid-1980s to attract international scuba divers to the Middle East to enjoy their coral reefs (Hawkins and Roberts 1994). Heron Island opened in the late 1960s, as a marine research station and one of Australia's earliest dive resorts. In the late 1970s and early 1980s, Pacific Island locations, such as Vanuatu, became synonymous with scuba diving for divers who learned of the *SS President Coolidge*, 'the world's largest accessible shipwreck', through articles published in scuba diving magazines and the establishment of organised dive travel services to facilitate specialised dive tourism holidays (Stone 2006).

### *Equipment for adventure*

Now scuba diving tourism is complemented by other advances including using Nitrox 'enriched air' (a nitrogen/oxygen mix which contains a higher percentage of oxygen than normal air) which helped diving become less of an effort and divers less susceptible to decompression illness. The advancement of technical diving added a further dimension to the recreational diving phenomenon. Technical diving incorporates rebreather equipment (a more complex closed circuit diving system) and uses mixed gas (tri-mix: nitrogen, helium and oxygen) which allows recreational divers to safely dive deeper, in search of new underwater sights at various scuba diving destinations. The term *technical diving* was first coined in 1991 by Michael Menduno (former editor and publisher of aquaCORPS magazine) as 'a discipline that uses special tools and methods to improve underwater safety and performance enabling a diver to conduct operations in a wide range of environments and perform tasks beyond the scope of recreational diving' (Strike and Cummins, 2012:15). Among features which distinguish technical from recreational diving are:

- allows water depths greater than 40 metres;
- provides breathing mixtures other than compressed air (i.e. Nitrox and Helium);
- allows diving in an overhead/closed environment (e.g. cave or wreck);
- incurs decompression obligations;
- requires specialised equipment and training.

Initially, technical diving was not seen as a recreational pursuit, even though early technical divers considered themselves to be recreational divers (Strike and Cummins 2012). With time, increased interest and a diving market searching for new horizons, technical diving generated its own appeal. Training organisations such as American Nitrox Divers International (ANDI), International Association of Nitrox and Technical Divers (IANTD) and Technical Diving International (TDI) specialised in technical diving education and provided the direction for a growing number of technical divers with ongoing demand for technical training. Many features identifying technical diving overlapped with aspects of recreational diving. The result has been a blurring of the boundaries which is evidenced by recreational training agencies developing technical training divisions in their business operations (e.g. PADI's Technical Diving Division, TDD) and technical training agencies developing recreational divisions (Global Underwater Explorers [GUE], TDI).

However, the complexities evident in technical diving demand commitment and discipline, which perhaps recognises a point of difference separating a casual leisure diver from a technical diver. One technical diving pioneer noted that 'Technical diving is . . . a philosophy, a mindset . . . to do it well you have to live, eat and breathe technical diving' (Deans 1995, cited in Strike and Cummins 2012:33). Today, there are destinations and associated events promoted specifically for technical diving. For example, Inner Space is an annual technical diving convention in the Cayman Islands. Thailand and the Philippines are also promoted as technical diving destinations in the Asia Pacific region.

Meanwhile, novel and innovative products continued to become available and offer convenience for those with no time or interest in diving training to enter the marine world. These were an alternative to products offered by the mainstream scuba training agencies. One can try snuba which is a shallow water diving system and a compromise between snorkelling and diving, requiring less equipment. Snuba divers breathe through a regulator which is attached via a long hose to an air tank, on the surface (Anon. n.d.c). Alternatively, Seawalker is a diving system allowing participants to walk on the bottom, rather than swim. Using a large full face window in the Seawalker helmet, participants view the underwater world at a maximum depth of 15 feet (Anon. n.d.d).

For dive tourists travelling with their own scuba gear, airline travel continues to bring challenges because of weight restrictions on luggage, especially for travel to remote locations on small aircraft. One response to increased diving demand has seen resorts and operators stock improved quality gear for hire, helping travellers to reduce their equipment load. As well, equipment manufacturers have developed small and lighter BCDs for travelling.

### Service and adventure

With increasing demand for and participation in dive tourism, there are expectations for quality service and experiences (O'Neill *et al.* 2000). Internationally, the prominence of the Asia Pacific region as a host to many pristine and exotic scuba diving destinations is being noticed. Papua New Guinea, Fiji, the Solomon Islands, the Philippines, Malaysia, Vanuatu and Thailand are internationally recognised as dive destinations. These locations began to offer a range of dive tourism facilities, sites and services which were widely promoted to the diving public and travellers to the region. Thailand has been especially successful in capturing the interest of the backpacker diving market which was formerly attracted to the Great Barrier Reef destinations. In response, destinations are encouraging interested tourists to undertake additional and professional level scuba diving training (e.g. Divemaster and Instructor).

The popularity of scuba diving tourism became evident in the number of travelling divers and dive travel promotions and the quantity of dedicated scuba diving retailers and resorts with scuba diving facilities worldwide. By the end of 2011, PADI alone registered more than 6100 retail and resort members globally, with services and facilities available to support the diving public (Anon. n.d.a). At the turn of the century, more than 10 million divers had been certified, with 2011 figures in the vicinity of 24 million. Scuba diving tourism has become a real and legitimate tourism sector.

## Conclusion

In bringing this chapter to a conclusion, it is possible to consider the development of scuba diving as a leisure interest and its progression to become scuba diving tourism through the convergence of critical factors which can be organised as reflecting autonomy, access and availability. The interest and motivation of individuals to improve the situation of the day in some small way has resulted in a phenomenal transformation and growth in an industry which, surprisingly, is based around the use of equipment which remains largely unchanged, compared with changes which have taken place elsewhere in other industries. Quite simply, the fundamental scuba diving 'kit' at the heart of a multi-billion dollar industry has changed little. The technological thread has been constant in the evolution of the scuba diving tourism industry.

### *Autonomy*

The impetus for the activity is to swim independently underwater and look at the marine world. The uncomplicated compactness of the open circuit scuba system allows this, and the design popularises the appeal. Scuba diving has enabled destinations, particularly developing nations in tropical locations, the opportunity for autonomy and financial independence by way of hosting scuba divers to witness and enjoy their marine resources. Countries such as Malaysia, Papua New Guinea, Vanuatu and Fiji have been successful in developing tourism infrastructure, including specialised hotels, resorts and marinas, which in turn generates employment and career opportunities for host communities (Cummins 2008).

### *Access*

The scuba diving industry is internationally accessible and has been legitimised through the establishment of national committees such as the Recreation Training Council (US) and ISO Standards Australia, which identify a uniform measure of operation to maintain consistency and safety. At the same time, they offer comfort and assurance for scuba divers in the training and supervisory quality which can be expected on site, regardless of the destination.

Technology has played an active role in extending interest as popular culture brought pioneers and heroes, including Cousteau, and created fictional heroes through television. Television gave access to environmental education and awareness about the marine world through documentaries narrated by public figures such as Sir David Attenborough.

### *Availability*

Scuba diving tourism is possible through various operators providing a combination of retail, equipment and education who are part of an international tourism industry with access to appealing and attractive destinations. When combined with transport and tourism infrastructure, there is a broad and varied range of scuba diving tourism opportunities throughout the world. In the past six to seven decades, human fascination in witnessing what lies beneath the watery surface has been transformed into a global billion dollar industry which is managed and delivered according to standards, laws and procedures as they apply to particular destinations and businesses. There are opportunities to pursue scuba diving in all climatic zones by entering a diversity of diving environments (reef/cave/wreck/ice) using the services of operators who can be found on every continent.

### *To the future*

Technology has been a central feature of scuba diving and, from early inventions, has extended opportunities for people to spend time underwater. These advancements have subsequently shifted the emphasis from diving for food and survival into the development of a multimillion dollar leisure industry which has firm links with tourism. Earlier sections of this chapter identified the importance of technology to initial design and later improvements to scuba equipment as life support, and then enhancements to comfort. The arrival of the *e*-age has also markedly transformed some of the critical elements of scuba diving tourism, particularly diver education and training and dive travel.

## References

Anderson, L. E. and Loomis, D. K. (2011) 'Scuba Diver Specialisation and Behaviour Norms at Coral Reefs', *Coastal Management*, 39(5):478–491.

Anderson, R. C., Adam, M. S., Kitchen-Wheeler, A. M. and Stevens, G. (2011) 'Extent and Economic Value of Manta Ray Watching in Maldives', *Tourism in Marine Environments*, 7(1):15–27.

Anon. (n.d.a) 'Worldwide Certification History'. Online. Available HTTP: <http://www.padi.com/scuba/about-padi/PADI-statistics> (accessed 13 March 2012).

Anon. (n.d.b) 'The Ocean Pays Tribute to a Hero'. Online. Available HTTP: <http://www.projectaware.org/node/11619> (accessed 10 July 2012).

Anon. (n.d.c) 'Welcome to the World of SNUBA'. Online. Available HTTP: <http://www.snubaturksandcaicos.com> (accessed 25 June 2012).

Anon. (n.d.d) 'What Is Seawalker?' Online. Available HTTP: <http://www.seawalker-diving.com> (accessed 25 June 2012).

Anon. (2003) 'The International Diving Market', *Travel and Tourism Analyst*, (December):1–39.

Arin, T. and Kramer, A. (2002) 'Divers' Willingness to Pay to Visit Marine Sanctuaries: An Exploratory Study', *Ocean and Coastal Management*, 45:171–183.

Badalamenti, F., Ramos, A., Voultsiadou, E., Sanchez, L., D'Anna, G., Pipitone, C. Mas, J., Ruiz Fernandez, J., Whitmarsh, D. and Riggio, S. (2000) 'Cultural and Socio-economic Impacts of Mediterranean Marine Protected Areas', *Environmental Conservation*, 27(2):110–125.

Bell, C., Needham, M. D. and Szuster, B. W. (2011) 'Congruence among Encounters, Norms, Crowding, and Management in a Marine Protected Area', *Environmental Management*, 48:499–513.

Bitterman, N., Ofir, E. and Ratner, N. (2009) 'Recreational Diving: Re-evaluation of Task, Environment, and Equipment Definitions', *European Journal of Sport Science*, 9(5):321–328.

Brown, K. G. and Cave, J. (2010) 'Marketing Cultural and Heritage Tourism: The Marshall Islands', *International Journal of Culture, Tourism and Hospitality Research*, 4(2):130–142.

Brown, M. (1988) 'Brief History of Sports Diving in Australia', in T. Cummins (ed.) *Diving Accident Management in Australia*, North Ryde, Australia: PADI: 1–6

Buckley, R. (2004) 'Skilled Commercial Adventure: The Edge of Tourism', in T.V. Singh (ed.) *New Horizons in Tourism*, Lucknow, India: CABI Publishing: 37–48

Byron, T. (n.d.) *The History of Spearfishing and Scuba Diving in Australia: The First Eighty Years 1917 to 1997*, Padstow Heights, Australia: Tom Byron Publishers.

Carleton Ray, G. (1999) 'Coastal-marine Protected Areas: Agonies of Choice', *Aquatic Conservation: Marine and Freshwater Ecosystems*, 9:607–614.

Cater, C. (2006) 'Playing with Risk? Participant Perceptions of Risk and Management Implications in Adventure Tourism', *Tourism Management*, 27:317–325.

Cousteau, J. Y. and Dumas, F. (1989) *The Silent World*, Oxford: Clio Press.

Coxon, C. (2006) 'Safety in the Dive Tourism Industry of Australia', in J. Wilks, D. Pendergast and P. Leggat (eds.) *Tourism in Turbulent Times: Towards Safe Experiences for Visitors*, Amsterdam: Elsevier: 199–216

Cummins, T. L. (2008) 'Recreational Scuba Diving and the Travel Experience' paper presented at the Commonwealth Conference on Sport Tourism, Kota Kinabalu, Malaysia.

Davis, D. (1996) 'The Development and Nature of Recreational Scuba Diving in Australia: A Study in Economics, Environmental Management and Tourism', unpublished thesis, University of Queensland.

Davis, D. and Tisdell, C. (1995) 'Recreational Scuba-diving and Carrying Capacity in Marine Protected Areas', *Ocean and Coastal Management*, 26(1):19–40.

de Groot, J. and Bush, S. (2010) 'The Potential for Dive Tourism led Entrepreneurial Marine Protected Areas in Curacao', *Marine Policy*, 34:1051–1059.

de Latil, P. and Rivoire, J. (1956) *Man and the Underwater World*, trans. E. Fitzgerald, London: Jarrolds.

Diole, P. (1953) *The Undersea Adventure*, trans. A. Ross, London: Sidgwick and Jackson.

Dimmock, K. (2009) 'Finding Comfort in Adventure: Experiences of Recreational Scuba Divers', *Leisure Studies*, 28(3):279–296.

Dimmock, K. Taplin, J. and Jenkins, J. (2012) 'Freshwater Systems and Tourism', in A. Holden, and D. Fennell (eds.) *A Handbook of Tourism and the Environment*, Amsterdam: Routledge: 155–169.

Driml, S. (1994) 'Protection for Profit: Economic and Financial Values of the Great Barrier Reef World Heritage Area and other Protected Areas', Research Publication No. 35, Townsville: Great Barrier Reef Marine Park Authority.

Ecott, T. (2001) *Neutral Buoyancy: Adventures in a Liquid World*, New York: Grove Press.

Edney, J. (2006) 'Impacts of Recreational Scuba Diving on Shipwrecks in Australia and the Pacific', *Micronesian: Journal of the Humanities and Social Sciences*, 5(1/2):201–233.

Ewert, A. (1989) *Outdoor Adventure Pursuits: Foundations, Models and Theories*, Scottsdale, AZ: Publishing Horizons Inc.

Eyles, C. (2005) *Last of the Blue Water Hunters*, New York: Aqua Quest Publications Inc.

Garrod, B. (2008) 'Market Segments and Tourist Typologies for Diving Tourism', in B. Garrod and S. Gössling (eds.) *New Frontiers in Marine Tourism: Diving Experiences, Sustainability, Management*, Amsterdam: Elsevier: 31–39.

Hawkins, J. and Roberts, C. (1994) 'The Growth of Coastal Tourism in the Red Sea: Present and Future Effects on Coral Reefs', *Ambio*, 23(8):503–508.

Hockings, M. (1994) 'A Survey of the Tour Operator's Role in Marine Park Interpretation', *The Journal of Tourism Studies*, 5(1):16–28.

Holyfield, L. (1999) 'Manufacturing Adventure: The Buying and Selling of Emotions', *Journal of Contemporary Ethnography*, 28(1):3–32.

Hutchison, G. (1996) 'Threats to Underwater Cultural Heritage: The Problems of Unprotected and Historical Sites, Wrecks and Objects found at Sea', *Marine Policy*, 20(4):287–290.

Leiper, N. (1995) *Tourism Management*, Melbourne: RMIT Publishing.

McCook, L., Ayling, T., Cappo, M., Choat, J., Evans, R., De Freitas, D., Heupel, Michelle, Hughes, Terry P., Jones, Geoffrey P., Marsh, Helene, Mills, Morena, Molloy, Fergus J., Pitcher, C. Roland, Pressey, Robert L., Russ, Garry R., Sutton, S., Sweatman, H., Tobin, R., Wachenfeld, D.R. and Williamson, D.H. (2010) 'Adaptive Management of the Great Barrier Reef: A Globally Significant Demonstration of the Benefits of Networks of Marine Reserves', *Proceedings of the National Academy of Sciences*, 107(43):18278–18285.

McGillivray, D. and Frew, M. (2007) 'Capturing Adventure: Trading Experiences in the Symbolic Economy', *Annals of Leisure Research*, 10(1):54–78.

Moscardo, G., Saltzer, R., Galletly, A., Burke, A. and Hildebrandt, A. (2003) 'Changing Patterns of Reef Tourism', Technical Report No. 49. Townsville: CRC Reef Research Centre.

Musa, G. (2003) 'Sipadan: An Over-exploited Scuba-diving Paradise?: An Analysis of Tourism Impact, Diver Satisfaction and Management Priorities', in B. Garrod and J. Wilson (eds.) *Marine Ecotourism: Issues and Experiences*, Clevedon, UK: Channel View Publications: 122–137.

Nash, M. (ed.) (2007) *Shipwreck Archaeology in Australia*, Crawley: University of Western Australia Press.

O'Neill, M., Williams, P., MacCarthy, M. and Groves, R. (2000) 'Diving into Service Quality: The Dive Tour Operator Perspective', *Managing Service Quality*, 10(3):131–138.

Page, S. and Connell, J. (2009) *Tourism: A Modern Synthesis* (3rd edn), Andover, Hampshire: Cengage Learning.

Parker, S. (2001) 'Marine Tourism and Environmental Management on the Great Barrier Reef', in V. Smith and M. Brent (eds.) *Hosts and Guests Revisited: Tourism Issues of the 21st Century*, New York: Cognizant Communication: 232–241.

Peters, H. and Hawkins, J. (2009) 'Access to Marine Parks: A Comparative Study in Willingness to Pay', *Ocean and Coastal Management*, 52:219–228.

Petreas, C. P. (2003) 'Scuba Diving: An Alternative Form of Coastal Tourism for Greece?', in B. Garrod and J. Wilson (eds.) *Marine Ecotourism: Issues and Experiences*, Clevedon, UK: Channel View Publications: 215–232.

Schott, C. (2007) 'Selling Adventure Tourism: A Distribution Channels Perspective', *International Journal of Tourism Research*, 9(4):257–274.

Stolk, P., Markwell, K. and Jenkins, M. (2007) 'Artificial Reefs as Recreational Scuba Diving Resources: A Critical Review of Research', *Journal of Sustainable Tourism*, 15(4):331–349.

Stone, P. (2006) *The Lady and the President: The Life and Loss of the SS President Coolidge*, Yarram, Victoria: Oceans Enterprises.

Strike, D. and Cummins, T. (2012) 'Technical Diving: Evolution or Revolution?', presentation delivered at DivTeK Conference, Marina Bay Sands, Singapore 13–15 April.

Thur, S.M. (2010) 'User Fees as Sustainable Financing Mechanisms for Marine Protected Areas: An Application to the Bonaire National Marine Park', *Marine Policy*, 34:63–69.

Tisdell, C. and Broadus, J. (1989) 'Policy Issues Related to the Establishment and Management of Marine Reserves', *Coastal Management*, 17:37–53.

Tongson, E. and Dygico, M. (2004) 'User Fee System for Marine Ecotourism: The Tubbataha Reef Experience', *Coastal Management*, 32:17–23.

Tschapka, M. (2006) 'Involvement, Motivations and Setting Preferences of Participants in the Adventure Tourism Activity of Scuba Diving', unpublished thesis, University of Canberra.

Uyarra, M., Gill, J. and Cote, I. (2010) 'Charging for Nature: Marine Park Fees and Management from a User Perspective', *Ambio*, 39:515–523.

Wielgus, J., Sala, E. and Gerber, L. (2008) 'Assessing the Ecological and Economic Benefits of a No-take Marine Reserve', *Ecological Economics*, 67(1):32–40.

Wilks, J. (1992) 'Introductory Scuba Diving on the Great Barrier Reef', *Australian Parks and Recreation*, (Summer):18–23.

Wilks, J. and Davis, R. (2000) 'Risk Management for Scuba Diving Operations on Australia's Great Barrier Reef', *Tourism Management*, 21(6):591–599.

Williams, I. and Polunin, N. (2000) 'Differences between Protected and Unprotected Reefs of the Western Caribbean in Attributes Preferred by Dive Tourists', *Environmental Conservation*, 27(4):382–394.

Zakai, D. and Chadwick-Furman, N. E. (2002) 'Impact of Intensive Recreational Diving on Reef Corals at Eilat, Northern Red Sea', *Biological Conservation*, 105:179–187.

# 3    A world geography of recreational scuba diving

*Alan A. Lew*

## Introduction

The world's oceans cover 69 per cent of the planet. Freshwater lakes and rivers comprise an additional 2 per cent of its surface. Life and landscape are very different below the reflected surface of these waters. As a terrestrial animal, humans know very little about that life, although we have found many ways to fish and trawl the oceans for food, to extract its mineral and fossil resources, and to use it as a common sewage dump. It is estimated, for example, that the oceans today contain only a third of the number of large fish that they had a century ago due to overfishing, with 54 per cent of their decline taking place since 1970 (Sheridan 2011). At the same time, the number of small fish in some species has more than doubled (Choi 2011). Among the many ways that we litter both ocean and freshwater areas, plastic refuse can be fatal to marine life and takes many decades to decay. Coastal tourist destinations tend to be the most noticeably affected by plastic litter, though remote parts of both the north Pacific and north Atlantic oceans have large areas with plastic garbage circulating thousands of miles from land (Berton 2007; Gill 2010).

Great strides have been made in recent years to educate the public about the precarious state of our oceans, and marine protected areas have grown considerably in number and size in recent decades, comprising 1.2 per cent of the world's oceans as of 2010 (IUCN 2010). However, much more needs to be done. One way to educate people about the diversity and value of marine life is to give them direct exposure to the underwater world in a recreational setting. This is mostly done through snorkelling and scuba diving experiences. Although mostly undertaken for recreational purposes, scuba diving can lead to a transformative experience that deeply changes one's perception and attitude toward sea life and the conservation ocean resources (Arin and Kramer 2002; Lück 2003; White 2008).

## Popularity of scuba diving

SCUBA is an acronym for 'self-contained underwater breathing apparatus'. The apparatus consists of a tank with compressed air (though other special gasses are sometimes used to help extend the amount of time that people can stay underwater) and additional gear to access the air and to help the diver maintain buoyancy underwater. Scuba diving has its roots in military applications, and early US Navy medical guidelines for diving are still followed by certified recreational divers today. There are also many professional divers who work for commercial, scientific and government agencies. They, along with recreational divers, have been increasing in number as ocean resource issues and awareness have grown in recent decades (Ong and Musa 2011).

Recreational diving is a specialty niche sport activity. The detailed discussion on scuba diving training and education is presented in Chapter 5. Dive experiences can range from uncertified 'Discovery Dives' (Davison 2012) to advanced technical dives for highly experienced and trained divers (Meduno 2001). Recreational diving generally started in the 1960s when NAUI (National Association of Underwater Instructors) and PADI (Professional Association of Diving Instructors) were founded. It did not really become widespread until the early 1980s when advances in equipment and training started to bring diving within reach of the middle classes of Europe and North America (Davison 2007). Estimating the number of divers in the world is a challenge, due to the great diversity and dispersed nature of this self-regulated industry. While most recreational dive companies require formal certification to participate in anything beyond a discovery dive, that certification can come from a number of different private organizations. These organizations do not provide data on the number of certifications that their member dive instructors issue each year, with the exception of 2002 when PADI, Scuba Schools International (SSI), the National Association of Underwater Instructors (NAUI) and Scuba Diving International (SDI) together claimed to have certified 177,000 divers in the US (Davison 2007). Worldwide, the largest certification organization, PADI is believed to issue about 500,000 new certifications each year, and it claimed to have certified 17.8 million divers as of 2008 (PADI 2009, cited in Ong and Musa 2011). PADI no longer discloses its certification numbers, but even if they did, there are at least ten other internationally recognized scuba certification organizations to consider, half of which are country or region based, and half of which are international.

An additional challenge is that only a fraction of certified divers are actually active in any given year. Some are very active, diving many times a year, while others never do another dive after they receive their certification (which they probably received while on holiday in the tropics). Anecdotally, scuba dropout rates have been estimated to range from 40 to 80 per cent of certified divers each year (Davison 2007), and even the most active divers will gradually dive less over time. The number of active divers probably does not change significantly from year to year, as new entrants roughly equal those who drop out of the sport.

Based on these numbers and a few other industry sources, it is estimated that at least 30 million people have been certified to dive worldwide as of 2012, while perhaps 6 million have actually dived at least once beyond certification, and about 3 million are somewhat more active divers, taking one or more dive trips a year. About a million people probably learn to dive each year, but about a million people drop out of diving, as well.

One way that the diving market is changing, however, is the increase in diving activity in less developed regions of the world. A search of Google Trends, which tracks the relative frequency of search terms on Google.com, showed a decline in searches for the word 'scuba' since 2004. This largely reflects the pattern dominance of searches from North America (the US and Canada), the UK and Australia, all of which had the same pattern of decline, with searches in 2012 comprising half the value of those in 2004 (in comparison with all Google searches). On the other hand, a significant increase in 'scuba' as a search term appears in recent years in Malaysia, Singapore and South Africa (since 2011) and the Philippines (since 2012).

While there may be some national or regional idiosyncrasies in these patterns, the Google data, which show the countries from which searches are originating, point to South Africa and Southeast Asia as the most prominent emerging growth areas for scuba diving. This can be considered true for these regions both in terms of new domestic divers (locals searching for scuba information), as well as international visitors who are looking for diving information after they have arrived in South Africa and Southeast Asia.

## Scuba diving environments

Almost any underwater location can be a diving spot. Most diving, however, is done either near continental or island coastlines, or on shallow reefs that are very close to the surface of an ocean or other body of water. Warm water coral reefs throughout the world are the most popular diving destinations. They attract the largest numbers of divers, by far, because their comfortable waters combine colorful diving with a sun, sand and sea holiday vacation experience. Though significantly less popular, adventurous diving experiences are common in cold waters off the coasts of North America, northern Europe, Australia, New Zealand and in freshwater lakes far from any ocean.

The geographic distribution of diving locations can be approached in two fundamental ways, both of which contain a degree of subjective interpretation. The first is by determining the location and range of potential dive sites around the world. One way to do this is to simply map all of the world's coastlines, or the estimated distribution of the world's coral reefs and marine biodiversity hot spots. At best, these provide a baseline against which we can assess where dive tourism is actually taking place. A second approach is to examine published lists of the most popular dive destinations around the world.

Figure 3.1 shows how most of the world is covered with water, and the vast extent of ocean coastlines that provide significant opportunities for scuba diving on every continent. Not every continent has tropical waters, but they all have waters suitable for recreational diving experiences. In general, destinations that are farther removed from the warm sun, sand and surf of the tropics receive fewer divers, while those at the far northern and southern extremes require considerable more technical equipment to overcome cold temperature challenges.

Areas of the globe with extensive and complicated coastlines, including Southeast Asia, Europe and the Caribbean, potentially have a greater diversity of

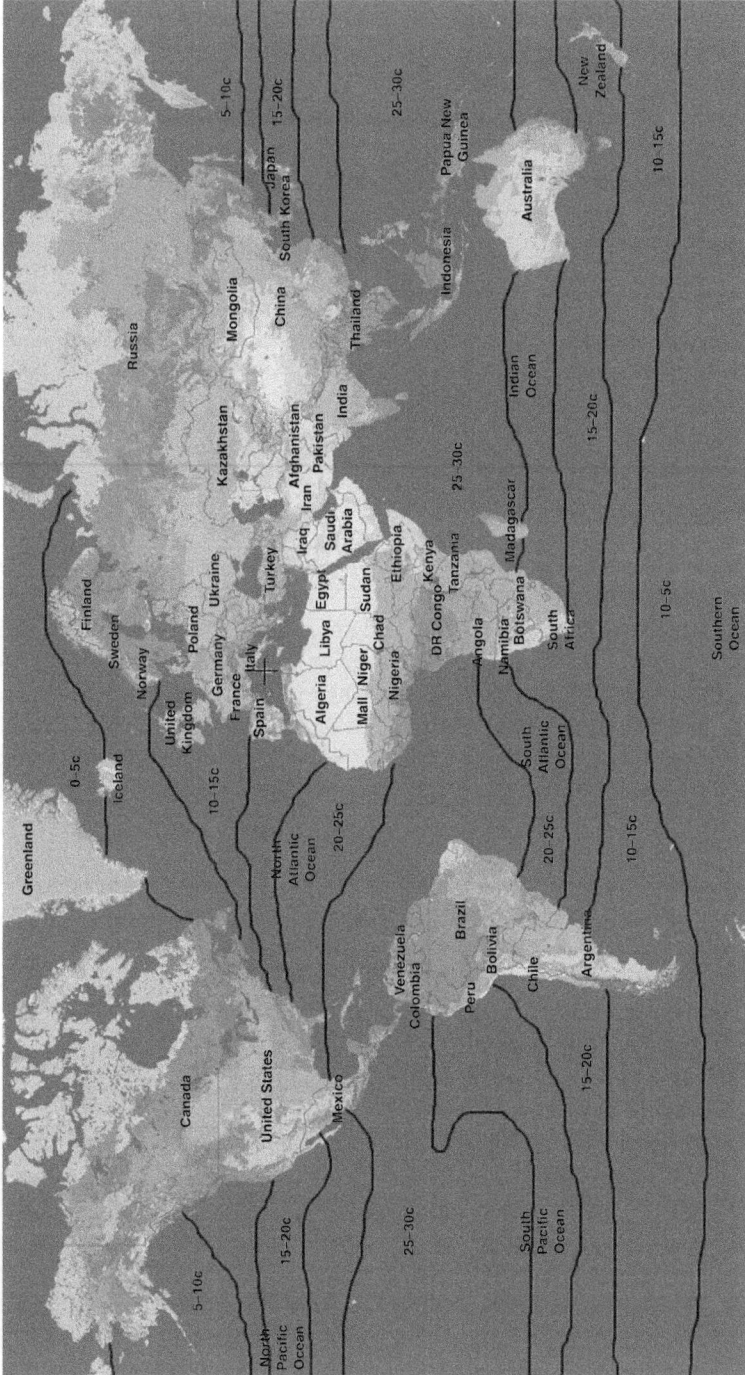

*Figure 3.1* World ocean coastlines and sea surface temperatures.

experiences to offer divers than do comparable areas with fewer bays, inlets and peninsulas. Indeed, all three of these regions, as will be shown below, are rich in the number of dive sites that they offer. These three regions, however, also tend to have larger populations living along their coasts and who are dependent on coastal resources. As such, their marine resources, including coral reefs, are among the most threatened on the planet (Burke *et al.* 2011).

### Warm water coral reefs and divers

As noted above, warm water coral reefs are the most popular destinations for scuba divers. Figure 3.2 shows the distribution of the world's warm water coral reef sites. The optimal temperature for tropical coral reefs is 26–27°C (79–81°F), though some, such as those in the Persian Gulf, have adapted to much lower winter temperatures (13°C; 55°F) (Wells and Hanna 1992). Most coral, however, is found in a band that extends between 30 degrees north and south latitude, which is somewhat larger than that of the tropics (between 23 degrees north and south latitude); it is rare in the eastern portions of the Atlantic and Pacific oceans due to the cooler waters found there. About 41 per cent of the coral reef area of the world is in the South Pacific (including Australia); an additional third is in Southeast Asia; and 7.6 per cent is in the Caribbean (Spalding *et al.* 2001).

In addition to their warm waters and colorful coral, warm water reefs are also attractive for divers because of their high diversity of fish and other sea life (Figure 3.3). Tropical corals are uniquely adapting to warm, sun soaked waters where temperatures decrease significantly at lower depths. Under these conditions, deeper water nutrients are not easily circulated to the surface to sustain fish populations. Coral, which is a small animal with a hard exoskeleton, becomes the primary nutrient source for fish and other animals of the higher food chain. As such, coral reefs are known as the 'rainforests of the oceans' because of their rich biodiversity (Mulhall 2007). Although they account for only 1 per cent of the entire ocean underwater land area, they support about 25 per cent of all known sea life, with many new species being discovered on a regular basis.

Both of these maps show that the greatest concentration of underwater reef and fish biodiversity is centered on insular Southeast Asia, especially in the 'Coral Triangle' area, which stretches from Luzon in the Philippines, Bali in Indonesia, and to the Solomon Islands on the east side of Papua New Guinea (Briggs 2005). Beyond Southeast Asia, adjacent areas of East Asia, Australia and the South Pacific, and large parts of the Indian Ocean, are also rich in coral and sea life. Other popular concentrations for diving include the Caribbean Sea region and the Red Sea between the Arabian Peninsula and Africa.

Corals reefs are among the most endangered ecosystems on the planet. Increasing ocean acidification is occurring as atmospheric carbon dioxide levels have increased from human industrial activities (CRA 2010). Acidification, along with increasing sea temperatures, is causing 'coral bleaching', which is the death of algae that live symbiotically with the coral and gives them nutrients and their

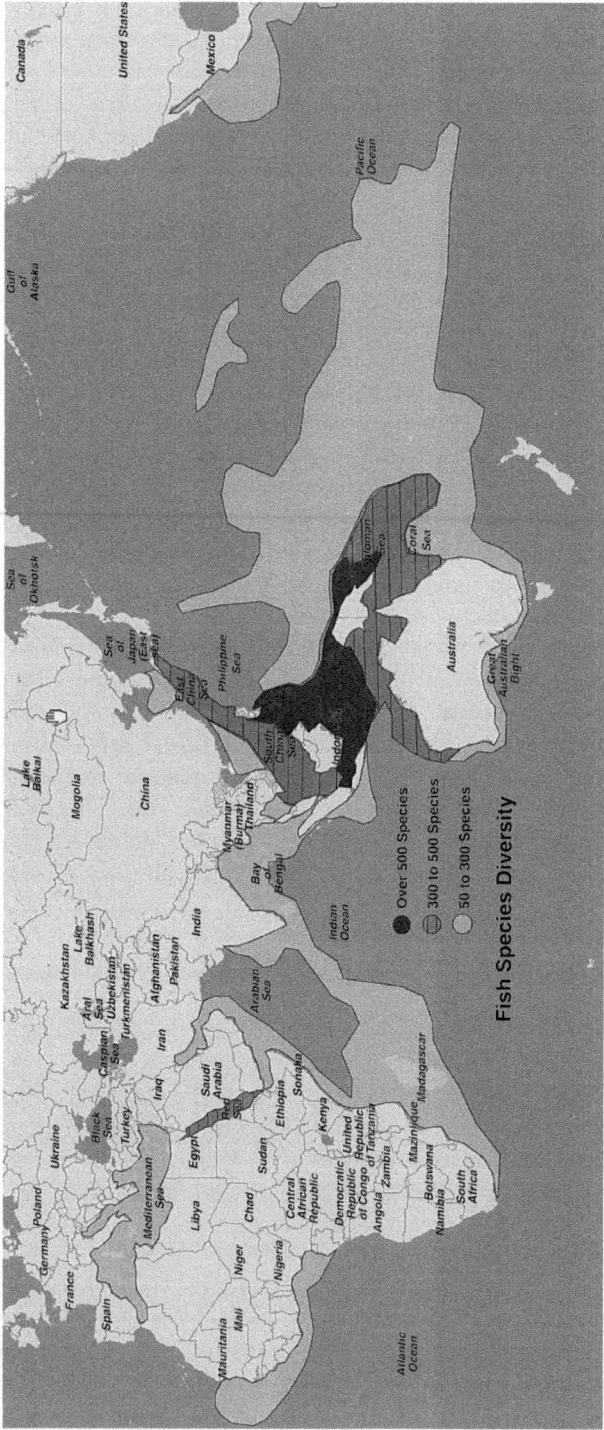

*Figure 3.2* Global distribution of coral reefs.

colorfulness. Most bleached coral dies, though some have recovered from a bleaching event.

The diversity of sea life in coral reefs also makes them popular local fishing grounds. With growing populations and increasing demands for seafood, these coral reefs have come under growing stress. Overfishing, blast fishing (using explosives to kill fish, and coral), and cyanide fishing (to stun and catch fish for the tropical fish trade) have resulted in significant decrease in the number of fish in many coral areas since the 1980s. This has been especially true for the large pelagic species. Coastal development that often results in water pollution and sediment runoff, as well as raw sewage, are also major threats to coral reefs in a growing number of island and coastal areas in the tropics.

Divers have also been accused of damaging coral reefs (Ong and Musa 2011). This can occur if a diver bumps the coral, stands on it, or possibly even touches it. In highly dived locations, especially those frequented by novice and uncertified divers, coral can show damage in this way. However, threats from divers are far smaller than those from fishing and land development activities. A single abandoned fishing net may destroy more coral than all of the divers that a dive resort receives over its lifetime.

Scuba dive shops, dive resorts and individual divers are increasingly becoming involved in environmental conservation programmes to address local reef quality issues. They will participate in cleanup dives to remove fishing nets and other accumulated litter from highly affected dive areas, and they will help with reef surveys to monitor environmental change in reef ecosystems (Richardson 2012). More responsible dive resorts in developing countries will also take extra efforts to hire local residents and source their foods and other supplies from local providers. In this way, they can help to educate local residents on the importance of the dive industry and, more importantly, the coral reefs and underwater life on which it is dependent. There is also evidence that dive services can have a significant impact by taking a proactive stance in educating and encouraging environmental responsibility by the divers they serve (Lück 2007; Ong and Musa 2011).

## Cold water diving

Cold water corals also exist, especially in northernmost Europe, around the Atlantic Ocean and near New Zealand, but these are mostly at depths below recreational diving (about 200 to 1000 meters, or 656 to 3280 feet, below sea level). But new discoveries are finding some even in less deep waters (as shallow as 40 meters, or 131 feet). With temperatures of 4 to 13°C (39 to 55°F), divers require dry suits to protect themselves from hypothermia. As with warm water coral, cold water coral areas are also threatened by destructive fishing practices and pollution from land and sea sources (Burke *et al.* 2011).

While most cold water corals are not in appropriate diving locations, almost all of the cooler coastal waters of the world do have high potential as specialty dive sites. The market for these sites is much smaller than for warm water destinations, but they still represent a significant segment of recreational diving. This is especially true for Europe and North America. Dive enthusiasts who live in colder climates can spend a lot on equipment and occasional colder water dives between their warm water diving holidays (Graefe and Todd 2001).

Cold water diving generally covers any type of diving that does not take place in warm waters (i.e. generally below 20°C, 68°F), and which may require some form of dry suit. A dry suit is designed to keep the diver's body dry and prevent hypothermia (which is caused by prolonged exposure to cold water). Sometimes the head, hands and feet are allowed to get wet, though the colder the water is, the less likely that any part of the body is exposed to water. Some dry suits look like a wetsuit, though many look more like military jet pilot or astronaut suits. Thicker suits help regulate body temperature better.

Some cold water destinations require divers to cut a hole in the ice to access the water below (known as 'ice diving') (Jackson 2012). A rope is used to find the hole at the end of the dive. Cold water diving is often much darker and murkier than warm water tropical dives, though they can also see unique and colorful forms of underwater life not found in warmer waters, including sea lions, harbor seals, and a variety of plants and fish (Hall 2011). Taking photos of them with large gloves covering one's hands, however, can be a challenge.

Not all cold water diving involves icy waters. However, when it does, it is considered a form of 'extreme scuba diving'. Antarctica is one of the newest extreme scuba diving destinations. The cold waters of the Antarctic are incredibly clear, with visibility up to 300 meters (1000 feet). Only a small amount of sunlight penetrates the ice above, but once their eyes adjust, divers 'describe the experience as flying over a darkened landscape of hills, valleys and sheer cliffs and if one were to look up a spectacular glowing blue cover with a moon like crater that is the ice and hole' (Noreen 2009).

### Other scuba diving environments

As important as water temperature is to the diving experience, the division of dive destinations into warm and cold water environments only touches the surface of the many different types of diving experiences that are possible. Salt water and freshwater diving is another major distinction, with salt water diving being far more popular than the often cooler freshwater destinations. Avid divers, however, will seek out underwater destinations in almost any possible environment. Other types of specialty diving experiences are presented in Table 3.1.

## Geographic distribution of the world's dive sites

A recreational dive destination, such as an inland lake or a coral atoll, typically consists of anywhere from two or three to a couple of dozen specific dive sites. A day of diving will usually include two to four dives, each of which is done at a different dive site. The selection of sites on any given day is determined by a dive guide based on the water and weather conditions on that day. Certified divers will also dive on their own, without a guide, though they still usually go to designated

*Table 3.1* Types of speciality diving experiences

*Night diving* – Night diving can reveal nocturnal underwater life that is hidden in the day time. It usually requires a strong underwater torch (flashlight), or two. Other than that, it does not require any other special equipment and in calm waters it can be undertaken by recently certified divers. A good guide is recommended, however, to keep one from getting lost.

*Cave diving* – Caves that are partially or fully filled with water are of interest to some recreational divers and cavers because so few people experience them. Cave diving, however, is a form of technical diving that requires advanced equipment, including special breathing systems (sometimes including two oxygen tanks that are strapped to the diver's stomach for visibility), a rope to help trace one's route to get out of the cave, torches for seeing and propulsion devices for when it is not possible to paddle one's feet (Exley 1981). A *rebreather* (which processes exhaled air so part of it can be used a second time) and a dry suit may also be necessary. As with ice diving, the diver cannot swim to the surface in an emergency, but must retrace their path to where they entered before surfacing.

*Wreck diving* – Wrecks (including both shipwrecks and plane wrecks) at the bottom of the seas are often teaming with underwater life, which makes them of interest both visually and historically to divers. Warmer water wrecks tend to have more coral life, though the boats deteriorate faster, while colder water wrecks have fewer fish, but are in better historical condition. Wrecks comprise some of the world's more popular dive sites, especially those that are in shallower waters. Most wrecks, however, are in deeper waters and recommended only for more experienced and advanced divers.

*High altitude diving* – This is any diving that takes place in a body of water that is 300 meters (984 feet) or higher above sea level. The activity is an extreme form of diving because it involves higher physical risk to the diver, with a greater chance of experiencing decompression sickness (also known as *the bends*) (Wienke 1994). High altitude diving usually takes place in alpine lakes and gives divers an opportunity to see underwater life that is seldom encountered at lower elevations.

*Shark or predator diving* – Diving with sharks and other large predator pelagic fish has become popular in recent years because of the adrenaline experience they provide. As with ice, caves and high altitude lakes, shark diving is a form of extreme activity. Large predator fish include tiger sharks, great white sharks (usually with the diver protected by a cage), orcas, belugas, striped marlin, sailfish and leopard seals (DAT 2012). Less threatening, though still large, are dive experiences with humpback whales, manta rays and whale sharks.

*Liveaboard diving* – A 'liveaboard' is a boat on which divers stay for one or more nights while traveling from one dive site to another. It does not require additional special equipment and allows divers to visit more and possibly a greater variety of dive sites. Liveaboards are a common option in the more popular dive regions of the world.

*Muck diving* – Muck diving is diving in mostly gravel and mud areas with little or no coral reef or rocky outcrops. In the Coral Triangle region, muck diving sites have a wide diversity of colorful life that is often quite different from coral environments. They tend to be very small, however, and are best observed with the assistance of a skilled guide.

*Free diving, snuba and Scuba-doo* – Free diving is a form of skin diving (which includes snorkeling) but involves breathing techniques that allow divers to stay underwater for long periods of time without air. These techniques have medical implications, and so training is required. Snuba is similar to scuba diving, except that the air source is on a small raft at the water's surface, instead of in a tank on the diver. It is often used for introductory dive experiences in calm water areas. Scuba-doo is a commercial brand for an underwater submersible device that includes an oxygen tank, a hood that keeps a seated user's head dry and without a mask or mouthpiece, and a propulsion source. It enables non-certified divers to experience calm water locations with a guide.

dive sites as these have been identified for having the greatest potential for inter-esting sightings.

Divetime.com is a website that contains a large list of dive sites and allows users to enter and review additional recreational dive sites from around the world (Divetime 2012). As of March 2012, Divetime.com contained over 13,000 dive sites, some of which were user entered, though most appear to have been provided from published sources. No matter the source, any listing of dive sites is subjec-tive because a 'dive site' is, in practice, any site that is of interest to divers. It is subjective also because diving destinations that are more popular will naturally have more designated dive sites than places that are less popular, mostly to meet higher demand. A third issue with the Divetime.com database is that it is poten-tially biased toward the opinions and knowledge of the website's users, who are mostly likely European or US based divers who have a good command of English and have Internet access.

The resulting regional distribution of Divetime.com's recreational dive sites (Table 3.2) shows a considerable over-representation of sites located in Europe (mostly western Europe), North America (the US and Canada), and Australia and New Zealand. Together, these three regions comprise 46 per cent of all the dive sites in the database. Despite its limitations, however, this source provides one of the better publically available listings of recreational dive sites and largely reflects the general knowledge and market orientation of the global recreational dive industry today.

*Table 3.2* Global distribution of recreational dive sites in the Divetime.com database

| Region | Number | % |
|---|---|---|
| Europe | 2583 | 19.6 |
| North America | 2176 | 16.5 |
| Asia | 1814 | 13.8 |
| Middle East and Africa | 1729 | 13.1 |
| Caribbean | 1394 | 10.6 |
| Australia and New Zealand | 1278 | 9.7 |
| South Pacific | 1113 | 8.4 |
| Middle and South America | 1094 | 8.3 |
| Antarctica | 0 | 0.0 |
| Total | 13,181 | |

Source: Divetime.com (2012)
Notes:
– Europe includes Russia
– North America is the US (including Hawaii) and Canada
– Asia includes East Asia, Southeast Asia and South Asia
– Asia excludes Southwest Asia (the Middle East)
– Middle America includes Mexico and Central America
– The South Pacific excludes Hawaii
– The Divetime.com website shows a total of 13,181 dive sites

On a positive side, the bias in the Divetime.com database points to the enormous potential that still exists in other parts of the world for the identification and development of new dive destinations. Almost every country in Europe and 46 US states, for example, have at least one recreational dive site. On the other hand, China, which had only two dive sites listed (excluding Hong Kong and Taiwan), has an enormous potential for future growth as a dive tourism region, given its enormous coastline and mostly warm to temperate waters. China is a rapidly emerging market for scuba diving certifications, which has become a status symbol for the country's upwardly mobile middle class.

Not all dive sites are the same. Just because Europe and North America are at the top of the list in total designated dive sites, does not necessarily mean that they are considered major recreational diving destinations. As mentioned above, tropical destinations tend to be the most popular, drawing dive tourists from around the world. The colder waters of Europe make it more of a local or domestic dive experience that give divers a chance to 'get wet', although there are also interesting underwater experiences to be had.

Table 3.3 summarizes the distribution of the Divetime.com dive sites around the world based on general water temperatures. Water types include (1) warm waters (roughly 25°C, or 77°F, and above), (2) temperate waters that are colder in winter and warmer in summer, and (3) cold waters (generally 15°C, or 59°F, and below). The division of dive sites into warm, temperate and cold water environments somewhat dilutes the regional bias in the data, as most of the over-represented sites are located in temperate and cold waters. Europe, for example, is not on the list of tropical water sites at all, while it dominates the list of cold water dive sites. Because of its great climatic range and number of dive sites, the US is divided into warm, temperate and cold water sites based on individual states listed on Divetime.com. Hawaii and Florida comprise the warm water states in the US and together have 43 per cent of the country's 2,176 dive sites. Among the temperate water dive sites in the US, 47 per cent are in the state of California. Australia and New Zealand are similarly divided regional into warm, temperate and cold water parts.

Overall, warm water dive sites, most of which are within the tropics, clearly predominate (59 per cent of Table 3.3 dive sites). These are mostly found in Florida and Hawaii in the US, northern Australia, insular Southeast Asia, the islands of the South Pacific, the Caribbean basin and the Red Sea. Potential emerging areas for warm water scuba diving development include Africa, from its southern to eastern coasts, and East Asia, from Vietnam to southern China.

In more temperate waters, where scuba diving is more likely in the summer season than other times of year, identified dive sites are primarily in southern and central Europe, followed by the US and Australia. South America and East Asia are potential regions for new temperate water diving opportunities. In general, temperate water diving is most popular in the home regions of certified divers. So if a temperate country has a larger number of certified divers, then a larger number of dive sites will be found and developed to meet domestic demand. This is the main reason for the large number of designated dive sites in the US and Europe.

Table 3.3 Number of reported dive sites worldwide by water temperature, on Divetime.com

| | | | |
|---|---|---|---|
| **Warm waters** | 623 | Cuba | 28 |
| United States: Florida | | Puerto Rico | 26 |
| Australia: tropical states | 506 | St Vincent and the | 25 |
| Philippines | 483 | Grenadines | |
| Egypt | 418 | India | 24 |
| Indonesia | 343 | La Reunion | 24 |
| Fiji | 314 | Madagascar | 23 |
| United States: Hawaii | 311 | Sint Maarten | 23 |
| Cayman Islands | 265 | Colombia | 22 |
| Honduras | 232 | Norfolk Island | 22 |
| Thailand | 232 | Venezuela | 22 |
| Malaysia | 231 | Antigua and Barbuda | 21 |
| Bahamas | 225 | Sudan | 21 |
| French Polynesia | 175 | Jamaica | 20 |
| Mexico: tropical | 173 | Martinique | 20 |
| Maldives | 170 | Saba | 20 |
| Papua New Guinea | 170 | Trinidad and Tobago | 19 |
| Micronesia | 148 | Cape Verde | 18 |
| Malawi | 141 | Comoros | 18 |
| Virgin Islands | 139 | Tonga | 17 |
| Belize | 117 | Anguilla | 16 |
| Mozambique | 117 | Eritrea | 15 |
| Sri Lanka | 110 | Saint Lucia | 15 |
| Bonaire | 96 | Other tropical Asia | 15 |
| Brazil | 94 | Guadeloupe | 14 |
| Seychelles | 90 | Nevis and St Kitts | 14 |
| Panama | 87 | Samoa | 14 |
| Mauritius | 78 | Singapore | 14 |
| Costa Rica | 72 | Myanmar | 13 |
| Dominica | 71 | Nicaragua | 12 |
| Tanzania | 68 | Yemen | 10 |
| Vanuatu | 68 | Other warm Africa | 10 |
| Vietnam | 67 | Other warm M+S | 10 |
| The Solomon Islands | 63 | America | |
| Ecuador | 57 | Other warm South Pacific | 5 |
| The Cook Islands | 52 | Total tropical water dive | 7729 (58.6%) |
| Barbados | 49 | sites | |
| Curacao | 49 | | |
| Aruba | 44 | **Temperate waters** | |
| Bermuda | 43 | United States: temperate | 625 |
| East Timor | 40 | states | |
| Dominican Republic | 39 | Australia: temperate | 466 |
| Turks and Caicos | 38 | states | |
| Kenya | 36 | France | 354 |
| Palau | 36 | South Africa | 325 |
| Sint Eustatius | 36 | Spain | 190 |
| Grenada | 33 | Cyprus | 152 |
| New Caledonia | 31 | New Zealand: North | 152 |
| Saudi Arabia | 30 | Island | |
| Oman | 29 | Greece | 124 |
| | | Mexico: temperate | 120 |

| | | Cold waters | |
|---|---|---|---|
| Turkey | 114 | *Cold waters* | |
| Denmark | 111 | United States: cold states | 366 |
| Italy | 105 | Ireland | 273 |
| Croatia | 87 | Norway | 260 |
| Germany | 76 | Canada | 251 |
| Malta | 51 | Netherlands | 199 |
| Portugal | 45 | United Kingdom | 193 |
| Israel | 41 | New Zealand: South | 152 |
| Argentina | 40 | Island | |
| Other temperate | 39 | Scotland | 131 |
| Europe | | Finland | 53 |
| Tunisia | 35 | Poland | 22 |
| Jordan | 31 | Belgium | 20 |
| Chile | 30 | Faroe Islands | 15 |
| Japan | 27 | Sweden | 13 |
| Gibraltar | 26 | Switzerland | 13 |
| Other temperate Middle | 22 | Estonia | 12 |
| East | | Russia | 11 |
| Taiwan | 18 | Other cold | 10 |
| Other temperate Asia | 14 | Europe | |
| United Arab Emirates | 13 | Other cold | 4 |
| Hong Kong | 10 | Asia | |
| Other temperate M+S | 6 | Other cold M+S | 2 |
| America | | America | |
| Other temperate Africa | 4 | TOTAL cold water | 1999 (15.2%) |
| Total temperate water | 3453 (26.2%) | dive sites | |
| dive sites | | **Total** | **13,181** |

Source: Divetime.com (2012)

Cold water diving sites are mostly in northern Europe, followed by the US, Canada and New Zealand's South Island. As with temperate water dive sites, their predominance in these areas is a reflection of the larger number of divers in Europe and North America, although even here cold water diving is a highly niche activity. The southern cone of South America, Northeast Asia and Antarctica are potential new areas for cold water diving, though the smaller coastlines and difficult accessibility to these areas will likely limit significant expansion.

## The top dive destinations

The dominance of Europe, North America and Australia in Tables 3.2 and 3.3 most likely reflects the large proportion of divers living in those regions. Despite the growing numbers of domestic divers in the global south, the overall pattern remains one of divers from the developed upper latitudes (north and south) traveling to the warmer destinations. The dive sites listed in Tables 3.2 and 3.3 comprise selected locations from among the vast underwater terrain of ocean coastlines, shallows areas, and inland lakes. Although there is some correlation, we cannot infer that countries with more dive sites have more people diving at them. While some warm water destinations can have a dozen or more visitors to a specific dive site on a busy day, most cold and temperate water destinations are considered busy if they have that many recreational divers in a month.

In addition to listing the numbers of identified dive sites in a country or destination, another way to assess the geographic distribution of recreational diving is to look at the popularity of dive sites. Dive enthusiast magazines and websites and travel magazines and websites often list the 'best' scuba dive sites in the world. These are compiled by editorial boards or professional writers who have a good exposure to the wider range of global diving destinations. As such, they might be considered as 'expert' recommendations. While such listings are still biased toward the readership of the websites and magazines that publish them, there is at least an effort toward a degree of objectivity, if only to maintain legitimacy among the reading public.

Most of these sources list the top ten dive sites in the world, though a few list fewer than ten, and others list up to 100 sites. Some list the top ten sites overall, but then include separate tables for the top 10 sites in terms of visibility (how clear the water is), variety of sea life, and environmental conservation efforts (cf. cyber-diver.com). Some sites list their top 10 in rank order, others give each an overall score, and others just list them without any ranking.

The publishers also tend to mix geographic scales, with countries, dive destinations and specific dive sites within a destination all in the same list. They also mix a considerable variety of different kinds of sites, each of which may have strengths that other do not have. Dive sites, for example, may be outstanding in one or more of the following characteristics:

- diversity and type of underwater life, with greater diversity and more rare species being most desired;
- topography, with a diversity of cliffs, walls, rocks and other drop offs being desired by more advanced divers;
- historical or cultural significance of underwater features, such as wrecks;
- water quality, as measured by clarity or underwater visibility distance;
- temperature, with comfort being desired by most divers;
- currents, which can be desired if gentle, but dangerous if strong.

With an awareness of these considerations, Table 3.4 presents a compilation of 15 listings of the top ten dive destinations in the world. The listings were all found online and were judged to have been based on some effort at objectivity. One site (scuba travel 2012b) was based on user votes for the best dives sites. There was also an effort to obtain some variability, with one listing based on dive site visibility and one based on the diversity of sea life. The others, however, were general best dive site listings. Sites (and countries) that were listed only once in the 15 sources were excluded from Table 3.3. Different geographic scales are shown, as sometimes an individual dive site was listed, sometimes a destination (with many sites) was listed, and at other times only the country was listed. In addition, these mixed geographic scales would sometimes appear on the same list. For Table 3.3, the country was the basis for comparison.

*Table 3.4* Compilation of 'Top Ten Dive Destinations in the World' lists

| Country | Region | Listed | Dive destinations |
|---|---|---|---|
| Australia | S Pacific | 10 | Great Barrier Reef, Heron Island |
| Indonesia | SE Asia | 10 | Sulawesi, Raja Ampat |
| Mexico | M America | 10 | Baja California, Riviera Maya and Cozumel |
| Thailand | SE Asia | 10 | Koh Tao Island, Phuket Island |
| Malaysia | SE Asia | 9 | Sipadan Island, Mabul Island |
| Egypt (south) | Africa/M East | 9 | Ras Mohammed Nat. Park, Red Sea |
| Belize | M America | 8 | Barrier Reef Reserve, Great Blue Hole |
| Fiji | S Pacific | 7 | |
| Ecuador | S America | 6 | Galapagos Islands |
| US – Hawaii | S Pacific | 5 | Kona Coast |
| Maldives | Indian Ocean | 5 | |
| Micronesia, F.S | S Pacific | 5 | Chuuk (Truk) Lagoon |
| Bonaire | Caribbean | 4 | |
| Cayman Islands | Caribbean | 4 | Grand Cayman Island |
| Costa Rica | M America | 4 | Cocos Island |
| Palau | S Pacific | 4 | |
| Turks and Caicos | Caribbean | 4 | Grand Turk Island |
| Cuba | Caribbean | 3 | |
| Papua New Guinea | S Pacific | 3 | |
| South Africa | Africa/M East | 3 | |
| US (excl Hawaii) | N America | 3 | |
| Canada | N America | 2 | |
| Honduras | Caribbean | 2 | |
| Marshall Islands | S Pacific | 2 | Bikini Atoll |
| Mozambique | Indian Ocean | 2 | Bazaruto Archipelago |
| Philippines | SE Asia | 2 | |
| Solomon Islands | S Pacific | 2 | |

Sources: Scubaguide 2012; DTW 2012; Cyberdiver 2012; Regenhold 2009; Basinski 2008; Noreen 2011; Marks 2005; Hillman 2012; Travelocafe 2010; TakePart 2012; Scuba Travel 2012b; Cimarosti 2011; Cheapflights 2011

Notes:
- Compiled from 15 online listings of the top ten dive sites in the world. Countries and sites that were only mentioned on one list were excluded.
- Countries and dive sites listed on only one of the 15 lists were excluded.
- No dive sites in Europe and East Asia appeared on any of the 15 lists, although Lake Baikal in eastern Russia was on one list.
- Region explanations: 'C Pacific' = Central Pacific Ocean; 'SE Asia' = Southeast Asia; Australia is listed as 'S Pacific' here because its most popular dive sites border the South Pacific realm; South Africa is in the 'Indian Ocean' because most of its dive sites are on the country's southeast coast.

Insular Southeast Asia, Australia's Great Barrier Reef, Mexico and Egypt's Red Sea were the most cited dive destinations among the 15 top ten lists included in Table 3.4. Notably, no single country appeared on more than 10 of the lists, reflecting the considerable variability in opinion of just what constitutes the best dive sites in the world. In addition no European country appears on this list at all, and the only temperate dive sites listed were in Canada and the US.

Based on their lower sea life diversity, the Caribbean and Middle America destinations, most notably Mexico, may be ranked a little higher on this list than they should be, due to their proximity to the North American market. Similarly, the islands of the South Pacific may be ranked a little lower overall due to their geographic remoteness from the major markets of North America and Europe. This is because fewer certified divers would be personally familiar with these dive sites.

From a recreational diver perspective, the list represents the general perception of what are the considered the top dive destinations in the world. This is reflected on scuba diving websites, which Table 3.4 largely represents, but also in dive industry print magazines, with which some of the websites are associated. If one were to open a dive enthusiast magazine, the countries and sites listed here would dominate the stories and advertisements, although occasionally there will also be some other, more exotic or obscure, destinations.

An alternative approach to identifying the top dive sites of the world is to have divers vote on them. This approach can be problematic because it is even more biased by the idiosyncrasies of website users than is the simple posting of dive sites. A North American user base, for example, is mostly exposed to Caribbean island destinations, Mexico and Hawaii. Another issue is that experiences of any one dive site can vary enormously from one day to the next based on water and weather conditions. Cloudy weather makes for less colorful coral and sea life. Therefore, two people voting on the same site may have had very different experiences.

One limitation with the compilation of the top 10 dive site lists is that they are limited to only ten sites. With these caveats in mind, the results of dive site voting on scubatravel.co.uk (Scuba Travel 2012a) were consulted as one of two major sources for compiling the top 50 dive sites in the world (Table 3.5). This is one of the more comprehensive online voting systems for dive sites, listing the top 100 vote-getting sites. The scubatravel.co.uk listing was combined with a 2012 ranking of the top 50 dive sites by CNNGo.com (Brenmer 2012). To compile their ranking, CNNGo consulted with dive industry professionals associated with four major diving enthusiast websites. Rankings for the top 50 sites on the nonprofessional voters list were averaged with those on the professionals' list to compile Table 3.5. Fourteen sites were only listed on one of the two tables. Mean rankings for 14 dive sites that were only listed on one of these two sources were averaged with the number 75, which is derived from being halfway between 50 and 100, making it comparable with the scubatravel.co.uk's full listing of 100 sites.

Table 3.5 differs from Table 3.4 in that it is based solely on specific dive sites. Thus, some destinations, like the small island of Sipadan in Sabah, Malaysia, is listed twice because two of its dive sites made the list. To help make the resulting list more comprehensible, the dive sites have been sorted by major global regions, which are then sorted by the top ranked sites listed in each region.

The results in Table 3.5 are very different from those in Tables 3.2 and 3.3, and even to some degree from Table 3.4. This reflects that fact that, while temperate dive destinations are plentiful, they do not attract the large numbers of

*Table 3.5* Top 50 dive sites in the world, by rank and region

| Rank | Dive site | Country |
| --- | --- | --- |
| **South Pacific** | | |
| 1 | Yongala Wreck | Australia |
| 3 | Blue Corner Wall | Palau |
| 8 | Navy Pier, Western Australia | Australia |
| 10 | Manta Ray Night Dive, Kona, Hawaii | US |
| 15 | North Horn, Osprey Reef, Coral Sea | Australia |
| 15 | Tiputa Pass, Rangiroa | French Polynesia |
| 19 | President Coolidge | Vanuatu |
| 20 | Middle Arch, Poor Knights Islands | New Zealand |
| 24 | Great White Wall, Tavieuni | Fiji |
| 24 | Ulong Channel | Palau |
| 27 | Cod Hole, Great Barrier Reef | Australia |
| 37 | Grand Central Station, Gizo | Solomon Islands |
| 39 | Perpendicular Wall, Christmas Island | Australia |
| 49 | Cocklebiddy Cave | Australia |
| 49 | Fish Rock, South West Rocks, NSW | Australia |
| 55 | Yonaguni Jima, Yaeyama Islands, Okinawa | Japan |
| 61 | Molokini Crater Wall, Maui, Hawaii | US |
| **Southeast Asia** | | |
| 1 | Barracuda Point, Sipadan | Malaysia |
| 5 | Richelieu Rock | Thailand |
| 11 | Tubbataha, Palawan | Philippines |
| 13 | Liberty Wreck, Bali | Indonesia |
| 27 | Elephant Head Rock, Similan Islands | Thailand |
| 29 | Raja Ampat, West Papua | Indonesia |
| 31 | The Canyons, Puerto Galera | Philippines |
| 42 | South Point, Sipadan | Malaysia |
| 47 | Banua Wuhu, Mahengetang | Indonesia |
| 49 | The Point, Layang Layang | Malaysia |
| 56 | Bunaken, Manado, Sulawesi | Indonesia |
| 57 | Castle Rock, Komodo | Indonesia |
| 57 | Cannibal Rock, Komodo | Indonesia |
| 61 | Drop Off, Verde Island | Philippines |
| 63 | Batu Bolong, Flores | Indonesia |
| 63 | Japanese Gardens, Koh Tao | Thailand |
| **Middle East, Africa and the Indian Ocean** | | |
| 4 | Thistlegorm, Red Sea | Egypt |
| 7 | Big Brother, Red Sea | Egypt |
| 8 | Shark and Yolanda Reef, Red Sea | Egypt |
| 13 | Elphinstone Reef, Red Sea | Egypt |
| 15 | Antons, Sodwana Bay | South Africa |
| 21 | Sha'ab Rumi South | Sudan |
| 23 | Manta Reef, Tofo | Mozambique |
| 30 | Aliwal Shoal, Umkomaas | South Africa |
| 32 | Maaya Thila | Maldives |
| 33 | Jackson Reef, Straits of Tiran | Egypt |
| 35 | Aquarium, Mnemba Island | Tanzania |

(*continue overleaf*)

*Table 3.5* Continued

| Rank | Dive site | Country |
|---|---|---|
| 35 | Ras Mohammed, Red Sea | Egypt |
| 40 | Blue Hole, Dahab, Red Sea | Egypt |
| 44 | The Cathedral, Flic-en-Flac | Mauritius |
| 44 | South Ari Atoll | Maldives |
| 49 | Straits of Tiran, Red Sea | Egypt |
| 59 | Daedelus, Red Sea | Egypt |
| ***Caribbean, Middle America and South America*** | | |
| 5 | Great Blue Hole | Belize |
| 12 | Gordon's Rock, Galapagos | Ecuador |
| 18 | Bloody Bay Wall, Little Cayman | Cayman Islands |
| 21 | Dos Ojos (Los Cenotes), Playa del Carmen | Mexico |
| 26 | Darwin Arch, Galapagos | Ecuador |
| 33 | Scotts Head Pinnacle | Dominica |
| 41 | Bajo Alcyone, Cocos Island | Costa Rica |
| 42 | Darwin Island, Galapagos | Ecuador |
| 44 | Wolf Island, Galapagos | Ecuador |
| 47 | Manchones Reef, Cancun | Mexico |
| 49 | La Dania's Leap to Karpata | Bonaire |
| ***Europe*** | | |
| 37 | Silfra, Thingvellir | Iceland |
| 49 | Blue Hole, Gozo | Malta |
| 60 | The Zenobia | Cyprus |
| 65 | Buroo Ned, Isle of Man | UK |

Notes:
- Each dive site listed above was in the top 50 of either scubatravel.co.uk (ranking of 100 sites based on reader votes) (Scuba Travel 2012a) or CNNGo.com (ranking of 50 sites based on consultation with dive industry professionals) (Bremner 2012).
- Rankings in this table are based on mean of these two sources.
- Rankings for dive sites listed on only one of the two sources (14 sites) were averaged with a second rank of 75 (half way between 50 and 100).
- Fractional differences were rounded to full numbers.
- Ties were given the same rank, resulting in rank duplications.

recreational divers that tropical destinations attract. For this reason, the South Pacific and Southeast Asia are clearly the most important dive destinations in terms of having the best dive sites in the world, at least as of 2012. Australia tends to dominate the South Pacific region, mostly due to its size. The Yongala Wreck in the Great Barrier Reef is one of the two top ranked dive sites in the world. The *SS Yongala* was a passenger steamer that sank near Townsville, Queensland, in a cyclone in 1911 with 122 people on board (MMT 2008). While the Great Barrier Reef is a major dive destination, Australia's other top dive sites are located on its southern and western coasts, as well as one (Christmas Island) which is clearly more of an Indian Ocean destination.

Southeast Asia, which is where the core of the Coral Triangle is located, has top dive sites sprinkled across most of its insular countries. Malaysia's Sipadan (which had the other top ranked dive site in Barracuda Point) and Tubbataha Reef in the Philippines are both Coral Triangle destinations. Thailand's top sites, on the other hand, are on its Indian Ocean side. Africa, the Middle East and the Indian Ocean (which are often combined as a single region from a diving perspective) are dominated, by far, by Egypt's Red Sea. Seven of the top 20 sites voted upon at scubatravel.co.uk were in this region, probably reflecting a UK bias among the readers and voters on that site. The Red Sea is the closest warm water diving area for people who live in the UK. For the most part, these results support the expert recommendations in Table 3.4. Several African dive sites may be an indication of potential growth in scuba diving along the Indian Ocean coast of that continent.

The Caribbean, Middle America and South America form the fourth major dive region of the world. The top dive sites in this region are shared among the Caribbean Sea destinations and a cluster of major dive sites in the Galapagos in the Pacific Ocean. Europe has four sites, including cold water dive sites in Iceland and the UK, though they rank fairly low on the list. There are no temperate destinations in North America, Asia or South America that ranked in the top 50 dive destinations on either of sources used to compile Table 3.5. The inclusion of temperate European sites and the exclusion of those from any other part of the world most likely reflect a UK bias among the voters of scubatravel.co.uk. Recognizing that every dive listing source is biased in some manner, the 50 dive sites listed in Table 3.5 gives a broader range and understanding of dive sites and destinations than simply looking at the top ten recommendations (Table 3.4) or at a listing of all dive sites by country and region (Tables 3.2 and 3.3).

## Summary and conclusions

An overall summary of recreational diving destinations today can be approximated by combining the results of the three dive sites and destination datasets examined above, and discounting the clear North American and European biases of Tables 3.2 and 3.3, the possible North American bias of Table 3.4, and the possible UK bias of Table 3.5. The results show:

1   The Coral Triangle region of insular Southeast Asia is the world's leading recreational dive destination region that combines accessibility (numbers of divers) and imageability (known for outstanding dives). This region is primarily centered on Indonesia and Malaysia, with Thailand as a secondary destination and the Philippines as an emerging dive destination. The region benefits from a strong western European dive market (Europe is closer to Southeast Asia than is North America), a strong Australian dive market, and a rapidly growing domestic Southeast Asian dive market. Unfortunately, large areas of Southeast Asia's coral reefs are also endangered due to over overfishing, pollution and development, and global warming (Burke *et al.* 2011).

2   Australia's Great Barrier Reef, the South Pacific (including Hawaii), the Red Sea and the Indian Ocean are also major global dive destinations, with highly

rated dive sites. However, they appear to serve somewhat more limited or narrow markets due to their accessibility and relatively smaller base of total dive sites. The South Pacific and the Great Barrier Reef are geographically remote from both Europe and North America. The Indian Ocean and the Red Sea are far-off destinations for most North Americans. All of these sites could, however, benefit from growth in the number of recreation dive enthusiasts in emerging countries of Asia. The remote coral islands of the Pacific and Indian Ocean are threatened by rising sea levels, while coral reefs along the African coast suffer from overfishing and pollution.

3    The Caribbean and Middle America are also major dive regions, although their top sites are not as well ranked internationally. Florida could also be included in this region. The countries in these regions benefit enormously from their close proximity to a large population of North American divers, for whom the Caribbean and Middle America are the most warm water economical dive destinations. Europe and an emerging South America serve as secondary markets for these regions. The coral reefs in the Caribbean suffer from major human impacts and coral bleaching from rising water temperatures.

4    Europe, most of the US (excluding Hawaii and Florida), and southern Australia and New Zealand comprise the major temperate and cold water dive regions of the world. They all benefit from large domestic diver markets, many of whom are not able to escape to warmer climates on a regular basis. They are generally not considered international dive destinations, though certified recreational divers may dive in their cooler waters on an occasional or regular basis. Some of their colder water areas offer challenging opportunities to see unique underwater life forms. Because these are in the more developed regions of the world, these dive sites tend to be better protected than those in more tropical regions. Temperate and cold climate regions elsewhere in the world, such as East Asia and South America, could potentially develop similar domestic dive activities.

5    Sub-Saharan Africa, especially on its Indian Ocean side, and the Arabian Peninsula are the two regions that may have the greatest potential for future grown as international dive destinations. South Africa, being the most developed country in Sub-Saharan Africa, is currently that region's leading dive destination. As other countries develop, and as political and military hostilities become settled, it is likely that Africa and the Middle East will see significant growth in their numbers of domestic and international divers, their number of dive sites, and the international renown of their diving destinations. Efforts should be taken now to better protect these reefs as a future economic resource.

Some significant patterns that emerge from the world geography of international dive tourism are that (1) there is a clear distinction between warm and cold water recreational scuba experiences and expectations on the part of divers; (2) only a very small part of the world's underwater resources have become recreational scuba destinations; and (3) most recreational scuba dive destinations are under threat from overfishing and the mismanagement of ocean resources. These patterns have significant implications for product development (finding and expanding new dive resources) and marketing (growing the population of dive tourists), as well as resource management, which includes the conservation of species diversity in an era of sea level change and warming, and ocean education for both destination residents and tourists.

## References

Arin, T. and Kramer, R. A. (2002) 'Divers' Willingness to Pay to Visit Marine Sanctuaries: An Exploratory Study', *Ocean and Coast Management*, 45:171–183.

Basinski, B. (2008) 'Top 10 Dive Destinations', *Matador Network*. Online. Available HTTP: <http://matadornetwork.com/trips/top-10-dive-destinations/> (accessed 15 March 2012).

Berton, J. (2007) 'Continent-size Toxic Stew of Plastic Trash Fouling Swath of Pacific Ocean', *The San Francisco Chronicle*, 19 October. Online. Available HTTP: <http://www.sfgate.com/cgi-bin/article.cgi?f=/c/a/2007/10/19/SS6JS8RH0.DTL> (accessed 6 April 2012).

Bremner, J. (2012) 'Into the Deep: World's 50 Best Dive Sites', *CNNGo*, 6 April. Online. Available HTTP: <http://www.cnngo.com/explorations/escape/outdoor-adventures/worlds-50-best-dive-sites-895793> (accessed 28 May 2012).

Briggs, J. C. (2005) 'The Marine East Indies: Diversity and Speciation', *Journal of Biogeography*, 32:1517–1522.

Burke, L., Reytar, K., Spalding, M. and Perry, A. (2011) 'Reefs at Risk Revisited', Washington, DC: World Resources Institute. Online. Available HTTP: <http://www.wri.org/publication/reefs-at-risk-revisited> (accessed 30 March 2012).

Cheapflights (2011) 'Top 10 Dive Sites, Cheapflights.co.uk', December. Online. Available HTTP: <http://www.cheapflights.co.uk/travel-tips/top-ten-dive-sites/> (accessed 15 March 2012).

Choi, C. (2011) 'Little Fish Exploding in Number, Models Show', *National Geographic News*. Online. Available HTTP: <http://news.nationalgeographic.com/news/2011/02/110225-little-fish-oceans-environment-fishing> (accessed 6 April 2012).

Cimarosti, G. (2011) 'A Look at the Top Scuba Diving Destinations for 2012', *Travel Reportage*, December. Online. Available HTTP: <http://blog.travelreportage.com/2011/12/11/a-look-at-the-top-scuba-diving-destinations-for-2012/> (accessed 15 March 2012).

CRA (2010) 'Threats to Coral Reefs Coral, Reef Alliance'. Online. Available HTTP: <http://www.coral.org/resources/about_coral_reefs/threats_to_coral_reefs> (accessed 5 April 2012).

Cyberdiver (2012) 'Scuba Diving Best Choice', *Cyber Diver*. Online. Available HTTP: <http://www.cyber-diver.com/best.html> (accessed 15 March 2012).

DAT (2012) 'Extreme Diving', *Dive Advice Travel*. Online. Available HTTP: <http://diveadvice.com/Extreme_Diving_Expeditions.html> (accessed 6 April 2012).

Davison, B. (2007) 'How Many Divers Are There?', *Undercurrents* 22(5). Online. Available HTTP: <http://www.undercurrent.org/UCnow/dive_magazine/2007/HowManyDivers200705.html> (accessed 30 March 2012) (paid subscriptions site).

Davison, B. (2012) 'The "Discover SCUBA Diving" Programs', *Undercurrents* 27(3). Online. Available HTTP: <http://www.undercurrent.org/UCnow/dive_magazine/2012/

DiscoverSCUBADiving201203.html> (accessed 30 March 2012) (paid subscriptions site).

Divetime.com (2012) 'Scuba Diving Sites', *Divetime*. Online. Available HTTP: <http://www.divetime.com/divesites/> (accessed 15 March 2012).

DTW (2012) 'The World's Best Dive Sites', *Dive The World*. Online. Available HTTP: <http://www.dive-the-world.com/destinations-diving.php> (accessed 15 March 2012).

Exley, S. (1981) *Basic Cave Diving: A Blueprint for Survival*, Jacksonville, FL: National Speleological Society Cave Diving Section.

Gill, V. (2010) 'Plastic Rubbish Blights Atlantic Ocean', *BBC News*, 24 February. Online. Available HTTP: <http://news.bbc.co.uk/2/hi/science/nature/8534052.stm> (accessed 6 April 2012).

Graefe, A. R. and Todd, S. L. (2001) 'Economic Impacts of Scuba Diving on New York's Great Lakes', *Proceedings of the North Carolina Coastal Plains Paddle Trails Initiative Conference*, Autumn 2001. Online. Available HTTP: <http://nrs.fs.fed.us/pubs/gtr/gtr_ne289/gtr_ne289_107.pdf> (accessed 8 April 2013).

Hall, D. (2011) *Beneath Cold Seas: The Underwater Wilderness of the Pacific Northwest*, Seattle: University of Washington Press.

Hillman, H. (2012) 'Top 10 Dive Destinations', *Hillman Wonders – Hillman's Top Ten*. Online. Available HTTP: <http://www.hillmanwonders.com/top_10_dive_destinations/top_10_dive_destination.htm> (accessed 15 March 2012).

IUCN (2010) 'Global Ocean Protection: Present Status and Future Possibilities', Gland, Switzerland: International Union for Conservation of Nature. Online. Available HTTP: <http://www.iucn.org/knowledge/publications_doc/publications/?6500/Global-ocean-protection--present-status-and-future-possibilities/> (accessed 6 April 2012).

Jackson, J. (2012) 'Scuba Diving in Stone Quarries Don't Compare with the Experience Divers Get in Blue Water Submersion', *Idea Marketers*. Online. Available HTTP: <http://www.ideamarketers.com/?articleid=1462018> (accessed 5 April 2012).

Lück, M. (2003) 'The "New Environmental Paradigm": Is the Scale of Dunlap and Van Liere Applicable in a Tourism Context?', *Tourism Geographies*, 5(2):228–240.

Lück, M. (2007) 'Managing Marine Wildlife Experiences: The Role of Visitor Interpretation Programmes', in J. Higham and M. Lück (eds.) *Marine Wildlife and Tourism Management*, Wallingford, UK: CABI: 334–346.

Marks, H. (2005) 'Top 10: Scuba Diving Destinations', *Scuba Centre*. Online. Available HTTP: <http://www.scuba-diving-articles.scuba-centre.com/articles/20050712001.html> (accessed 15 March 2012).

Meduno, M. (2001) 'PADI Brings Tech Diving to the Masses', *Undercurrents* 16(3). Online. Available HTTP: <http://www.undercurrent.org/UCnow/dive_magazine/2001/PADIBringsTech200103.html> (paid subscriptions site) (accessed 8 April 2013).

MMT (2008) 'SS Yongala. Maritime Museum of Townsville'. Online. Available HTTP: <http://www.townsvillemaritimemuseum.org.au/the_yongala/ss_yongala.php> (accessed 5 April 2012).

Mulhall, M. (2007) 'Saving Rainforests of the Sea: An Analysis of International Efforts to Conserve Coral Reefs', *Duke Environmental Law and Policy Forum*, 19:321–351.

Noreen, N. (2009) 'Extreme Diving: Ice Diving in Antarctica', *Aquaviews*. Online. Available HTTP: <http://aquaviews.net/scuba-dive-destinations/extreme-diving-ice-diving-in-antarctica/#> (accessed 6 April 2012).

Noreen, N. (2011) 'Top 10 Summer Scuba Diving Destinations', *Aquaviews*. Online. Available HTTP: <http://aquaviews.net/scuba-dive-destinations/top-10-summer-scuba-diving-destinations-2/> (accessed 15 March 2012).

Ong, T. F. and Musa, G. (2011) 'An Examination of Recreational Divers' Underwater Behaviour by Attitude-behaviour Theories', *Current Issues in Tourism*, 14(8):1–17.

PADI (2009) 'Statistics, Professional Association of Dive Instructors'. Online. Available HTTP: http://www.padi.com/scuba/about-padi/PADI-statistics/ (accessed February 20, 2009), cited in G. Musa and K. Dimmock (2012) 'Scuba Diving Tourism: Introduction to Special Issue', *Tourism in Marine Environments*, 8(1/2):1–5.

Regenhold, S. (2009) 'World's Greatest Diving Spots', *Travel + Leisure*, March. Online. Available HTTP: <http://www.travelandleisure.com/articles/worlds-greatest-diving-spots> (accessed 15 March 2012).

Richardson, V. (2012) 'How Divers Can Give Back: Part II', *Undercurrent*, 27(4). Online. Available HTTP: <http://www.undercurrent.org/members/UCnow/dive_magazine/2012/DiversCanGiveBack201204.html> (accessed 6 April 2012).

Scuba Travel (2012a) '100 Best Dive Sites of the World', *Scuba Travel*. Online. Available HTTP: <http://www.scubatravel.co.uk/topdiveslong.html> (accessed 15 March 2012).

Scuba Travel (2012b) 'Top 10 Dives in the World', *Scuba Travel*. Online. Available HTTP: <http://www.scubatravel.co.uk/topdives.html> (accessed 15 March 2012).

Scubaguide (2012) 'Top Ten Scuba Destinations', *Scubaguide*. Online. Available HTTP: <http://www.thescubaguide.com/godiving/topten.aspx> (accessed 15 March 2012).

Sheridan, K. (2011) 'Fewer Big Fish in the Sea', *Discovery News*. Online. Available HTTP: <http://news.discovery.com/animals/big-fish-oceans-overfishing-110218.html> (accessed 6 April 2012).

Spalding, M., Ravilious, C. and Green, E. (2001) *World Atlas of Coral Reefs*, Berkeley, CA: University of California Press and UNEP/WCMC.

TakePart (2012) 'Top 10 Scuba Diving Destinations', *Take Part*. Online. Available HTTP: <http://www.takepart.com/photos/top-10-scuba-diving-destinations> (accessed 15 March 2012).

Travelocafe (2010) '10 Best Scuba Diving Destinations', *Travelocafe*. Online. Available HTTP: <http://www.travelocafe.com/2010/08/best-scuba-diving-destinations-in-world.html> (accessed 15 March 2012).

Wells, S. and Hanna, N. (1992) *Greenpeace Book of Coral Reefs*, New York: Sterling.

White, L. (2008) 'See the Value: Quantifying the Value of Marine Life to Divers', unpublished Master's thesis, Duke University, Durham, US.

# Review 1: wreck diving

*Joanne Edney and Jonathon Howard*

Wreck diving is a form of scuba diving where shipwrecks are explored. These can be found all around the world in salt and freshwater environments. These wrecks may be the result of conflict, tragedy or misadventure, although more recently they may also have been deliberately sunk as artificial reefs for tourism or other purposes (Edney 2006, 2012). They provide divers with a sense of discovery, mystery, history and beauty.

Shipwrecks are becoming increasingly popular and important recreational and tourism resources (Edney 2006). The plethora of articles in popular dive magazines is testament to their popularity and attraction. Some notable wreck diving hotspots include Chuuk Lagoon in the Federated States of Micronesia, Scapa Flow in the UK, the Graveyard of the Atlantic in the US and the Great Lakes in Canada and the US (PADI 2007). Such sites typically provide divers with an opportunity to explore something interesting and different: divers can visit different types of vessels, ranging from cargo ships and passenger ships to warships and aircraft. They can see vessels of different ages and construction, in a range of different environments and, as shipwrecks make great habitats, people can see a huge variety and abundance of marine life (Edney 2012). This combination of factors, and the seascapes in which they occur, creates interesting and evocative experiences of considerable appeal to divers (Edney 2006).

Studies of wreck divers visiting Chuuk Lagoon, in the Federated States of Micronesia (FSM), and of wreck divers in Australia (Edney 2011, 2012), show that wreck divers seek particular types of experiences, notably, seeing historically significant shipwrecks, artefacts, marine life and enjoying the peace and tranquillity of the underwater environment.

The socio-demographic profile of wreck divers is broadly similar to that of scuba divers in general (Musa *et al.* 2010; Stolk *et al.* 2005; Thapa *et al.* 2005), although wreck divers tend to be older and more experienced divers, who hold higher levels of certification. Given that wreck diving is more challenging and demanding than regular scuba diving, wreck divers require higher levels of training, skill and experience to safely participate in this activity (Edney 2011, 2012).

Many wreck divers could be classed as 'exploration' tourists, that is, as these divers gain more experience, they seek new and more challenging experiences (Cater 2008; Tabata 1992). The least challenging are those sites where the divers swim around the outside of a wreck. By contrast, penetrating a wreck provides additional challenge. Divers may confine their penetration to within the limit of natural light, or undertake full penetration beyond the limit of natural light.

Divers may also challenge themselves by visiting shipwrecks located in deeper water, such as those beyond 40 metres, rather than those in shallow water. Doing so adds to the challenges common to all forms of scuba diving, including negotiating environmental conditions such as visibility, temperature and currents. As wreck divers become more skilled and experienced, they tend to progress onto more challenging sites.

While there is no formal requirement to hold wreck diving certification, divers who visit and penetrate wrecks at depths greater than 40 metres require the skills and experience to be comfortable and competent to perform these types of dives. With increasing depth comes the challenges associated with increased pressure, including nitrogen narcosis and the need for the technical knowledge and discipline to safely undertake decompression diving. To safely penetrate wrecks, divers need the skills to be able to minimise silting, which are proficiency in buoyancy control and correct fin kicking techniques. For some wreck penetrations, divers need to be proficient in the use of a penetration reel.

The diving community is active and mobile. Dive tourism makes an important contribution to some local economies, particularly in Pacific Island and Southeast Asian nations, such as the Federated States of Micronesia, Palau, Vanuatu and Thailand (Dearden *et al.* 2006; Dimmock 2007; Edney 2006, 2012; Howard 1999; Tabata 1992; Vianna *et al.* 2012). In locations such as Chuuk Lagoon, wreck diving is the most important component of the dive tourism industry and the focus of tourism in the region.

There are more than 50 shipwrecks and 12 aircraft wrecks resting on the bottom of Chuuk Lagoon, in depths ranging from the surface to around 65 metres. The wrecks are the result of Allied air attacks on the Japanese fleet based there during World War II. The majority of the 6,000 tourists who visit Chuuk each year are wreck divers (Division of Statistics 2008). These divers are attracted by the warm tropical waters, abundant marine life, the history associated with the wrecks and the quality of the wreck diving experience (Jeffery 2003, 2004a, 2004b). Chuuk Lagoon also has deep wrecks, such as the *San Francisco Maru* and the *Oite*, which have maximum depths of around 60 metres and 65 metres respectively. These wrecks appeal to the more experienced and dedicated wreck divers.

Another popular Pacific Island wreck diving destination is Vanuatu. Here, on the island of Espiritu Santo, commonly referred to as Santo, the *SS President Coolidge* and Million Dollar Point can be found less than a kilometre apart. The *SS President Coolidge*, a luxury liner which was converted to a troop carrier during World War II, is one of the largest and most easily accessible wreck dives in the world. Divers are able to see luxury fixtures and features from its time as a cruise liner alongside World War II artefacts and equipment on board when it sunk transporting troops and equipment in 1942. Million Dollar Point is a logistics dump and divers can see thousands of tonnes of US military equipment, such as trucks, bulldozers and barges, which were dumped into the water after the War.

Renowned around the world as exceptional dive sites, these wrecks provide a major source of revenue for local economies (Howard 1999; Klint *et al*. 2012; Stone 1997). Tourism accounts for almost 40 per cent of Vanuatu's gross domestic product and diving attracts around one quarter of Vanuatu's visitors, with Santo being a key destination for divers (Edney 2012; Howard 1999; Klint *et al*. 2012).

The popularity of diving on shipwrecks has seen governments and non-government organisations in many countries increasingly sink ships to create new sites and attract dive tourists, as their potential economic benefits are being recognised. This is particularly the case in Australia and North America, where ex-military vessels are popular. Notable examples include the ex-navy vessels sunk off the coast of Australia in recent years, such as the ex-*HMAS Swan* and ex-*MAS Brisbane*, and in the US the ex-*USS Orsikany* and ex-*USS Spiegel Grove* (Dowling and Nicol 2001; Edney 2012; Morgan *et al*. 2009; Pendleton 2005; Stolk *et al*. 2005).

Many wrecks have archaeological, anthropological, historic, social and cultural values (Delgado 1988a, 1988b; Edney 2006, 2012). For example, they may be gravesites, and some, such as those at Chuuk, are significant gravesites for other nations, as many contain the remains of Japanese servicemen who fought in World War II. Wreck sites are fragile, and any disturbance or damage diminishes both their recreational and cultural heritage values.

Damage associated with scuba diving can be caused by boat anchors, deliberate and accidental contact with wrecks, divers searching for, touching, or removing artefacts, or even exhaled air bubbles touching the wrecks. In the case of diver contacts, it may simply be from poor buoyancy control or unsecured equipment (Edney 2006). For example, in Vanuatu, research recorded unintentional contact rates of up to 24 times per minute (Howard 1999). In other cases, contact is deliberate, including when divers hold onto a wreck to steady themselves or when they touch artefacts to photograph or examine them more closely. Although such contact is often not a major threat to shipwrecks, these impacts can cause significant damage – especially when they combine with high diver visitation levels. More significant human impacts to shipwrecks occur from activities such as fishing, anchor damage from large ships, commercial salvage or looting. Management controls are important tools which can be used at wreck diving destinations to ensure cultural heritage values are not compromised. For example, there are laws which protect the wrecks of Chuuk Lagoon, and divers can be fined for removing artefacts from the wrecks. These laws also require all divers to be accompanied by licensed dive guides when diving on the wrecks, with the aim of preventing illegal behaviour. At the same time, they continue to provide divers with a sense of discovery and beauty (Edney 2006).

Management controls which are considered acceptable and reasonable by the diving community are likely to succeed in conserving shipwreck sites. Research on wreck divers in Chuuk Lagoon and Australia has found that controls such as penalties, permits, special certification and the use of underwater guides are favoured over methods like exclusion (Edney 2012). Interestingly, divers from different countries can have different attitudes towards management controls

(Edney 2011). Managing sites to protect their cultural heritage, and recreation values should involve managing them in a manner which is culturally relevant to all people involved: the communities where the wrecks are located, the nations with an interest in the shipwrecks and the circumstances which brought about the shipwreck event, and the divers who now enjoy the experiences these sites provide (Edney 2006).

## References

Cater, C. (2008) 'Perceptions of and Interactions with Marine Environments: Diving Attractions from Great Whites to Pygmy Seahorses', in B. Garrod and S. Gössling (eds.) *New Frontiers in Marine Tourism: Diving Experiences, Sustainability, Management*, Amsterdam: Elsevier Ltd: 49–64.

Dearden, P., Bennett, M. and Rollins, R. (2006) 'Implications for Coral Reef Conservation of Diver Specialization', *Environmental Conservation*, 33(4):353–363.

Delgado, J. P. (1988a) 'Historical Overview', in J. W. Murphy (ed.) *Historic Shipwrecks: Issues in Management*, Washington, DC: Partners for Liveable Places and National Trust: 11–20.

Delgado, J. P. (1988b) 'The Value of Shipwrecks', in J. W. Murphy (ed.) *Historic Shipwrecks: Issues in Management*, Washington, DC: Partners for Liveable Places and National Trust: 1–10.

Dimmock, K. (2007) 'Scuba Diving, Snorkelling, and Free-diving', in G. Jennings (ed.) *Water-based Tourism, Sport, Leisure, and Recreation Experiences*, Amsterdam: Elsevier: 128–147.

Division of Statistics (2008) *Statistical Yearbook: Federated States of Micronesia 2008*, Pohnpei: Government of the Federated States of Micronesia.

Dowling, R. K. and Nichol, J. (2001) 'The *HMAS Swan* Artificial Dive Reef', *Annals of Tourism Research*, 28(1):229–232.

Edney, J. (2006) 'Impacts of Recreational Scuba Diving on Shipwrecks in Australia and the Pacific: A Review', *Micronesian Journal of the Humanities and Social Sciences*, 5(1/2):201–233. Online. Available HTTP: <http://marshall.csu.edu.au/MJHSS/> (accessed 15 February 2012).

Edney, J. (2011) 'Understanding Wreck Divers: Case Studies from Australia and Chuuk Lagoon', paper presented at the Asia-Pacific Regional Conference on Underwater Cultural Heritage: 8–12 November 2011, Manila, Philippines. Online. Available HTTP: <http://www.themua.org/collections/archive/files/da439e635611426bb9bb32a8d-ab0f9ac.pdf> (accessed 15 February 2012).

Edney, J. (2012) 'Diver Characteristics, Motivations and Attitudes: Chuuk Lagoon', *Tourism in Marine Environments*, 8(1–2):7–18.

Howard, J. L. (1999) 'How do Scuba Diving Operators in Vanuatu attempt to Minimise their Impact on the Environment?', *Pacific Tourism Review*, 3:61–69.

Jeffery, B. (2003) *War in Paradise: World War II Sites in Truk Lagoon, Chuuk, Federated States of Micronesia*, Weno, Chuuk: Chuuk Historical Preservation Office.

Jeffery, B. (2004a) 'World War II Shipwrecks in Truk Lagoon: The Role of Interest Groups', *CRM Journal*, 1(2):51–67.

Jeffery, B. (2004b) 'World War II Underwater Cultural Heritage Sites in Truk Lagoon: Considering a Case for World Heritage Listing', *The International Journal of Nautical Archaeology*, 33(1):106–121.

Klint, L. M., Jiang, M., Law, A., Delacy, T., Filep, S., Calgardo, E., Dominey-Howes, D. and Harrison, D. (2012) 'Dive Tourism in Luganville, Vanuatu: Shocks, Stressors, and Vulnerability to Climate Change', *Tourism in Marine Environments*, 8(1/2):91–109.

Morgan, A. O, Massey, M. D. and Huth, W. L. (2009) 'Diving Demand for Large Ship Artificial Reefs', *Marine Resource Economics*, 24:43–59.

Musa, G., Seng, W. T, Thirumoorthi, T. and Abessi, M. (2010) 'The Influence of Scuba Divers' Personality, Experience, and Demographic Profile on their Underwater Behavior', *Tourism in Marine Environments*, 7(1):1–14.

PADI (2007) *Wreck Diver Manual*, Rancho Santa Margarita, CA: Professional Association of Diving Instructors (PADI).

Pendleton, L. H. (2005) 'Understanding the Potential Economic Impacts of Sinking Ships for Scuba Recreation', *Maritime Technology Society Journal*, 39(2):47–52.

Stolk, P., Markwell, K. and Jenkins, J. (2005) 'Perceptions of Artificial Reefs as Scuba Diving Resources: A Study of Australian Recreational Scuba Divers', *Annals of Leisure Research*, 8(2–3):153–173.

Stone, P. (1997) *The Lady and the President: The Life and Loss of the* SS President Coolidge, Yarram, Victoria: Oceans Enterprises.

Tabata, R. S. (1992) 'Scuba Diving Holidays', in B. Weiler and M. C. Hall (eds.) *Special Interest Tourism*, London: Belhaven Press: 171–184.

Thapa, B., Graefe, A. R. and Meyer, L. A. (2005) 'Moderator and Mediator Effects of Scuba Diving Specialization on Marine-based Environmental Knowledge–Behaviour Contingency', *The Journal of Environmental Education*, 37(1):53–66.

Vianna, G. M. S., Meekan, M. G., Pannell, D. J., Marsh, S. P. and Meeuwig, J. J. (2012) 'Socio-economic Value and Community Benefits from Sharkdiving Tourism in Palau: A Sustainable Use of Reef Shark Populations', *Biological Conservation*, 145(1):267–277.

# Part II

# Issues of health and education

# 4 Safe scuba diving: health and safety essentials

*Douglas G. Walker*

## Introduction

Personal safety in any situation is ultimately dependent on the interplay of a number of independent factors. The first necessity is to have a realistic level of awareness of the basic problems and possible dangers which are inescapably associated with the environment and the proposed activity. Allied to this is the need to have an adequate level of both training and experience to avoid incurring problems, and to successfully respond if they do occur before they reach a critical level – and to have a willingness to do both. There must be no medical, physical, or personality factors capable of impairing the correct response to any adverse circumstances.

If equipment is involved, it must be suitable for the proposed task and its use understood. Where there are other people involved, they also should meet these standards. Equipment nowadays should rarely, if ever, be an adverse factor if equipment is functioning correctly and the diver is competent in its use. The additional external factor is the management of the dive itself.

This chapter is a reminder of what every diver has been told during basic training, but space does not allow discussion of every single opinion or detail of the physiology, pathology, or the detailed management of recreational scuba diving problems. The tables are based on coronial documents concerning scuba diving related deaths in Australian waters. All medical conditions documented, whether apparently significant or not, are noted. The available records are not regarded as having identified all the medical conditions present or detailed the true, rather than claimed, experience of the victims. Potentially adverse medical conditions may be present for a significant period before displaying an adverse effect, 'silent' cardiovascular disease being frequently an unsuspected danger. Immersion in water, whether fresh or salt, involves risks as it is irrespirable, 'steals' heat from the diver, and has rapid change in ambient pressure with small changes in depth. Contact with marine creatures can cause morbidity or death, but the basic marine environment poses a far greater danger. Flying after diving is an accepted risk factor for decompression sickness.

## Fatality report

The potential for accident and/or fatality can apply equally to crossing a busy road, operating a chainsaw, climbing stairs, or diving. In the case of scuba diving, the diver's ability and fitness are critical. Commonly the major significant elements identified in reviews of the critical paths in diving-related incidents are health factors, inadequate experience on the part of the diver, and imperfect decision making. Fatality reports (Walker 1998; Walker 2002; Walker 2009; Walker and Lippmann, 2009; Walker *et al.* 2009; Walker *et al.* 2010; Lippmann *et al.* 2011) are the basis for understanding the causes of deaths of divers (see Table 4.1).

In the 345 cases reviewed, there were cardiac factors of significance in 55 of them, and 74 where pulmonary barotrauma (PBT)/cerebral arterial gas embolism (CAGE) was the clinical diagnosis, based on the described course of events. This condition is usually associated with a hurried ascent. Trauma was a cause in 12, and a finding of 'drowning' or 'uncertain cause' (and other factors) in the remainder. Where there was cardiac risk, the divers were usually apparently unaware of this, although a small number were aware and chose to accept this.

## Basic scuba diving physiology

The problems associated with immersion are well described and taught to all during their initial training courses, though it takes time to fully appreciate the full import of the information. Basic, and known to all, is that water is irrespirable –

*Table 4.1* Medical diagnosis of cause of death 1955–2007

| Cause of death | Period (years) | | | | | | |
|---|---|---|---|---|---|---|---|
| | 1955–64 | 1965–74 | 1975–84 | 1985–94 | 1995–04 | 2004–07 | Total |
| Drowning | 11 | 35 | 49 | 35 | 34 | 7 | 171 |
| PBT/CAGE* | 2 | 1 | 3 | 25 | 29 | 14 | 74 |
| Cardiovascular | 1 | 1 | 5 | 24 | 17 | 7 | 55 |
| Trauma | | 1 | 3 | 5 | 1 | 2 | 12 |
| Cause not stated | | 4 | 6 | 2 | 8 | 2 | 22 |
| Asphyxiation vomit | | 1 | 1 | 1 | | | 3 |
| Suicide | | | | 2 | | | 2 |
| Acutely ill | | | | 2 | | | 2 |
| $O_2$ or $CO_2$ | | | | 2 | | | 2 |
| Acute DCI** | | | | | | 1 | 1 |
| 'Anoxia' | | 1 | | | | | 1 |
| Total | 14 | 44 | 67 | 98 | 89 | 33 | 345 |

Notes:
* PBT/CAGE – pulmonary barotrauma/cerebral arterial gas embolism
** Decompression illness

drowning is the final stage in a high proportion of diving-related fatalities. It is far denser than air, seawater more so than fresh, which results in significant ambient pressure changes being experienced during both descent and ascent in the water column. The changes in the ambient pressure are particularly rapid during passage through the first 10 meters below the surface, where there is a change from 1 bar at the surface to 2 bar at 10 metres below the surface; after that, the rate of change is proportionately slower, though still clinically significant to a diver.

Although the body's solid tissues are largely fluid in content, so readily adapt to changing ambient pressure, problems arise with air-filled body spaces. During the descent, significant pain can occur if there is failure to equalise the pressure in sinuses or the middle ears, and incorrect attempts to forcefully introduce more air can lead to permanent damage to the ear. If sufficient air is not introduced, there will be bleeding into the affected sinus(es) or middle ear, nature's attempt to reduce the space to that appropriate to the reduced gas volume. In the majority of instances during ascent, the expanding air vents and causes no problem, although if the sinus lining mucosa has been torn, some of the expanding air may enter the tissues, resulting in subcutaneous or 'surgical' emphysema; if it fails to vent, there will be significant pain.

Unfortunately, on occasions the lung alveolar linings may be torn and air may enter the circulation; the resultant air emboli can be fatal. This can occur with an ascent of a few metres when close to the surface but can also occur during ascents while at depth. This may result from inadequate expiratory venting during ascent, but it may also occur if a local area of the lung is out of venting phase with adjacent areas. This is why a history of asthma or lung disease is of relevance when assessing fitness to dive safely.

There is also the well known narcosis effect of nitrogen at depth. This is particularly of importance because, as when becoming drunk, the person affected is slow to recognise the impairment in decision making ability which is occurring.

Water power can easily be far more powerful than anyone can resist, be it in a river or the sea, whether wading, swimming, in a boat, or as a diver. Both waves and currents can be encountered unexpectedly, although usually there are warnings to those who look for them. A serious but often forgotten or disregarded fact is that even a person wearing protective clothing will lose heat steadily, even when immersed in seemingly warm water. Sudden immersion in cold water can so affect respiration that the victim becomes unable to control their breathing or to continue to swim, so drowns.

There remains one occasionally beneficial consequence of facial immersion, the dive reflex (Brick 1966). This is a slowing of the heart which can be clinically beneficial when used in cases where there is uncontrolled tachycardia – episodes of excessively rapid heart beat which can imperil life.

Fortunately the human body systems include an ability to circumvent and thereby to adapt to problems, though this is of a limited degree. These include: the dive reflex on submersion; heat conservation by restriction of the circulation to tissues close to the surface when exposed to cold while prioritising flow to critical organs like the brain; and the circulatory changes to adjust to the effect of immersion on the body. There is a change from the surface situation (where the ambient pressure is essentially the same whatever the body's posture) to the aqueous environment (where the ambient pressure rapidly changes with even relatively small depth differences, altering the volumes of the gases within the body spaces). This can be considered Nature's G Suit.

There is one particular and critical difference between the basic rules of existence in air and water environments. In the former, falling may result in suffering injury from contact with a solid object, while in the latter, the critical factor is not the person's weight and height of the fall but the consequences of the difference in ambient pressure between initial and final depths and how successful is the adjustment of air volumes within the body spaces. Full appreciation of this may be inadequate in less experienced divers.

## Health factors of possible significance

According to the information published in UKSDMC (http://www.uksdmc.co. uk/), some medical conditions are absolute contraindications to safe diving while others, possibly less often considered or apparent, greatly reduce the safety margin. The former include all conditions which limit, either permanently or intermittently, physical function, endurance, or alertness, to a significant degree. The diver's personality and willingness/ability to follow safe diving protocols are matters which can have a critical influence on the outcome of a diving-related problem.

### Age

The minimum age at which children are permitted to learn and practice scuba diving is not universally agreed (Walker 2003). There are two special factors involved in considering this matter. The first is whether the child has sufficient maturity to be capable of understanding in full the reasons which govern the rules a diver must follow, particularly while making an ascent. Impulsiveness is not restricted to the young but is more likely to govern actions in this age group. The other is the possibility that the small gas bubbles which are present in the circulation asymptomatically after surfacing from even very modest depth dives may lodge in the growth plates of the bones. Nobody wishes to be responsible for providing case evidence of the validity of this possibility. Different opinions exist on this matter between authorities in different jurisdictions.

The question of whether there should be an upper age limit requires consideration on a case by case basis, determinants being the alertness and physical reserve of the diver, the presence or absence of cardiac or other adverse factors, and whether the type of diving practiced takes account of the physiological changes of ageing (which make decompression of tissue gases slower) and allows of an increased safety margin when entering the dive depth and duration. Dive tables have an expected failure rate even when carefully followed because every body's physiology is influenced by input from a multitude of data sources – such as fatigue, cold, tissue blood flow, drugs, alcohol, exertion – which continually create a different background to body response which mathematical calculations based on theory cannot possibly match. They are calculated on the dive being in seawater by a physiologically perfect male diver, with an initial ambient of 1 atmosphere pressure (1 ATA).

### *General health*

There will be occasions when extra physical exertion is required or a stressful situation arises during a dive. For this reason obesity, poor physical status, or easily provoked shortness of breath, will impair responding rapidly and adequately.

### *Mental health and personality*

These critical elements are not necessarily among the factors considered at a medical assessment of fitness to dive. However it should be considered by the diving instructor when he decides to evaluate a pupil's fitness as a diver (Bachrach 1978). Nevertheless, the instructor has been paid to give a prescribed course, usually short, and supply a certificate of the candidate's success in the completion of the course. It is difficult for the instructor to tell the trainee they are too stupid, impulsive, or unlikely to follow safe diving practices, to dive safely. Some instructors do give such advice on occasion but such would-be divers, if very determined, are then likely to seek, and find, another instructor who can be persuaded, either by prolonging the training, or by being kept in ignorance of the full health details, to provide the desired certification.

There is another factor, organisational in nature, in that the novice often believes they are now safe to dive unsupervised, particularly if their certificate is titled 'advanced diver'. It is vital to accept the necessity to obtain experience in the use of newly acquired skills, particularly in any inhospitable environment.

## Medical conditions

Here we consider only factors which have been noted in fatal incidents.

### *Cardiovascular*

Any cardiac history – angina, coronary artery surgery, heart attack, or arrhythmia – is reasonably considered a significant warning of increased risk, though a cardiologist may agree to the applicant's desire to accept the risk. Indicators of requiring health advice include hypertension which requires medication, palpitations, episodes of breathlessness, or faints. However, experience shows that 'silent' heart attacks (myocardial infarcts), disregarded chest pains, and silent coronary artery disease are far from rare.

## Respiratory

The ability to efficiently ventilate all areas of the lungs, particularly to vent in phase with adjacent areas, is vital. This cannot be recognised by a routine medical examination, and may be intermittent and due to a respiratory infection or as a consequence of an asymptomatic asthma/allergic reaction. Unimpeded venting of the expanding air during ascent is vital to avoid the occurrence of any pulmonary barotrauma during ascent. This is the reason for questioning everyone hoping to learn to dive about whether they have a history of asthma, lung disease, emphysema, lung cysts, or chest surgery. While it is possible for those with such a medical history to dive without any problem developing, its presence reduces the safety margin and may one day lead to a fatal air embolism. If lung efficiency is sufficiently reduced to cause breathlessness, this will be an obvious sign of inadequate fitness to dive.

## Asthma

Asthma is a vexed subject in connection with diving because this condition's main manifestation is an inability to freely vent inspired air. It is however a condition which large numbers of active divers admit to having been told they had when they were younger, with many still requiring either regular or occasional medication, yet none appear to admit experiencing ill effects during diving (http://www.brit-thoracic.org.uk). As both a fine spray of sea water and inhaling cold air are known factors capable of provoking an acute asthma episode, and each is present while using a regulator, this is somewhat surprising, but apparently true. Asthma has been demonstrated as a possible significant element in few fatal diving incidents in Australia, though not the sole factor in any case. Undoubtedly it has a high potential to be a significant adverse factor. While the recent availability of efficient asthma prophylaxis medications is obviously a beneficial change, there is no way to guarantee their correct pre-dive use. It is possible that those most at risk avoid taking up this sport, as the level of non-disclosure of this condition is believed to be high.

## Nervous system conditions

These can be considered to fall into several groups – personality, mental health, and epilepsy or other neurological diseases. The diver's personality is of significance as it determines responses to dive discipline and wise evaluation of the sea conditions, the need to cancel or abort a dive, the recognition and acceptance of true level of ability, and respect for others' needs. Both a lack of determination and its excess have a relevance, as they can result in making fatally inappropriate decisions, including failure to reveal significant past diving events (e.g. panic) or health problems (e.g. blackouts). A habit of separating from buddies, or of exceeding dive plan times and depths, and continuing diving while significantly low on air, are warning signs of divers dangerous to themselves, and sometimes others.

Mental problems may be severe (a history of 'breakdown' or suicide attempt is a warning rather than a bar to diving) while the more common conditions of anxiety, apprehension, tendency to panic, lack of confidence, or claustrophobia are of obvious interest to buddies – and dive masters. Unfortunately it is more likely that the diver will downplay or conceal such conditions, so observation by instructors, dive masters, or fellow divers is required.

### *Epilepsy*

Epilepsy is obviously of particular risk in an aqueous environment, whether at the surface or while immersed (Alamada *et al.* 2007). While anyone experiencing recent fits, or taking regular medication for their condition, is clearly unacceptable as a diver, or indeed for other risk situations, problems arise when there have been no (reported) fits for several years without medication and the person wishes to undertake diving. This is a decision a neurologist will find hard to make, balancing the person's right to accept the risk against the blame which will follow if permission is followed by a drowning. Naturally, the buddy must be made aware of any potential problem condition.

### *Diabetes*

There are great differences in medical opinions on the risk posed by this condition, particularly if on insulin treatment. If the condition is poorly controlled, the answer is simple – no aquatic activities are safe. If the condition is well managed and the early phase of low blood sugar always recognised, a responsible diver with a responsible and well instructed buddy may be accepted after specialist advice. However, low blood glucose may result in the diver believing he is well and so refusing warnings from his buddy. It is not known how many insulin dependent divers are diving in Australia because, fortunately, they do not appear among the fatal incidents. The only diabetic diver known to have died in Australian waters suffered a heart attack despite a recent cardiologist's check which showed no apparent cardiac abnormality. Here, the need to swim against a strong current proved to be the critical factor, not his diabetes.

### *Dental*

Of occasional importance is the wearing of dentures. If these are loose, it is possible for them to become dislodged and either be swallowed, choking their owner, or be spat out leaving the face unsupported. This can make it impossible for the diver to retain the regulator, or for others to adequately apply a face mask to provide oxygen during resuscitation efforts. Although such events are indeed rare, they can and do occur. Preventive management is to ensure good fixation of the dentures or through use of a customised mouthpiece. Dental pain can result if air is present under a filling, an ascent barotrauma problem.

*Vision*

It is important to be able to see around to be aware of dangerous surroundings, the best exit point, the location of the dive boat. The disorientating effect of a sudden blackout from disturbed mud or silt can be both sudden and unexpected. Poor sight may have played a part in a few incidents but wearing a 'prescription' mask will obviate any such problem.

*Physical disability*

While some disabilities clearly make independent diving injudicious, raising the risk level excessively, it is possible for blind or severely mentally impaired people to have a 'diving experience'. The safety factor is that those running the dive have received special training in how to conduct the dive. In fact the situation has some degree of resemblance to a 'resort dive experience', where an instructor shepherds several persons, minimally instructed, totally untrained, and previously unknown to the instructor, on a dive.

Indeed, if assisted to don and remove their equipment and with both entry into and exiting from the water, paraplegic people can dive in a semi-independent manner, although they should have buddy assistant in attendance, ready and able to give help in case of any difficulties or an emergency situation. Buddies require special training.

Where there is a missing lower limb, use of a prosthetic limb, or a custom-made aid to attach a fin, may compensate adequately. In all such cases, it is the attitude and the ability of the diver that is critical to a successful outcome.

There are innumerable medical conditions and problems where decisions on fitness (i.e. safety) to dive require informed 'diving medicine' based discussion. This requires the involvement of people with special experience in such difficult decision making. There is no such official group to referee this situation in Australia, though there was at one time in the UK. Nowadays there is nothing, save desire to avoid disablement or death, to prevent any person in Australia who holds a certificate of training from ignoring all advice and continuing to dive. The situation varies from country to country.

*Pregnancy*

There is no definitive answer to whether diving poses any risk to a pregnancy, only a cautious statement that nobody wished to accept blame should any abnormality or pregnancy failure follow diving. The theoretical risk arises from the possibility that post dive venous bubbles may by-pass the lung capillary bubble filtering function, a real risk if there is a functionally active opening (foramen ovale) in the wall between the two auricles (St Ledger-Dowse *et al.* 2007). This condition is diagnosable but not by a test suitable for the routine examination of every diver seeking to combine diving with pregnancy. The fear is that the bubbles may damage the placenta, or form in the baby while the mother is decompressing and embolise in vital growth areas. Nothing is known of the risk to the baby if the mother required treatment in a recompression chamber (RCC).

There have been no attempts to research this question for several decades and there are no reports of adverse consequences despite the likelihood that many women dive while unaware they are pregnant, and others continue during their pregnancy but restrict their dive duration and depth profiles. However, symptoms associated with a normal pregnancy may lead to a cessation of diving. There is always a risk that the 'normal' occurrence of foetal abnormalities will be blamed, incorrectly, on the diving.

### *Medications*

The influence of both legal and illegal chemicals on diver safety is a potentially significant matter but there are problems with research (Campbell 2010). First, few divers offer information and usage; this is usually only revealed during the formal investigation by police of a fatal incident, and even here there is minimal volunteering of details. In cases where prescription medication is being taken, there is also usually a lack of investigation of the medical records of the deceased.

Because every person's body processes have some differences from those of others – 'one man's meat is another man's poison' – no more than some general guidelines are offered. Alcohol, mind altering drugs, legal or otherwise, and some medications for medical conditions (called 'side effects') are potential causes of trouble to the diver, though few adverse effects are recounted. If in doubt, seek expert advice, though the factor of individual sensitivity is not an uncommon problem encountered with new medicines

## The environmental factors

The environment totally governs the existence of the diver at all times, a fact which a diver must understand as vital to survival. The physical power exerted by waves and currents necessitates awareness of these factors and necessitates care to monitor water conditions to be aware of changes before they become critical. Omitting to regularly check the contents gauge can result in a sudden awareness of a signifi-cantly low air status and trigger an impulsive ascent to the surface, the only viable air resource. Only very experienced and practiced divers are justifiably confident of success in sharing air on ascent in a panic situation. Early recognition of low-air status allows the performance of a calm relaxed ascent. If panic can be avoided, a safe ascent can be made to the surface by allowing the expanding air to escape through the mouth, greatly reducing the risk of air embolism when the diver attempts to control the process. It is not, however, a situation any diver should permit to develop through their inadequate monitoring of their contents gauge.

### *Water power*

This is an obvious potential danger but not always afforded the respect it deserves. Currents can be very compelling and waves, either at the surface in open water or in association with rocks, can be lethal to boats and humans. Awareness of the local conditions – tides, weather forecasts – is a prudent element in any dive.

## Fresh water diving

The lesser density of fresh compared to salt water not only has as a consequence a need to adjust dive tables, it also significantly changes the buoyancy of the diver. Anyone making a lake or quarry dive without making a reduction in the weights they are carrying will rapidly and alarmingly descend deeper, faster, and possibly with far less control, than they expect.

## Hypothermia

Hypothermia impairs efficiency, physical and mental, and will ultimately develop in almost every diving situation in time (Keatinge 1969; Nasrabach *et al.* 2011; Alan-Steinman 2002). Although tolerance to cold develops in some, this merely delays its clinical impact. Protective suiting delays heat loss but cannot prevent it. Here again, avoidance is better as it can become critical even where the water does not appear cold. It was the major cause of death in the sinking of the cruise liner *Lakonia* (Polak and Adams 1932). A wetsuit, or alternative wear, protects both against rapid heat loss, slowing but not preventing it. It also protects against injury from contact with rocks and marine life.

Rewarming requires care, as sudden external warming dilates the peripheral blood vessels, resulting in a flood of cold blood entering the central body circulation, which has adverse consequences. Warm drinks and wrapping in blankets are basic first aid, but hospitalisation may be essential for survival.

## Visibility

The diver should be aware of any possibility of the occurrence of a low or nil visibility event by recognising the significance of the presence of silt, and be capable of avoiding a panic response to a 'silt out' caused disorientation. This can also occur in an enclosed area but no diver should enter any area which has an obstructed ascent route to the surface, unless trained for such situations. Any entry into a wreck invites disaster.

## Drowning

Drowning is most frequently the cause of death in association with immersion and is a consequence of inhaling water. A reflex response to inhalation of water is thought to be responsible for some sudden deaths, leaving doctors uncertain whether the official cause of death should be certified as cardiac or drowning, a difference of little value to the victim. It is vital to re-establish circulation with oxygenated blood to the brain without delay – it becomes a drawn-out tragedy where brain damage occurs due to the length of time before restoration of respiration, even should some circulation persist. Brain damage from lack of oxygen can be irreversible and a vegetative ('brain dead') state continue, leaving relatives to make a decision on whether to continue life support, or a person may continue to live with severe limitations. It is important for everyone, and especially those who are involved in aquatic activities, to be trained, able, and willing to apply Cardio Respiratory Resuscitation (CPR).

### Pulmonary barotrauma

Pulmonary barotrauma can directly damage the lungs, a tear of its surface leading to escape of air into the chest space (pneumothorax), possibly with bleeding (haemo-thorax); these are associated with breathlessness. The more usual result will be entry of air into the tissues, making them feel crackly (crepitus) and distended. If this is severe, the pressure within the neck tissues of the chest (mediastinum) may result in change in the voice or clinically significant chest symptoms.

The commonest serious problem arising from lung barotrauma is the entry of air into the blood stream, arterial gas embolism (Pollock 1976; Wikipedia 2012). Within the heart, the air can block a coronary artery or part fill one of the ventricles, preventing proper pumping of the blood. It can also, critically, continue to the brain, which has priority call on blood from the heart. The consequences range from a momentary impairment in alertness to sudden death, either on surfacing or shortly afterwards. Remarkably, there can be a lucid interval during which the victim is able to swim and act in a normal manner before collapse and death occur.

### Ears and sinuses

By far the commonest problem encountered by divers is the equalisation of the ears. The middle ear space is connected by the Eustachian tube to the back of the nose, and this opens to enable equalisation of air pressure between the middle ear and nose when swallowing occurs. The nasal space is itself equalised at each breath with the pressure at the diver's depth. Pain is significant if equalisation of pressure is inadequate, and if this cannot be corrected, the relative vacuum in the ear will 'lock' it and make it impossible to open the tube. The use of excessively forceful raising of the intra nasal pressure will exacerbate the problem. The correct response is to immediately cease the descent, ascend a short amount, and gently use the method taught in training, usually to swallow while mildly raising the intranasal pressure. Any too forceful method can seriously damage the ear. Toleration of ear pain is a foolish option. If pain persists during and after surfacing, medical advice is required.

When one of the sinuses fails to equalise, the pain can be severe and may not resolve on ascent. Indeed this problem can occur during ascent if a sinus had been irritated by the tolerance of a problem, or its over-vigorous management, during the descent. This problem may be a consequence of nasal congestion due to a 'head cold', as is the case with middle ear equalisation problems. If there is pre-existing sinus disease, it should be treated.

### Nitrogen narcosis

Nitrogen narcosis is a famous long recognised danger to divers. It is an anaesthetic-type effect of nitrogen dissolved in the blood (Sheffield and Vann 2002). Nitrogen is chemically called an 'inert' gas but, when its partial pressure is raised by increased ambient during a deep dive, it has an increasingly 'intoxication' effect leading to reduction, then loss, of awareness of vital survival protocols. The only remedy is ascent to a lesser depth. This response is more likely when an alert buddy is with the diver and recognises what is occurring.

### Decompression illness (DCI)

It is the partial pressure of the gas (nitrogen) which is the determinant of how much of the gas dissolves in the blood in a given time at the local (ambient) pressure. The duration and depth of the dive are critical factors, and guide calculations are the basis of the dive tables. However, many additional factors also have an influence – each person is different physically if considered with respect to their complexity of physiological processes, and continually adapting (changing) in response to the flow of internal and external factors such as health factors, fatigue, drugs, activity, stress, cold and hot shower. It is impossible to make allowance for all these. A pragmatic approach to the problem is followed, an acceptance of a low level of failure even if the dive tables are followed very closely. As recompression treatment is not always fully successful, a careful diver will add in a (hopeful) safety factor to the depth and dive time used in the calculation. The need to avoid dehydration is correctly stressed to all divers, as this increases decompression illness risk.

With the above in mind, it will be apparent that any dive tables offering longer and deeper dives with less need for decompression stops are even less safe. It is always the most prudent option to choose the more conservative table, particularly in this unforgiving environment.

Minimisation of risk is through close attention to using 'conservative' dive tables and increasing the safety margin by adding such factors as cold, fatigue, age, health, any medications, activity, and so on – whether before, during, or following the dive. Also it is important to always guard against possible dehydration.

### Altitude

The calculation of dive tables assumes, unless otherwise stated, that the dive starts at sea level with a healthy man fully acclimatised to living at the 1 atmosphere ambient pressure assumed to be present there. This explains the need to pay attention to any dive commencing at a lower ambient pressure environment, such as a quarry or lake on a mountain. Such modified dive tables require professional development, and any created by simple amendments to regular dive tables are not advised. As dive tables assume a use in salt water, this factor also requires consideration.

### Flying after diving

The common advice of no flying or crossing of high mountains for at least 24 hours after diving is based on the observation that it requires at least that length of time for body tissues to off-gas till reaching equilibration with surface ambient (Vann *et al.* 1993; Edmonds 1984). This does not necessarily imply there are now no nitrogen bubbles present in the body but only that they are adequately controlled by the lung filter. There being a natural variation between people, as noted in considering dive tables, some divers are unfortunate and can experience decompression illness symptoms despite following this advice, particularly if they have been active or altered the body response by some other action since surfacing. Anyone who has performed long or deep dives requires a longer delay before flying. If there are any post-dive symptoms, there is need to obtain advice concerning a possible 'lurking' decompression problem (DCI) before deciding to fly.

### Marine life

In addition to the problems already discussed, there are those which result from contact with marine life (coral, rocks, sea urchins) or contact initiated by marine life (sharks, sting rays, cone shells, 'blue bottles', box jellyfish, and even crocodiles). The list is almost endless but rarely serious. Remember, you are visitors in a totally alien world and must respect its rules of survival. The best-known risk is the shark, though in truth it rarely attacks divers if they are not in a 'bait fish' or seal area. The practice of seeking to attract sharks by 'burleying' (emptying blood, meat, offal, or fish into the water) is adverse to recreational diving in the area (Caruso *et al.* 1996).

Broken tips of sea urchin spines are best left to be dissolved by the body because they are friable and it is more traumatic to attempt to remove them. Stings from 'blue bottle' tentacles can be washed in vinegar or a commercial product but should not be rubbed or touched by unprotected fingers to remove them. Box jellyfish stings cause severe pain and require rapid trained attention for the shock and pain. There are many marine creatures capable of being injurious, so follow the 'if in doubt, keep clear' philosophy. It is useful to have a first aid booklet dealing with marine stings and bites. Naturally the correct response to a shark attack is removal from the water and attempt to control bleeding till emergency assistance arrives. And if there is a warning notice about risk of crocodiles or a rip current or other local danger, take it seriously.

But remember, serious injuries are rare and that rare quality, 'common sense' is the guide to keeping safe. This is particularly relevant in relation to trauma from contact with rocks or propellers. In the former case, respect the power of water and consider your safest exit point before making your water entry. In the second, look and listen and use a 'diver down' flag. This does not guarantee safety but it greatly improves your legal standing in cases of injury. Remember that the risk is greatest in any boat channel. A black suited diver at the surface, in choppy water, is very difficult for a boat's skipper to see.

## Training

It is essential not only to be trained but also to have sufficient experience and confidence in the aqueous world to correctly respond to the requirements of this

*Table 4.2* Experience level of scuba diving fatalities

| Experience | 1954–64 | 1965–74 | 1975–84 | 1985–94 | 1994–04 | 2004–07 | Total |
|---|---|---|---|---|---|---|---|
| Inexperience | 11 | 18 | 30 | 36 | 27 | 12 | 134 |
| Some experience | 2 | 10 | 18 | 14 | 19 | 4 | 67 |
| No relevant exp | – | 9 | 3 | 5 | 3 | 3 | 23 |
| Experienced | 1 | 4 | 14 | 39 | 36 | 13 | 107 |
| Not stated | – | 3 | 2 | 4 | 4 | 1 | 14 |
| Total | 14 | 44 | 67 | 98 | 89 | 33 | 345 |

environment. A correct awareness of one's true ability is vital as this reduces the temptation to claim greater experience and ability than is true, leading to exposure to situations beyond one's capacity to manage. There is a real danger in any belief that a certificate of completing a course denotes one is competent in applying the course's subject matter. There is need to remember that experience in one dive locality is no proof of adequate understanding of a different one – training in calm warm water is no preparation for cold rough water, or a drift dive. The temptation to dive far deeper than your experience justifies can lead to trouble, as similarly any attempt to continue your dive when low on air because your buddy wishes to continue.

The recording of the true experience level – an element of the investigation of diving-related fatalities on behalf of the Coroner – is often given low priority, and possibly there is generosity in ascribing the status of 'experienced' to the deceased (see Table 4.2) (Walker 1998; Walker 2002; Walker 2009; Walker and Lippmann 2009; Walker *et al.* 2009; Walker *et al.* 2010; Lippmann *et al.* 2011).

The implication of expertise may be undeserved if based on the number of dives, if their type is unknown. Mere duration of time without significant morbidity is an inadequate and misleading measure, particularly if making a type of dive differing from the diver's usual ones. It is important to remember that the process of transition from just-trained to being fully imprinted is one which takes time and practice.

## Equipment

While it is obvious that only equipment in good condition should be used, it is also of vital importance that one is familiar with its use. A different position of the buoyancy vest controls, or use of a poorly fitting wetsuit or fins, could be distracting at a critical time, while a tight fitting wetsuit jacket, buoyancy vest, or fins have been identified as significant adverse factors. It is important to remember that anyone used to wearing a stinger suit or thin wetsuit will find it strange to wear a thick cold-water suit.

The importance of a correct and easy to read contents gauge, and consulting it, is very obvious. Being faced with a low-air situation while diving severely limits options and increases the likelihood of a panic type (restricted exhaling) ascent with its associated risk of an air embolism.

Never accept leaking of air from hose connections, excessive weights, air with odour, or faulty regulator. As your buddy and the organisation of the dive are integral to your dive, they should receive strict appraisal also. There is a low margin for error underwater and penalties for mistakes can be deadly.

## Planning your trip

It is important to establish that the proposed dive holiday will be responsibly run and that you have the health, training, and experience to safely manage what is proposed. Remember to take evidence of training and diving experience (log book).

The local health requirements should be met. Suitable travel insurance which covers retrieval and treatment of such costly problems as decompression illness and of air embolism is essential. If the nearest medical support is distant, you should give serious consideration to this factor. You should inform the dive organiser of any significant personal factors – such as easy fatigue, claustrophobia, heavy air use – and always make the dive master aware of your actual diving experience and ability.

## Basic personal first aid kit

This should include anti-diarrhoea, anti-seasickness, and possibly anti-allergy tablets, in addition to skin cleanser and antiseptic to attend to small cuts and scratches and a mix of small wound dressings and alcohol swabs. Scissors and fine nosed forceps (for splinters, ticks, etc) are very useful. And you should always have an adequate supply of any medications you are required to take. An ability to perform CPR is a valuable accessory.

## Conclusion

Diving requires awareness and acceptance of the critical differences between the open air and aqueous environments. The basic medical requirements are a personality able to make calm judgements in an emergency situation, absence of conditions capable of impairing alertness or significantly reducing physical ability, and absence of cardiac or respiratory impairment. Any diver aware of having a possibly significant health factor should ask a doctor well informed about diving related medical problems for advice. This is especially important if chest discomfort or pain has been experienced. However, no medical check can guarantee against the presence of some 'silent' disease. The basic and most important safety factor is an understanding of the 'local rules', and having the training, experience, and determination, to follow them when visiting this amazing 'bring your own air' other world.

## References

Alamada, M. R., Bell, G. S. and Sander, J. W. (2007) 'Epilepsy and Recreational Scuba Diving: An Absolute Contraindication or Can there be Exceptions? A Call for Discussion', *Epilepsia*, 48(5):851–858.

Anon (n.d.) 'Nitrogen Narcosis', *Wikipedia the Free Encyclopedia.* Online. Available HTTP: <http://en.wikipedia.org/wiki/Nitrogen_narcosis> (accessed in 10 November 2012).

Bachrach, A. P. (1978) 'Psycho-physiological Factors in Diving', *Undersea and Hyperbaric Medicine Journal*, 1(29):2–8.

Brick, I. (1966) 'Circulatory Responses to Immersion of Face in Water', *Journal of Applied Physiology*, 21(1):33–36.

British Thoracic Society (2003) 'Guidelines on Respiratory Aspects of Fitness for Diving', *Thorax*, 58(1):3–13.

Campbell, E. (2010) 'Medications, Drugs and Diving', *Scubadoc's Diving Medicine.* Online. Online. Available HTTP:< http://www.scuba-doc.com/drugsdiv.htm> (accessed 10 November 2012).

Caruso, J. L., Hopgood, J. A., Uguccioni, D. M. and Bennett, P. R. (1996) 'Inexperience Kills: The Relationship between Lack of Diving Experience and Fatal Diving Mishaps', *Undersea and Hyperbaric Medical Society*, 23:60–62.

Edmonds, C. (1984) *Marine Animal Injuries in Man*, Melbourne: Wedneil.

Keatinge, W. R. (1969) *Survival in Cold Water: The Physiology and Treatment of Immersion Hypothermia and of Drowning*, Oxford: Blackwell Scientific Publications.

Lippmann, J., Walker, D., Lawrence, C., Houston, J. and Fock, A. (2011) 'Provisional Report on Diving-related Fatalities in Australian Waters 2006', *Diving and Hyperbaric Medicine*, 41(2):70–84.

Nasrabach, Z. N., Ghorbani, M. and Marashi, S. (2011) 'Sudden Death after Immersion in Cold Water', *Forensic Medicine*, 2(11):24–26.

Polak, B. and Adams, H. (1932) 'Traumatic Air Embolism in Submarine Escape Training', *US Navy Medical Bulletin*, 30:165–177.

Pollock, H. W. (1976) 'A Classic Case of Diver Air Embolism at the Surface from High Wave Action', *SPUMS Journal*, 6(4):10–13.

Sheffield, P. J. and Vann, R. D. (2002) 'Flying after Recreational Diving', *Workshop Proceedings*. Divers Alert Network. Online. Available HTTP: <http://www.diversalert-network.org/files/FADWkshpBook_web.pdf> (accessed 17 November 2012).

St Ledger-Dowse, Gunby, M., Moncad, A., Fife, C. and Bryson, P. (2007) 'Scuba Diving and Pregnancy: Can We Determine Safe Limits?', *Diving and Hyperbaric Medicine – South Pacific Underwater Medicine Society*, 37(1):47–50.

Steinman, A. (2002) 'Immersion in Cold Water', abridged from 'Cold-Water Immersion', A. Steinman and G. Giesbrecht, in P. Auerbach (ed.) *Wilderness Medicine* (4th edn), St Louis: C. V. Mosby, 2001. Online. Available HTTP <http://www.experts.com/Articles/Immersion-Into-Cold-Water-By-Dr-Alan-Steinman> (accessed 10 November 2012).

Vann, R. D., Denoble, P., Emmerson, M. N. and Corson, K. S. (1993) 'Flying after Diving', *Aviation Space Environment Medicine*, 64:801–807.

Walker, D. (1998) *Report on Australian Diving Deaths 1972–1993*, Divers Alert Network (DAN), S.E. Asia-Pacific, Melbourne: JL Publications.

Walker, D. (2002) *Report on Australian Diving Deaths 1994–1998*, Divers Alert Network (DAN), S.E. Asia-Pacific, Melbourne: JL Publications.

Walker, D. (2009) *Report on Australian Diving Deaths 1999–2002*, Divers Alert Network (DAN), S.E. Asia-Pacific, Melbourne: JL Publications.

Walker, D. and Lippmann, J. (2009) 'Provisional Report on Diving Related Fatalities in Australian Waters 2003', *Diving and Hyperbaric Medicine*, 39(1):4–19.

Walker, D., Lippmann, J., Lawrence, C., Houston, J. and Fock, A. (2009) 'Provisional Report on Diving Related Fatalities in Australian Waters 2004', *Diving and Hyperbaric Medicine*, 39(3):138–161.

Walker, D., Lippmann, J., Lawrence, C., Houston, J. and Fock, A. (2010) 'Provisional Report on Diving Related Fatalities in Australian Waters 2005', *Diving and Hyperbaric Medicine*, 40(3):131–140.

Walker, R. (2003) 'Assessing Children's Fitness for Scuba Diving', *Medical Journal of Australia*, 176(8):450.

# Review 2: scuba diving for people with disabilities

*Selina Khoo and Caroline Walsh*

The Convention on the Rights of Persons with Disabilities (United Nations 2006:23) states that countries are to take measures to ensure persons with disabilities 'have access to sporting, recreational and tourism venues' as well as 'have access to services from those involved in the organization of recreational, tourism, leisure and sporting activities'.

Tourism organisations too have called for equal access at tourism destinations for people with disabilities. The Manila Declaration on World Tourism (1980) stresses the importance of access and recognises tourism as a fundamental right for all. Meanwhile, the United Nations World Tourism Organization Declaration on the Facilitation of Tourist Travel (2009:51) calls for countries to make their tourism sites accessible for people with disabilities and provide special training to staff which prepares them to work with people who have disabilities.

People with disabilities have the right to travel. The Takayama Declaration defines accessible tourism as 'tourism and travel that is accessible to all people, with disabilities or not, including those with mobility, hearing, sight, cognitive, or intellectual and psychosocial disabilities, older persons and those with temporary disabilities' (United Nations Economic and Social Commission for Asia and the Pacific 2009:5).

Accessible tourism is an emerging market and there is definitely a demand for it. Unfortunately, not much has been done to address this group of people (Buhalis and Michopoulou 2011) and the potential of this market has not been fully explored. Darcy (2010) holds a similar view, and proposes the tourism industry should address the need for accessible tourism.

## Accessible scuba diving

Scuba diving is an adventure sport and is historically associated with those who are fit and young (Carin-Levy and Jones 2007). Diving for people with disabilities started in the late 1970s in the US (Walsh *et al.* 2012). Participation has grown since then, and is becoming more popular. Walsh *et al.* (2012) point out that most people with disabilities are introduced to diving as a part of rehabilitation. Today they also scuba dive for leisure. Social attitudes and personal experiences and personality do influence one's initial decision to dive.

Many types of disability do not hinder divers from safely embarking on scuba diving activities. However, a diver must meet a set of specific medical requirements before being allowed to engage in full training and diving activities. In the past, people with any medical condition, disability or impairment were not allowed to scuba dive. However, currently, the permission to scuba dive depends on the organisation and the national jurisdiction in which diving takes place. Often, medical requirements among divers with disability involves answering a simple set of questions related to their medical history. According to Disabled Divers International, the only medical condition which totally prevents an individual from diving is epilepsy (Walsh 2012).

As stated earlier, even though many disabilities do not prevent those affected from scuba diving, individuals must consider the potential medical problems which might be experienced during the dive. These include risk of osteoporosis and fractures, integrity of medical implants, thermal regulation, muscle atrophy and hypotrophy, cardiovascular issues, deep vein thrombosis, decompression sickness, seizures, pneumothorax, latex allergy, pressure ulcers, bladder management, ear barotrauma and asthma (Cheng and Diamond 2005). All these medical conditions, however, are manageable if one is determined to experience scuba diving activities. Cheng and Diamond (2005) stress the importance of people with disabilities checking with their doctors before taking up diving. They should be advised on the risk factors involved. Medical assessments require knowledge of both scuba diving and rehabilitation medicine (Williamson *et al.* 1984).

## Benefits

The benefits of physical activity for people who have disabilities include improvements of functional, musculoskeletal, cardio respiratory, mental and metabolic health (Rimmer *et al.* 2010). The nature of scuba diving has additional benefits for divers with disabilities, such as feeling weightless and free from physical impairment, feelings of accomplishment, and the thrill of participating in an adventurous activity (Carin-Levy and Jones 2007). Psycho-social benefits include improved self-perception and social experiences, and equality with other divers. Divers with disabilities participate in scuba diving because it is a challenging and enjoyable activity which promotes confidence, competence and independence (Cheng and Diamond 2005; Yarwasky and David 1996). The beauty and challenge of the marine environment also adds to their enjoyment. Friendship is another reason given by divers with disabilities. Walsh *et al.* (2012) observe that divers with disabilities who have support systems (social, physical, medical and physiological) and inclusive friendship groups are more likely to dive regularly. They dive to promote camaraderie, equality and empowerment.

**Barriers**

Unfortunately, it is not always possible for people with disabilities to scuba dive, as there are barriers to their participation. The constraints to diving are not so much medical but, in fact, are rather structural and social. There is a lack of information, equipment and facilities available for tourists with disabilities (Stumbo *et al.* 2011). Other considerations for divers with disabilities relate to their financial situations, social capital, and social networks (Walsh*et al.* 2012).

Many barriers associated with travelling for people with disabilities are associated with access. When discussing the issue of accessibility, both physical as well as information access need to be considered. Physical access includes access to transportation, accommodation, sights, restaurants and streets (Buhalis *et al.* 2005). At present, very little information is available on tourism opportunities for people with disabilities. Information access is important to make an informed decision about travel. In general, Information Communication Technologies (ICTs) provide the tools for disseminating information about tourism products and services. They also enable people with disabilities to express their opinions and needs regarding tourism (Buhalis and Michopoulou 2011), and use websites and blogs to share their travel experiences ith others.

The tourism industry needs to overcome barriers to make tourism accessible (Walsh *et al.* 2012). Buhalis *et al.* (2005) note the need for knowledge, effort and commitment to provide tourism opportunities for people who have disabilities, which should be available for the entire trip. There are three pertinent factors to consider when providing accessible tourism (Buhalis and Michopoulou 2011). These are physical/built environment, information regarding accessibility and accessible information online.

Physical barriers prevent full participation in tourism activities. Thus tourism services providers should ensure physical accessibility by either designing establishments which are accessible, or modifying their current facilities to be accessible. To cater for divers with disabilities, the planning process from selecting, booking and executing travel plans, as well as other needs, have to be considered. It is important for destinations, transportation, accommodation and other service providers to demonstrate what accessible services they currently provide and also their willingness to accommodate the needs of divers with disabilities (Walsh *et al.* 2012). Many operators feel it is expensive and complicated to make their destinations accessible. However, by doing so, they are likely to increase their market potential and create a positive image of themselves as operators who are concerned with equality and accessibility for all.

Accessibility to information through the Internet is also important. Reliable information about accessible tourism should be available to divers with disabilities. It is even more conducive if tourism operators are able to provide photographs, videos and maps of their facilities. Information which is available online should cater to the various types of disabilities. Buhalis and Michopoulou (2011) stress the importance of tourist destinations using technology to maximise their opportunities in providing for accessible tourism.

## Accessible diving organisations

The main accessible diving organisations are the International Association for Handicapped Divers (IAHD) and the Disabled Divers International (DDI) in Europe and the Handicapped Scuba Association (HSA) in the US. They regulate the rules on who can and cannot dive. They also train divers with disabilities, as well as instructors without disabilities, to work with persons with disabilities. The training programmes for scuba diving instructors for divers with disabilities cover a variety of topics including awareness of the needs of divers with disabilities, methods to assist divers with different disabilities as well as adapting and modifying scuba diving equipment. The Professional Association of Dive Instructors (PADI) and the British Sub-Aqua Club (BSAC) have disability advisors or adaptive techniques advisors.

The IAHD, DDI and HSA have established certification systems for divers with disabilities, based on their level of independence. There are three levels of certification. Depending on the level of certification, such divers are required to dive with one, two or three other certified divers.

Accessible tourism providers are either specialist operators or mixed providers who provide mainstream and specialised products and services. For example, Worldwide Dive and Sail provides services for divers who are hearing impaired. Walsh *et al.* (2012) loathe the fact there is very little integration between divers with and without disabilities. Most dive activities do not include both groups. Thus, potential opportunities in tourism and scuba diving for integration and access remain.

In conclusion, there should be more awareness and understanding of disability and the rights of persons with disabilities. By increasing public awareness about accessible tourism and inclusive practices, more persons with disabilities will be able to participate in scuba diving activities (Walsh *et al.* 2012).

## References

Buhalis, D., Eichhorn, V., Michopoulou, E. and Miller, G. (2005) 'Accessibility Market and Stakeholder Analysis', report completed for OSSATE (One-Stop-Shop for Accessible Tourism in Europe): 88, October, University of Surrey. Online. Available HTTP: <www.ossate.org> (accessed 18 April 2012).

Buhalis, D. and Michopoulou, E. (2011) 'Information-enabled Tourism Destination Marketing: Addressing the Accessibility Market', *Current Issues in Tourism*, 14(2):145–168.

Carin-Levy, G. and Jones, D. (2007) 'Psychosocial Aspects of Scuba Diving for People with Physical Disabilities: An Occupational Science Perspective', *Canadian Journal of Occupational Therapy*, 74(1):6–14.

Cheng, J. F. and Diamond, M. (2005) 'Scuba Diving for Individuals with Disabilities', *American Journal of Physical Medicine and Rehabilitation*, 84(5):369–175.

Darcy, S. (2010) 'Inherent Complexity: Disability, Accessible Tourism and Accommodation Information Preferences', *Tourism Management*, 31(6):816–826.

Manila Declaration on World Tourism (1980) 'Proceedings from the World Tourism Conference', 27 September–10 October, Manila, Philippines: 1–4. Online. Available HTTP: <www.univeur.org/CMS/UserFiles/65.%20Manila.PDF> (accessed 2 June 2012).

Rimmer, J. H., Chen, M. D., McCubbin, J. A., Drum, C. and Peterson, J. (2010) 'Exercise Intervention Research on Persons with Disabilities: What we Know and Where We Need to Go', *American Journal of Physical Medicine and Rehabilitation*, 89(3):249–263.

Stumbo, N. J., Wang, Y. and Pegg, S. (2011) 'Issues of Access: What Matters to People with Disabilities as They Seek Leisure Experiences', *World Leisure Journal*, 53(2):91–103.

United Nations (2006) *Convention on the Rights of Persons with Disabilities and its Optional Protocol*. Online. Available HTTP: <http://www.un.org/disabilities/documents/convention/convoptprot-e.pdf> (accessed 15 July 2012).

United Nations Economic and Social Commission for Asia and the Pacific (2009) *Takayama Declaration on the Development of Communities-for-All in Asia and the Pacific*, Takayama: UNESCAP.

United Nations World Tourism Organization (2009) 'Declaration on the Facilitation of Tourist Travel – Persons with Disabilities', *Resolutions Adopted by the General Assembly*, Eighteenth Session (51, Item 4.3), Estana, Khazakhstan, 5–8 October. Online. Available HTTP: <http://www.e-unwto.org> (accessed 22 August 2012).

Walsh, C., Haddock-Fraser, J. and Hampton, M. P. (2012) 'Accessible Dive Tourism', in D. Buhalis, S. Darcy and I. Ambrose (eds.) *Best Practice in Accessible Tourism: Inclusion, Disability, Ageing Population and Tourism*, Bristol: Channel View: 180–190.

Walsh. C. A. (2012) 'A Comparative Study of Non-disabled and Disabled Divers Exploring What Encourages Divers to Take Part in Volunteering as Part of their Diving Experience', unpublished Master's thesis, submitted to the University of Kent, UK.

Williamson, J. A., McDonald, F. W., Galligan, E. A., Baker, P. G. and Hammond, C. T. (1984) 'Selection and Training of Disabled Persons for Scuba-diving, Medical and Psychological Aspects', *The Medical Journal of Australia*, 141(7):414–418.

Yarwasky, L. and David, M. F. (1996) 'Motivation to Participate of Divers with and without Disabilities', *Perceptual and Motor Skills*, 82(3c):1096–1098.

# 5 Scuba diving education and training

*Kelsey Johansen*

## Introduction

The international scuba diving training sector occupies a central role in the global dive tourism industry. A number of organizations have grown to become international providers of the education and skill development required to access scuba diving. Through their efforts to ensure diver training remains relevant and contemporary, dive training and education has been a key feature in the development of scuba diving tourism and advanced diver training.

The standardized approach to education and training has supported a globalized approach to diving which also complements tourism as 'it is intended that, no matter where in the world a diver receives training, he or she will be able to visit other areas and be accepted as a diver with competence and experience equal to that indicated by the qualification held' (CMAS 2002:3). A diver's qualification and certification (C-card) is similar to an international driver's licence. As long as divers have proof of certification and proof of recent diving experience, they can travel and dive widely.

All sport divers (i.e. non-commercial non-military divers, including recreational divers and dive tourists) must be certified to purchase compressed gas cylinder refills for diving (Johansen 2011). Therefore, all active sport divers must be certified by a representative of the global scuba diving training industry. The industry is comprised of independent international and national scuba diving certifying agencies including the British Sub Aqua Club (BSAC), le Confédération Mondiale Des Activités Subaquatiques (CMAS) also known as the World Underwater Federation, the National Association of Underwater Instructors (NAUI), the Professional Association of Diving Instructors (PADI), and Scuba Schools International (SSI).

## Founding organizations

The commercialization and internationalization of scuba diving training can be traced back to the 1930s (Musa and Dimmock 2012). However, prior to the 1950s, diving training was conducted exclusively by the military or by the scientific community through organizations like the Scripps Institute of Oceanography and

Woods Hole Oceanographic Institute, based in California and New England, US, respectively (NAUI 2008a). Informal dive clubs were the only source of training available to civilian or sport divers. Interest in diving continued to grow and the number of 'uncertified' divers rose steadily. In the 1950s the need to create regulated civilian diver training programmes grew (NAUI 2008a).

## *The National Association of Underwater Instructors*

One of the first civilian scuba diving training and certification organizations in the world, NAUI, can trace its origins to 1951 when Neal Hess, NAUI co-founder, contributed a column on scuba instruction to *The Skin Diver* magazine. He called the column 'The Instructors Corner' (NAUI 2008a). As Hess became well known, he received requests to review course outlines and requests to certify instructors. Soon after, Hess started a new column called the 'National Diving Patrol' in which he published the names of the instructors he had certified (NAUI 2008a).

In 1952, NAUI's other co-founder, Albert Tillman, launched a training programme sponsored by the Los Angeles County to certify skin and scuba divers (NAUI 2008a). The following year, Tillman undertook diver training at the Scripps Institute. Subsequently, Los Angeles County held its first Underwater Instructor certification course and shortly began granting provisional instructor certifications across the United States. This programme was named the National Association of Underwater Instructors (NAUI 2008a). Meanwhile, Hess and others planned to offer their first large-scale instructor certification course the following year at the meeting of the Underwater Society of America in Houston, Texas. In 1956, NAUI was incorporated as a non-profit educational organization.

In 1995, NAUI redefined itself as NAUI Worldwide. The change allowed it to increase business support to affiliated members (NAUI 2008a). By 1998, NAUI Worldwide had established a network of international service centres forming a single membership association which promoted teaching to one worldwide standard of training (NAUI 2008a). In 2000 and 2001, NAUI released a new educational system for diver education and training.

It is possible to enroll in a NAUI scuba diver course as long as the individual is at least 10 years of age and in good physical health (NAUI 2008b:). The first level of training begins with Scuba Diver certification (see http://www.naui.org). Novices are taught the fundamental scuba diving knowledge and skills to dive safely in open water (NAUI 2008b).

Divers progress through Advanced Scuba Diver certification (12 years of age and above). This course involves a minimum of six open water dives which must include separate navigation, night/low visibility and deep (40 meters/130 feet) dives, plus three of the following specialty dives (NAUI 2008b):

- search and recovery;
- boat diving;
- light salvage;
- hunting and collecting;

- exploration and underwater mapping;
- wreck diving (non-penetration);
- observation and data collection;
- diving in surf or currents;
- altitude diving;
- fresh or salt water diving (opposite of student's natural environment);
- shore diving;
- diving for photos or video;
- using dive computers.

For NAUI divers, those who wish to advance further and pursue leadership roles must first achieve the Master Scuba Diver certification. This includes a minimum of eight open water dives related to: emergency procedures and rescue; deep/ simulated decompression diving; limited visibility or night diving; underwater navigation; search and recovery – light salvage (NAUI 2008b). A NAUI Master Scuba Diver can progress through leadership certifications including Assistant Instructor, Skin Diving Instructor, and Divemaster, to culminate in NAUI Dive Instructor certification.

NAUI offers advanced specialty and technical diving training courses in: deep; ice; dry suit; and confined space diving (Cave Diver I, II and III, Cavern Diver, Wreck Penetration Diver); diver rescue (Scuba Rescue Diver and Search and Recovery Diver); underwater skills (Navigation, Underwater Archaeologist, Underwater Ecologist, Underwater Environment, Underwater Photographer, Underwater Hunter and Collector); rebreather use (Semi-Closed Rebreather Diver and Closed Circuit Rebreather Diver); mixed gas use (Enriched Air Nitrox, Tri-Mix Diver I and II, CCR Mixed Gas Diver, Mixed Gas Blender and $O_2$ Service Technician); and technical diving (Intro to Tech, Decompression Technique, Heliair Diver, Helitrox Diver, Technical Nitrox Diver). These continuing education courses ensure NAUI divers have the skills needed to dive safely in the appropriate environments and diving conditions.

### The British Sub Aqua Club

Recognized as the National Governing Body for Underwater Activities in the UK (BSAC n.d.), the BSAC was founded in 1953 in London and aims 'to promote underwater exploration, science and safety' (Ellerby 2009:150). This organization is one of the world's oldest diving clubs, and home to more than 38,000 active club members (British Sub Aqua Club 2005). BSAC is one of the most respected diver training agencies in the world (Ellerby 2009) certifying an average of 15,000 divers a year (British Sub Aqua Club 2005).

BSAC qualifications begin with Ocean Diver, an internationally-recognized novice certification (BSAC n.d.). The certification allows individuals to dive recreationally up to 20 metres or 60 feet (Ellerby 2009). Training includes basic buddy rescue training but not decompression stops or unsupported dives (ibid). The subsequent BSAC Sports Diver certification is an extension which takes a diver's range to 35 metres (105 feet) including in-water decompression stops, basic first aid and diver rescue skills (Ellerby 2009). Beyond the Sports Diver certification BSAC qualifications are divided, with the choice to pursue recreational or professional certifications.

In addition to certifications, BSAC offers complementary skill development and specialist courses allowing divers to broaden their skills and experience in four areas: rescue techniques (lifesaving, first aid, oxygen administration); technical diving (mixed gas use and rebreathers, search and recovery, extended range diving, advanced techniques); seamanship (boat handling, chartwork, navigation, outboard maintenance); and scientific diving (marine life identification, underwater archaeology) (Ellerby 2009). Buoyancy standards are awarded with BSAC Qualification Cards issued after successful completion of a Buoyancy and Trim Workshop (ibid). To promote internationally accepted certifications, the company issues CMAS equivalency cards which recognize the CMAS equivalent of a BSAC qualification (Ellerby 2009).

## *La Confédération Mondiale des Activités Subaquatiques*

CMAS is another diving education and training organization which has been in operation for some time (see http://www.cmas.org). CMAS is an international non-profit federation founded in Monaco in 1959. CMAS acts as the global governing body for underwater sports including scuba diving, freediving and snorkelling. The head office is in Rome, Italy (CMAS 2012a).

The organization is established and operates as three distinct committees (Technical, Sport and Scientific). CMAS is an umbrella organization for recreational dive training and underwater sports (including fin swimming, spearfishing, sport diving). These activities are represented by the Technical and Sport Committees respectively. The Scientific Committee's mission is 'to bring into focus the important issues related to the marine environment: invasive species, coastal ecosystems, biodiversity observation and monitoring to divers around the world (CMAS 2012b), thus promoting divers' awareness of, and involvement in, marine conservation.

Through its Technical Committee, CMAS offers internationally recognized diver, snorkeller and instructor qualifications. The Technical Committee's goal is to promote safe diving through world class standards for all aspects of scuba diving and ensuring adherence by federation members and dive providers (CMAS 2012c). CMAS International Diver Certificates can be obtained in two ways: (a) a diver can undertake training through a diving school or centre recognized by the organization and be awarded the CMAS International Diver Certificate or (b) a diver can undertake diver training through a National Federation which is a CMAS Technical Committee member and be awarded a CMAS International Diver Certificate equivalent.

The three tiered CMAS diver training begins with one-star scuba diver certification (CMAS 2008). This entry level certification is for sport divers, and describes a diver as someone who is competent in the safe and correct use of all appropriate open water diving equipment in a sheltered water training area and is ready to gain open water diving experience in the company of an experienced diver (CMAS 2002). Certification requires 385 minutes of in class or theory training, 480 minutes of practical lessons, and 5 open water dives (CMAS 2002). The one-star diver certification allows sport divers to dive up to 21 metres (63 feet), but does not permit night diving or Nitrox use. In Nordic regions, the one-star Nordic diver training requires 6 open water dives; the extra dive is preparation for cold water diving (CMAS 2002).

CMAS divers progress through two-star and three-star scuba certifications before being eligible for elite four-star scuba diver certification. Three-star certification qualifies a diver as a dive leader (CMAS 2002). CMAS divers can pursue professional certifications, including scuba diver instructor levels (one-star, two-star and three-star). CMAS also offers specialty diving courses covering topics including cave, extended range and ice diving, rebreather (semi-closed and closed) and scooter use, Nitrox and Trimix (technical) diving, and underwater photography (CMAS 2012d).

## Newer players

### *The Professional Association of Diving Instructors*

PADI was founded in 1966 in Illinois, US (PADI 2008). The aim of its founding members was to increase the professional nature of diving instruction and promote state-of-the-art instruction. As of 2010, PADI had more than 5,700 affiliated dive shops and resorts throughout the world and enjoys the status of the world's largest diver training agency (PADI 2008; Shreeves 2007). With 130,000 Instructors, Assistant Instructors and Dive Masters teaching diving in 183 countries, it is no surprise PADI educational materials are available in 24 languages (Shreeves 2007; PADI 2008) or that the organization has certified an average of 900,000 divers a year since 2001 (PADI 2008).

The minimum age allowed by PADI to undertake scuba diving training is 10 years. The certification is called Junior Open Water Diver (PADI 2012a). To undertake novice training at Open Water Diver certification level, students must be 15 years of age. Candidates must also be able to float for 10 minutes, swim 200 metres without assistance, and 300 metres with a mask, fins, and snorkel (Shreeves 2007).

After finishing the PADI Open Water Course, a diver must complete five specialty courses including navigation and deep diving to qualify for Advanced Open Water Diver certification. From this point, divers can train in first aid and CPR to qualify as a Rescue Diver, after which there is the opportunity to progress towards Master Scuba Diver certification (with a minimum of 50 logged dives). This is the highest non-professional certification offered by PADI. Alternatively, a diver can pursue professional training culminating in Course Directorship (Shreeves 2007; PADI 2012a). Additional training opportunities exist for PADI divers, including specialty training in: Altitude Diver, AWARE Fish ID, Boat

Diver, Cavern Diver, Coral Reef Conservation Diver, Deep Diver, Digital Under-water Photographer, and many other topics (Shreeves 2007).

### Scuba Schools International

SSI is a worldwide diver certification and education organization founded in 1970. SSI has more than 30 regional offices and affiliated members in 2,400 international locations in 110 countries (Scuba Schools International 2003; Scuba Schools International 2009). In 1999 the organization merged with the National Association of Scuba Diving Schools (NASDS) (Scuba Schools International 2012a).

SSI has minimum requirements for entry-level training. They include being 16 years old with general in-water comfort and completion of a short medical ques-tionnaire. Beyond Open Water Diver certification, SSI recognizes experience levels and specialty training allowing divers to achieve higher certification (Scuba Schools International 2009). Beyond Open Water Diver, SSI levels are: specialty diver, advanced open water diver, master diver, century diver, gold diver, platinum diver, and platinum pro diver status.

To pursue leadership or instructor training, SSI divers first obtain Master Diver certification. This requires 50 logged dives, 5 completed specialty courses, and diver stress and rescue certification. Candidates then progress through a number of professional certification levels leading from dive guide to Instructor Trainer (Scuba Schools International 2009). Continuing education courses include: stress and rescue, navigation; photography; boat, dry suit, shark, deep, night/limit visibility diving; perfect buoyancy, and waves, tides, and currents (Scuba Schools International 2003). Divers can also undertake technical training through the Extended Range and Technical Extended Range Programmes.

## Non-profit versus for-profit organizations

Differences exist between scuba diver certification agencies including the busi-ness philosophy, the training philosophy, and involvement with travel and tourism. Some of the most striking differences are between the non-profit and for-profit organizations. Non-profit organizations (BSAC, CMAS, and NAUI) have fewer certification courses within their educational hierarchy compared to their for-profit counterparts. This difference can be seen in Table 5.1.

Other differences which exist between the organizations are found in their educational philosophies. For example, CMAS is an organization which started as a group of volunteer hobbyists and their training philosophy originates from professional or military diving backgrounds (CMAS 2012a). Furthermore, being the World Underwater Federation, CMAS courses reflect a wide range of Euro-pean and global diving standards. Due to the smaller number of overall CMAS certification levels compared with BSAC, PADI, and SSI (which offer 2–3 entry-level progressions), the CMAS single entry-level training course contains more

Table 5.1 Breakdown of international scuba diver certification levels by equivalency

International scuba diver certifications and their equivalents

| Levels of training | BSAC | CMAS | NAUI | PADI | SSI |
|---|---|---|---|---|---|
| Beginner Recreational | Ocean Diver<br>Sport Diver | One-Star Diver | NAUI Scuba Diver | PADI Scuba Diver<br>Open Water Diver | Scuba Diver<br>Open Water Diver<br>Indoor Diver |
| Intermediate Recreational | Dive Leader | Two-Star Diver | Advanced Scuba Diver | Adventure Diver<br>Advanced Open Water Diver | Specialty Diver<br>Advanced Open Water Diver |
| Advanced Recreational | Advanced Diver<br>First Class Diver | Three-Star Diver<br>Four-Star Diver | Master Scuba Diver | Rescue Diver<br>Master Scuba Diver | Master Diver<br>Dive Leader |
| Entry-level Professional | Assistant Diving Instructor | One-Star Instructor | Dive Master<br>Skin Diving Instructor<br>Assistant Instructor | Dive Master<br>Assistant Instructor | Dive Guide<br>Dive Master<br>Dive Control Specialist |
| Professional | Theory Instructor<br>Practical Instructor<br>Instructor<br>Open Water Instructor | Two-Star Instructor | NAUI Scuba Instructor | Open Water Scuba Instructor | Training Specialist<br>Open Water Instructor<br>Instructor<br>Specialty Instructor |
| Advanced Professional | Advanced Instructor<br>Instructor Trainer | Three-Star Instructor | Instructor Trainer | Master Scuba Diver Trainer<br>IDC Staff Instructor<br>Master Instructor<br>Course Director | Advanced Open Water Instructor<br>Dive Control Specialist Instructor<br>Master Instructor<br>Instructor Trainer |

Source: Adapted from Johansen 2011

classroom and in-water instruction aimed at producing more experienced, knowledgeable and skilled divers.

Non-profit organizations, such as BSAC, deliver their skill development and specialty courses at no cost to participants (Ellerby 2009). They tend to be the regulatory authority in their geographic area of coverage. For example, BSAC is recognized as the National Governing Body for Underwater Activities in the UK (BSAC n.d.), while CMAS acts as the international governing body for underwater sports (underwater hockey and rugby, skin diving, and scuba) (CMAS 2012a).

Unlike CMAS, BSAC began as a dive club. Its status as a social family-friendly club and centre network (BSAC n.d.) informs its educational goals and training philosophy. This differs greatly from NAUI, whose roots in community services and educational program delivery (NAUI 2008a) guided the development of their educational programming, values, and training practices. Other diving organizations (such as PADI or SSI) may be geared towards holiday and tropical water diving, and tend to bring divers into the water immediately (CMAS 2012a).

Lastly, while BSAC, CMAS, PADI, and SSI are affiliated with diver training facilities in a number of geographic regions, PADI and SSI operate resorts and even facilitate dive travel through groups such as the PADI Travel Network. For more than 20 years the PADI Travel Network has been working to connect would-be dive tourists with PADI dive shops and resorts (PADI 2012b). Furthermore, the PADI website (http://www.padi.com/scuba/scuba-diving-trips/default.aspx) provides information on a number of package vacations and travel specials and includes a 'spotlight' on several top dive destinations, providing information on what divers can expect upon arrival and examples of top dive sites. While a beneficial service for dive tourists, this type of website information illustrates some key differences between a for-profit company and agencies like BSAC and CMAS whose websites focus on informing divers of their educational services and how to locate facilities, clubs, and services in their home region.

## Scuba diving certification

Dive training agencies operate internationally and have regional branch offices which deal with the specific demands of their geographic area of responsibility (Johansen 2011). These agencies grant regional offices and local dive stores/operators the right to certify divers using standardized courses and examinations (Lindgren *et al.* 2008). Diver certifying organizations therefore make decisions about what is communicated to divers through their training courses. The scuba diver education and training industry can subsequently be illustrated using a top-down organizational diagram which comprises three levels. Level one represents the training organizations with diving operators at level two. Divers themselves are situated at level three (Lindgren *et al* 2008). From this it can be determined 'there is a hierarchy to the environmental knowledge and environmental management practices disseminated through certifying bodies to divers' (Johansen 2011:9). Nonetheless, the role of diver education 'is to inform, influence, and change divers' cognition, which is demonstrated in responsible behaviour' (Musa and Dimmock 2012:2).

'Education is [also] crucial to the scuba diving industry as a means of ensuring safety' (Musa and Dimmock 2012:2). Scuba diving is an adventure sport which has inherent risks (NAUI 2008b). Consequently, for liability and safety reasons, certifying bodies often prioritize safety and emergency procedures training (Johansen 2011) over environmental content. In addition to educational materials, dive instructors are a key component of the diver education process. They receive their training and certification from instructors of the organizations for which they teach (Johansen 2011). Therefore a diver's understanding and recognition of the importance placed on aspects of course content is shaped by established curricula, instructors' knowledge and values, and personal diving experiences (Lindgren *et al.* 2008).

The outcome of a diver's training depends to an extent 'on the individual dive instructor, his or her knowledge and interpretation of, and emphasis on, different parts of the educational process' (Lindgren *et al.* 2008: 121). The educational experiences of divers can and do subsequently vary in length of training, maximum student group size, content, and emphasis (Lindgren *et al.* 2008). The experience of divers whose theoretical and practical training is based on the educational materials provided by these certifying bodies, is then similar to that of their dive instructors.

The uniformity of diver certification courses is beneficial in facilitating international recognition of scuba diver certification and training, and thus international dive tourism. Thus an instructor's emphasis has the potential to lead to a reduction in the transmission of environmental content during novice diver certification courses (Lindgren *et al.* 2008; Johansen and Koster 2012). As a result, the dive industry has recognized the need for continuing education and training which places greater emphasis on environmental content and advanced skills and knowledge (Johansen 2011).

## Scuba diving continuing education

While basic scuba diving courses teach the skills and knowledge needed to dive safely to a limited depth (often up 20 metres or 60 feet), they do not provide instruction in the complete variety of skills an experienced diver will need throughout their diving career. As a diver gains experience, a range of underwater activities open up to them, including underwater photography, assisting with conservation research, and even international travel which exposes them to diving in unfamiliar environments. In this way, advanced divers need skills beyond those taught in entry-level courses.

Commonalities exist between the continuing education opportunities provided across the industry's training agencies. The courses often focus on key diving skills (buoyancy and navigation), or advanced skills such as technical diving, confined space diving (cave or wreck diving), and deep diving. Some courses provide insight into environmental principles related to scuba and low impact diving, as is evident in Table 5.2.

*Table 5.2* Breakdown of international scuba diver advanced certification courses

*International scuba diver advanced certification courses*

| BSAC | CMAS | NAUI | PADI | SSI |
|---|---|---|---|---|
| Accelerated Decompression Procedures (ADP) | Basic Nitrox Diver | Deep Diver | Altitude Diver | Altitude Diving |
| Buoyancy and Trim Workshop | Advanced Nitrox Diver | Enriched Air Nitrox | AWARE Fish ID | Boat Diving |
| Compressor Operation | Night Diving | Scuba Rescue Diver | Boat Diver | Deep Diving |
| Dive Planning and Management | Search and Recovery | Search and Recovery Diver | Cavern Diver | Digital Underwater Photography |
| Equipment Care | Photographer (Levels I, II, and III) | Training Assistant | Coral Reef Conservation Diver | Diver Stress and Rescue |
| Mixed Gas Blender/ Nitrox Gas Blender | Cave Diver (Level I and II) | Underwater Archaeologist | Deep Diver | Dry Suit Diving |
| Search and Recovery | Marine Science (Level I) | Underwater Ecologist | Digital Underwater Photographer | Enriched Air Nitrox |
| Wreck Appreciation | Rebreather Diver | Underwater Environment | Diver Propulsion Vehicle Diver | Equipment Techniques |
| Advanced Lifesaver Award | Free Diver (Apnea Level I, II, and III) | Underwater Photographer | Drift Diver | Ice Diving and Cavern Diving |
| Automated External Defibrillator (AED) | | Underwater Hunter and Collector | Dry Suit Diver | Navigation |
| First Aid for Divers | | Wreck Diver (External Survey) | Enriched Air Diver | Night and Limited Visibility Diving |

Lifesaver Award
Oxygen Administration
Practical Rescue Management
Boat Handling
Chartwork and Position Fixing
Outboard Engine and Boat Maintenance
Underwater Photography
Ice Diving

Mixed Gas Open Circuit Courses (3)
Rebreather and Mixed Gas Rebreather Course (4)

Equipment Specialist
Ice Diver
Multilevel Diver
National Geographic Diver
Night Diver
Peak Performance Buoyancy
Project AWARE Specialist
Rebreather Diver

Search and Recovery Diver

Semiclosed Rebreather
Sidemount Diver
Underwater Naturalist
Underwater Navigator
Underwater Videographer
Wreck Diver
Technical Courses
Emergency Training (Emergency Oxygen Provider)

Perfect Buoyancy
Science of Diving
Search and Recovery
Shark Diving
Waves, Tides, and Currents
Wreck Diving
SSI TechRx
Emergency Training (First Aid and CPR, Oxygen Provider, AED)

As divers advance to master scuba diving skills, they seek out new and more challenging diving opportunities. In North America, divers typically have a shorter diving season. This may lead them to acquire cold water or ice diving skills to extend their season. Or they may travel to warmer scuba diving destinations where there are more diverse underwater flora and fauna.

## Scuba diving discovery opportunity

Some of the certifying bodies offer 'try diving' experiences. These non-certification programs are one of the most popular ways people are introduced to the sport. With PADI and SSI training facilities available globally through professional retailers, resorts, and clubs, tourists have the chance to try scuba diving on vacation. These destinations are appealing dive sites because they usually offer warm water temperatures, abundant marine biodiversity and good underwater visibility. By contrast, North American and European divers 'backyard dive sites' may require additional diving skills to accommodate low visibility and colder water temperatures at home.

SSI's Try Scuba Diving programme is an introductory confined water/diving experience in which novices spend three to four hours in a body of water that has good visibility and conditions to get a feel for the excitement of scuba diving. Facilitated by an Instructor or Dive Master, on a 1:1 or 1:2 ratio, these 'Try Diving' experiences provide an overview of the proper knowledge and skills required to take their first look at the underwater world (Scuba Schools International 2012b). Club-based 'Try Diving' events, usually held at local pools, are an option prior to enrolling in a certification course. In the 'SSI Try scuba' programme, novices spend one to two hours in a pool getting a taste of the scuba experience in the safety of a familiar setting.

PADI's Discover Scuba® Diving Experience is a non-certification introductory programme which offers the chance to try scuba diving either in a pool or other body of water. This provides the basics you need to dive under the direct supervision of a PADI Professional (PADI 2012a). If one pursues a Discover Scuba Diving programme with an open water component, dive time can be counted toward a PADI Scuba Diver or Open Water Diver certification.

Other options include completing the theory component of training online or through a local training centre before leaving home. As discussed elsewhere in this volume (see Chapter 10), a diver can complete the open water dives in conjunction with a trip to an all-inclusive dive resort (Wally Peterson, personal communication, 15 October 2011). Opportunities to combine dive training with a scuba diving holiday can be facilitated through dive training agency websites. These opportunities partner novice divers with training agencies affiliated with the certifying body's network of resorts and dive centres.

Non-governmental organizations (NGOs), such as Frontier Conservation (www.frontier.ac.uk), provide opportunities for would-be divers to combine certification with travel, volunteer conservation work, vocational training, and/or career breaks. In this way, novice divers attain basic certification during their placement and then use the skills to assist with volunteer projects. Certified divers can advance dive training skills or build scuba facilitated research skills including underwater surveying and monitoring techniques.

Divers are able to combine Continuing Education with dive tourism. Courses may be one or two day Continuing Education programmes which teach regionally specific dive skills at dive tourism destinations. These courses may be part of a diver's professional training. PADI's Instructional Development Courses are offered around the world, including in Thailand, Florida, and Bali. The courses offer seasoned PADI instructors the opportunity to learn to teach instructor-level certification by becoming PADI Course Directors.

## Future issues in scuba diving tourism, and diver education and training

Scuba divers visit coral reefs in 91 countries and generate substantial economic revenue for destination communities (Spalding *et al.* 2001). Destinations such as the Great Barrier Reef Marine Park generate millions of dollars in income each year from reef-based tourism (Driml 1994), which illustrates the importance of the dive industry to the regional and global economy (Johansen 2011). Furthermore, 80 per cent of all certified divers hold a valid passport and many are regular overseas travellers (Moscardo *et al.* 2003). The growing popularity of the activity and size of the global diving population has raised a level of concern about diver impacts on sensitive marine environments.

Consequently, certification courses aim to raise regular divers' awareness of their impact on marine environments and encourage them to use low impact diving practices. But regular divers are not the only group requiring diver impact awareness. According to Lindgren *et al.* (2008:129), 'one large group of divers are holiday divers who [are] likely never to move beyond [their] first certificate'. As such, the skills and knowledge these divers receive related to buoyancy control and low impact diving practices is likely to have eroded (Lindgren *et al.* 2008) between their original certification and future engagement with dive tourism. Therefore the potential loss of diving knowledge and skills is high for holiday divers who are inactive in the diving community and do not use diving skills unless they take a dive tourism holiday (Johansen 2011: 2). The gap between skill acquisition, use, and knowledge reinforces the need for skills refresher courses. Refresher courses which include an emphasis on low impact diving practices and skills such as buoyancy control, proper weighting, and finning techniques allow dive tourists to regain skills in sheltered areas prior to visiting sensitive dive sites.

Pre-dive briefings and dive master interference are integral to minimizing diver impacts (Barker and Roberts 2004; Davis and Tisdell 1995; Dearden *et al.* 2007; Medio *et. al.*1997; Rouphael and Inglis, 1997) and provide dive tourism operators with the chance to deliver destination-specific environmental knowledge.

Global climate change is a related issue in the future of dive tourism and diver education and training (see Chapter 11). Increases in sea levels, aquatic and terrestrial temperatures, the frequency and severity of intense weather events

(Klint *et al.* 2012), instances of coral bleaching, the introduction of invasive species (Barker and Roberts 2004), and disturbances of the water body which leads to decreasing visibility and less favourable diving (Gössling *et al.* 2006: 427) – all can decrease the attractiveness of dive tourism sites. Meanwhile the threat of increased cyclones, coastal erosion, and flooding decrease the perceived safety of a destination. Dive tourism operators are confronted with decisions to mitigate threats and address tourists' fears to ensure the viability of destinations. One way to do this is through diver education. Using real world examples such as those experienced and witnessed on dive expeditions can be important to motivate broader dialogue about climate change and the relationship with tourism and dive tourism

## Conclusion

International scuba diving training organizations feature significantly in the history and development of the scuba diving industry. The major training providers offer a range of certification including progression from novice to advanced certifications. The growth of scuba diving as a niche tourism sector has led to a need for diver awareness and education related to environmental impacts. The response by dive training organizations includes low impact diving as one of a range of continuing education/specialty courses in the development of divers' skills and education. There are opportunities to partner scuba diving training and professional development with travel and volunteer experiences as well. This chapter concludes with consideration of some future issues facing scuba diving tourism, education and training.

## References

Barker, N. H. L. and Roberts, C. M. (2004) 'Scuba Diver Behaviour and the Management of Diving Impacts on Coral Reefs', *Biological Conservation*, 120:481–489.
BSAC (n.d.) 'History', British Sub Aqua Club. Online. Available HTTP: <http://www.bsac.com/page.asp?section=937&sectionTitle=History> (accessed 17 February 2012).
BSAC (2005) 'M5-Assistance with Study Projects Relating to Sports Diving Membership Information', British Sub Aqua Club, Cheshire, UK: British Sub Aqua Club.
BSAC (2010) 'Annual Report & Accounts 2010', British Sub Aqua Club. Online. Available HTTP: <http://www.bsac.com/page.asp?section=1697&sectionTitle=Council+reports> (accessed 17 February 2012).
CMAS (2002) 'Standards & Requirements Diver and Instructor', La Confédération Mondiale des Activitiés Subaquatiques. Online. Available HTTP: <http://www.cmas.org/documents_area.php> (accessed 21 November 2011).
CMAS (2008) 'CMAS Standard Touristic Diver Course Outline and Training Programme', La Confédération Mondiale des Activitiés Subaquatiques. Online. Available HTTP: <http://www.cmas.org/documents_area.php> (accessed 21 November 2011).
CMAS (2012a) 'About CMAS', La Confédération Mondiale des Activitiés Subaquatiques. Online. Available HTTP: <http://www.cmas.org/about_cmas.php> (accessed 6 January 2012).

CMAS (2012b) 'Scientific Committee – About the Committee', La Confédération Mondiale des Activitiés Subaquatiques. Online. Available HTTP: <http://www.cmas.org/114-40070.php> (accessed 6 January 2012).

CMAS (2012c) 'Technical Committee – About the Committee', La Confédération Mondiale des Activitiés Subaquatiques. Online. Available HTTP: <http://www.cmas.org/114-38727.php> (accessed 6 January 2012).

CMAS (2012d) 'CMAS International Diver Training Standards and Procedures Manual', La Confédération Mondiale des Activitiés Subaquatiques. Online. Available HTTP: <http://www.cmas.org/technique/cmas-international-diver-training-standards-and-procedures-manual> (accessed 16 November 2012).

Davis, D. and Tisdell, C. (1995) 'Recreational Scuba-diving and Carrying Capacity in Marine Protected Areas', *Ocean & Coastal Management*, 26:19–40.

Dearden, P., Bennett, M. and Rollins, R. (2007) 'Perceptions of Diving Impacts and Implications for Reef Conservation', *Coastal Management*, 35(2/3):305–317.

Driml, S. (1994) 'Protection for Profit: Economic and Financial Values of the Great Barrier Reef World Heritage Area and other Protected Areas', Research Publication No. 35, Townsville: Great Barrier Reef Marine Park Authority.

Ellerby, D. (2009) *The Diving Manual: An Introduction to Scuba Diving* (4th edn), Surrey, UK: Circle Books.

Gössling, S., Bredberg, M., Randow, A., Sandström, E. and Svensson, P. (2006) 'Tourist Perceptions of Climate Change: A Study of International Tourists in Zanzibar', *Current Issues in Tourism*, 9(4–5):419–435.

Johansen, K. (2011) 'The Effectiveness of Environmental Communication with Scuba Divers: A Case Study Comparing the Curricula of BSAC, PADI, and SSI Entry-Level Certification Courses', unpublished thesis, Lakehead University, Canada.

Johansen, K. M. and Koster, R. L. (2012) 'Forming Scuba Diving Environmental Codes of Conduct: What Entry-level Divers are Taught in their First Certification Course', *Tourism in Marine Environments*, 8(1/2):61–76.

Klint, L. M., Jiang, M., Law, A., Delacy, T., Filep, S., Calgaro, E., Dominey-Howes, D. and Harrison, D. (2012) 'Dive Tourism in Luganville, Vanuatu: Shocks, Stressors, and Vulnerablility to Climate Change', *Tourism in Marine Environments*, 8(1/2):91–109.

Lindgren, A., Palmlund, J., Wate, I. and Gössling, S. (2008) 'Environmental Management and Education: The Case of PADI', in B. Garrod and S. Gössling (eds.) *New Frontiers in Marine Tourism: Diving Experiences, Sustainability, Management*, Amsterdam: Elsevier, Ch. 6.

Medio, D., Ormand, R. F. G. and Pearson, M. (1997) 'Effect of Briefings on Rates of Damage to Corals by Scuba Divers', *Biological Conservation*, 79:91–95.

Moscardo, G., Saltzer, R., Galletly, A., Burke, A. and Hildebrandt, A. (2003) 'Changing Patterns of Reef Tourism', Technical Report No. 49, Townsville: CRC Reef Research Centre.

Musa, G. and Dimmock, K. (2012) 'Scuba Diving Tourism: Introduction to Special Issue', *Tourism in Marine Environments*, 8(1/2):1–5.

NAUI (2008a) 'NAUI History', National Association of Underwater Instructors. Online. Available HTTP: <http://www.naui.org/history.aspx> (accessed 14 December 2011).

NAUI (2008b) 'NAUI Recreational Courses', National Association of Underwater Instructors. Online. Available HTTP: <http://www.naui.org/recreational_divers.aspx#scuba> (accessed 14 December 2011).

PADI (2008) 'PADI History', Professional Association of Diving Professionals. Online. Available HTTP: <http://www.padi.com/scuba/about-padi/PADI-history/default.aspx> (accessed 11 January 2010).

PADI (2012a) 'Discover Scuba Diving', Professional Association of Diving Professionals. Online. Available HTTP: <http://www.padi.com/scuba/padi-courses/diver-level-courses/view-all-padi-courses/discover-scuba-diving/default.aspx> (accessed 28 March 2012).

PADI (2012b) 'Scuba Diving Trips', Professional Association of Diving Professionals. Online. Available HTTP: <http://www.padi.com/scuba/scuba-diving-trips/default.aspx> (accessed 28 March 2012).

Rouphael, A. B. and Inglis, G. J. (1997) 'Impacts of Recreational Scuba Diving at Sites with Different Reef Topographies', *Biological Conservation*, 82:329–336.

Scuba Schools International (2003) *SSI Open Water Diver Manual* (4th edn), Fort Collins, CO: Concept Systems, Inc.

Scuba Schools International (2009) 'About SSI'. Online. Available HTTP: <http://www.divessi.com/about_ssi> (accessed 12 January 2010).

Scuba Schools International (2012a) 'NASDS Divers'. Online. Available HTTP: <http://www.divessi.com/nasds> (accessed 6 September 2012).

Scuba Schools International (2012b) 'Try Scuba'. Online. Available HTTP: <http://www.divessi.com/ts> (accessed 15 February 2012).

Shreeves, K. (2007) *PADI Open Water Diver Manual*, Rancho Santa Margarita, CA: PADI.

Spalding, M. D., Ravilious, C. and Green, E. P. (2001) *World Atlas of Coral Reefs*, Berkeley, CA: University of California Press.

www.frontier.ac.uk (n.d.) *Background & Mission: Biodiversity & Livelihoods*. Frontier Conservation. Online. Available HTTP: <http://frontier.ac.uk/About-Us/Background-Mission.aspx> (accessed 15 January 2012).

# Review 3: international standards on recreational diving services

*Peter Jonas*

## History

Recreational scuba diving has developed to be a popular recreational activity, with a variety of different training service providers on offer to the divers. For a diver, it is not an easy task to choose the most suitable and reliable training organisations from the various dive centres. Often they may have to rely on their friends and the Internet. The price, and interesting packages attached to the training, may influence their decision making. With increasing concern about quality experience as well as the safety of divers, creating standards for recreational scuba diving seems to be an inevitable development.

Standardisation is important for recreational activities, such as scuba diving, for which training and experience is essential for the participants to be able to carry out the activity safely. Although recreational diving is potentially hazardous, the risks to the participants and to the natural and cultural resources of the dive destinations can easily be reduced to acceptable levels by the adoption of appropriate precautions.

From 1999 to 2004, scuba diving training organisations, dive centre operators, and representatives of consumers and authorities have jointly developed – under the auspices of the European Committee for Standardisation (CEN) – European standards for scuba diver and scuba instructor training programmes, as well as a standard for recreational scuba diving service providers (dive centres, dive schools).

Divers and diving professionals travel and operate worldwide, thus it is not surprising that interest in the standards is being shown by service providers engaged globally in dive tourism. Therefore the European Committee forwarded the European standards to the International Organisation for Standardisation (ISO) (ISO n.d.) for the adoption of international standards. Following a fast track procedure, the first series of international standards on recreational diving services was published in February 2007.

The standards were formally assigned to the newly created ISO Technical Committee 228 – Tourism and Other Services – which was established in 2006. Within the Technical Committee (TC) 228, Working Group (WG) 1 – Diving Services – is concerned with the maintenance and further development of standards in the sector of recreational scuba diving services. The secretariat service is provided by the Austrian Standards Institute (ASI).

## Objectives

The standards on recreational scuba diving services serve both recreational divers and scuba diving professionals, and have several objectives. The first objective is for the diver: The standards ensure a high level of quality and safety for an activity which demands proper training. They create internationally recognised diver qualifications which enable divers to purchase services from dive centres world-wide. The second objective is for the diving professionals (dive guides, scuba instructors): The standards provide a benchmark for their training organisations and service providers to prove that their services comply with the current state-of-the-art standards and thus be considered as safe. Standards provide scuba instructors with an internationally accepted qualification which opens the market for training by the service providers. The third objective is for tour operators who sell diving tours or diver training as part of their holiday packages: The standards provide a tool to select the proper partner for diving operations which could enhance their liability protection. The fourth objective is for governments and regulators: The standards are increasingly being used for regulatory purposes, making them a part of local licensing systems for dive centres.

The elaboration of standards is an extensive and sometimes a tiring exercise. However, it has been proven to be worthwhile. The adoption of the standards by several key international markets has fully opened up the scuba diving industry, which was rather limited in its operations in the past. For example, Greece used to have a more or less closed market for scuba diving. Now, the country has adopted the scuba diving standards as benchmarks for regulating scuba diving tourism, drawing on their guidelines for the industry to be established.

## Content of the standards

The International Organisation for Standardisation (ISO n.d.) provides ten standards for recreational scuba diving, in two categories. The two categories are (1) Training system standards, and (2) Service provision standards. All standards specify the required levels of experience and competency of scuba divers and scuba instructors as well as safety practices and requirements for recreational scuba diving service providers, appropriate to the different diving levels.

The requirements specified are a minimum. They do not preclude the provision of additional training or the evaluation of additional competencies by a service provider. These international standards are intended as a tool for comparison between existing (or future) scuba diver qualifications. They are not course programmes and do not require that course programmes and scuba diver qualifications must necessarily correspond to the levels they specify.

*Table 5.3* ISO standards of scuba diving

---

*ISO 24801-1* Requirements for the training of recreational scuba divers – Part 1: Level 1: Supervised Diver

*ISO 24801-2* Requirements for the training of recreational scuba divers – Part 2: Level 2: Autonomous Diver

*ISO 24801-3* Requirements for the training of recreational scuba divers – Part 3: Level 3: Dive Leader:

*ISO 24802-1* Requirements for the training of scuba instructors – Part 1: Level 1

*ISO 24802-2* Requirements for the training of scuba instructors – Part 2: Level 2

*ISO 11107* Requirements for training programmes on enriched air nitrox (EAN) diving

*ISO 11121* Requirements for introductory training programmes to scuba diving

*ISO 13970* Requirements for the training of recreational snorkelling guides

*ISO 13289* Requirements for the conduct of snorkelling excursions

*ISO 24803* Requirements for recreational scuba diving service providers

---

## Standards specifying requirements for diving training

As presented in Table 5.3, *ISO 24801-1* specifies requirements for the training of recreational scuba divers at Level 1: Supervised Diver. Scuba divers at Level 1 are qualified to dive in open water under the direct supervision of a dive leader within the following parameters:

- dive to a recommended maximum depth of 12 meters;
- no in-water decompression stops;
- dive only when appropriate support is available at the surface.

*ISO 24801-2* specifies requirements for the training of recreational scuba divers at Level 2: Autonomous Diver. Scuba divers at Level 2 are qualified to dive with other scuba divers of at least the same level in open water within the following parameters:

- dive to a recommended maximum depth of 20 meters;
- no in-water decompression stops;
- dive only when appropriate support is available at the surface.

In accordance with ISO 24801-2, this diver qualification level is the level which is commonly known as 'Open Water Diver' or in the CMAS (n.d.) system as '2*-Diver'. Scuba divers at this level are deemed to have sufficient knowledge, skill and experience to dive with other divers of at least the same level in open water without supervision by a scuba instructor. Nevertheless, the standard also states that if diving conditions are significantly different from those previously experienced, an 'autonomous diver' requires an appropriate orientation from a dive leader.

*ISO 24801-3* specifies requirements for the training of recreational scuba divers at Level 3: Dive Leader. Scuba divers at Level 3 are qualified to:

- plan, organise and conduct dives and lead other scuba divers in open water;
- conduct any specialised recreational scuba diving activities for which they have received appropriate training;
- plan and execute emergency procedures appropriate for the diving environment and activities.

This diver qualification level in accordance with ISO 24801-2 is the level which is commonly known as 'Dive Leader', 'Dive Master' or in the CMAS system as '3*-Diver'. Dive leaders according to this standard are competent to plan, organise and conduct their dives and lead other recreational scuba divers in open water.

*ISO 24802-1* specifies requirements for the training of scuba instructors at Level 1. Scuba instructors at Level 1 shall be trained such that they are qualified to:

- teach and assess students up to diver Level 1 on their theoretical knowledge;
- teach and assess students up to diver Level 1 in confined water.

This level is commonly known in the scuba diving industry as 'Assistant-Instructor'.

*ISO 24802-2* specifies requirements for the training of scuba instructors at Level 2. A Level 2 scuba instructor shall be trained such that they are qualified to:

- plan, organise and conduct dives and lead other recreational scuba divers of all levels in open water, including rescue activities;
- teach and assess students up to scuba diver Level 3;
- plan, organise and conduct scuba diver training courses.

Commercial diver training organisations often call this level the 'Open Water Instructor', whereas the CMAS training systems refer to this level as CMAS 2* instructor. The standard specifies the common body of knowledge and skills for the general diver training. With suitable additional training or experience, an instructor at this level is competent to plan, organise and conduct appropriate speciality training.

*ISO 11107* refers to requirements for training programmes on enriched air nitrox (EAN) diving: The training programme according to this standard shall ensure that scuba divers are qualified to plan, conduct and log EAN open-water no-decompression dives, and to procure EAN mixes, EAN equipment and other services to engage in recreational EAN diving without supervision. The training programme does not qualify divers to make dives which require mandatory in-water decompression stops or dives using more than one breathing gas and/or rebreathers.

*ISO 11121* refers to requirements for introductory training programmes to scuba diving. The training programme shall ensure that participants are able to participate safely in an introductory open water dive. Nevertheless, the completion of this programme does not qualify the participants to procure breathing gas, diving equipment or any other scuba diving services.

*ISO 13970* specifies requirements for the training of recreational snorkelling guides. In accordance with this standard, snorkelling guides shall be trained such to have sufficient knowledge, skill and experience to plan, organise and conduct snorkelling excursions and lead recreational snorkelers in open water.

## Standards specifying requirements for service provision

*ISO 13289* specifies requirements for the conduct of snorkelling excursions. This international standard specifies minimum requirements for service providers offering supervised recreational snorkelling excursions. It applies to activities that will include participants being taken into an open water environment.

*ISO 24803* specifies requirements for recreational scuba diving service providers. This international standard specifies requirements for service providers in the field of recreational scuba diving. It specifies three areas of service provision: (a) training and education, (b) organised and guided diving for certified divers, and (c) rental of diving equipment. Service providers may offer one or more of these services. This standard applies to all form of recreational scuba diving service providers such as traditional dive centres as well as liveaboard.

## Certification

The international standards on recreational diving services define the state-of-the-art for safety and quality of scuba diver and scuba instructor training services. However, there are two main questions remaining to be answered. First, how does the training organisation prove credibly that the training system meets all the requirements of the international standards? Second, how can the consumer or an authority be sure that the requirements of the relevant standards are really fulfilled by a training organisation?

Certification means that an independent body confirms that a service has been tested and that its quality is subject to a continuous surveillance. Soon after the publication of the European standards, the need to establish a certification process for training organisations and dive centres became apparent. This led to the establishment of the European Underwater Federation Certification International (EUF n.d.) which was jointly created by the European Underwater Federation (EUF) and the Austrian Standards (AS). This corporation ensures independent certification of scuba diving training organisations and dive centres.

Certification allows training organisations to prove convincingly that their training programmes are in full conformity with the requirements defined by the international standards. In the meantime, all major scuba diving training organisations have been certified according to the ISO standards on recreational diving services.

Important diving markets such as Egypt, Cyprus and Greece have endorsed the international standards within their national legislation (or have agreed that they will do so shortly). Their aim is to protect the interest of both domestic and inbound divers in the countries, by requesting certification of dive centres as a prerequisite for a licence.

In Egypt, from 2009 until the Revolution in 2011, there existed a cooperation agreement between the Egyptian Chamber of Diving and Water Sport (CDWS) and the EUF Certification International, in order to certify all dive centres in Egypt according to ISO 24803. The purpose of this cooperation was to assist Egypt in implementing the ISO standards in their dive centres, providing divers with an assurance of quality. Furthermore, the ISO 24804 certification was a prerequisite for a dive centre to gain a licence from the Ministry of Tourism in Egypt. The system was built on three major foundations. First, it was a certification scheme based on ISO 24803 with the criteria and the procedure to inspect dive centres, including annual audits at each centre. Second, the training of local inspectors was carried out by Austrian Standards. Third, regular surveillance visits by Austrian Standards were carried out in order to ensure the proper ongoing operation of dive centre inspection conducted by the inspectors of the Egyptian CDWS.

Unfortunately, the events of 2011 in Egypt have brought the promising and successful endeavour to an – at least temporary – end. The author is not able to say when the inspections of dive centres in Egypt according to ISO 24803 may resume again.

Figure 5.1 illustrates how the cooperation between the diving industry (represented by the CDWS), the authorities (i.e. the Egyptian Ministry of Tourism) and the certification body of the Austrian Standards implementing the ISO 24803

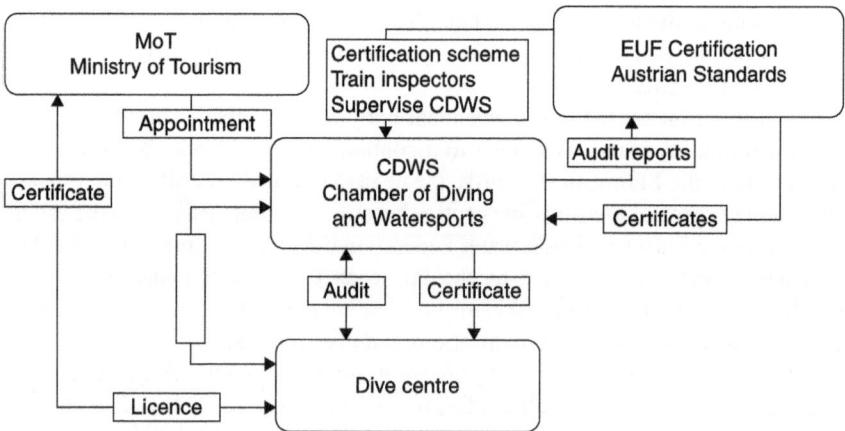

*Figure 5.1* Model of the cooperation between Egypt's CDWS and Austrian Standards to implement ISO 24803 certification of dive centres in Egypt.

has worked. The authorities (MoT) have appointed the CDWS as the sole representative of the diving industry in Egypt, with mandatory membership by all dive centres or operators. The CDWS employs a group of competent individuals with many years of experience in the scuba diving sector as inspectors in charge in carrying out the annual inspections on the dive centres. The inspections were carried out using the ISO 24803 requirements for dive centres. A certificate issued by the Austrian Standards attests the fulfilment of these requirements, and this was a prerequisite for the dive centre to be issued a licence by the MoT.

Using this approach, the authority refers to the international standards and endorses them within its national legislation rather than reinventing the wheel and creating its own specifications. There are two advantages. First, the ISO standards represent the state-of-the-art, as they have been created by competent persons from the scuba diving sector. Therefore the standards include the best knowledge available and result in the highest safety level possible at the time of publication. Second, the process of standardisation is usually much quicker, and it is able to react to changes in technology and be more flexible, compared with the process of legislation. Generally, standards have a wider acceptance than legislation by the business community at large.

Certification by an independent body (also referred to as 'third-party-certification') brings the advantage that the inspections are carried out by technical experts and that the examination is carried out in a neutral, unbiased and impartial manner; certification bodies have neither a stake in the service provider nor an interest of the users of the service.

## References

CMAS (n.d.) 'Confédération Mondiale des Activités Subaquatiques/World Confederation of Underwater Activities'. Online. Available <www.cmas.org> (accessed 14 July 2012).

EUF (n.d.) 'European Undewater Federation Certification International'. Online. Available <www.euf-certification.org> (accessed 15 July 2012).

ISO (n.d.) 'International Organization for Standardization'. Online. Available <www.iso.org> (accessed 15 July 2012).

# Part III

# Consumer behaviour of divers

# 6 Scuba diving motivation

*Kee Mun Wong, Thinaranjeney Thirumoorthi and Ghazali Musa*

## Introduction

The Travel Industry Association (1998) identifies scuba diving as a hard adventure activity that shares common characteristics with rock climbing, whitewater rafting, mountain biking, kayaking, skydiving, and snowboarding. The activity possesses elements of risk, danger, and uncertainty (Ewert 2001) in the interaction of divers with the marine environment. Nevertheless, divers travel from many parts of the world to distant places to experience the beauty of marine life (Tabata 1992). In the scuba diving industry, the state of coral reefs and the number and variety of marine creatures play important roles in its sustainability (Ngazy *et al.* 2001).

Scuba diving is a growing activity (Bennet 2003; Dignan 1990) as evidenced by the increase in the Professional Association of Diving Instructors (PADI) certifications. For example, in 1970, PADI issued 23,736 certifications, and the number increased to 930,941 in 2011. By that year, the total cumulative number of certifications issued by PADI was more than 20 million (PADI 2012). The increased demand for scuba diving spurs the interest among researchers to examine the motivations of scuba divers to embark in the activity.

Motivation is a crucial element in consumer behaviour study and a major determinant of scuba divers' behaviour (Ong and Musa 2012). It provides in-depth understanding of divers' actual expectations, requirements, and aims when involved in the activity. Motivation is an inner state of an individual that drives and directs behaviour (Kassin 1998; Murray 1964), to satisfy both psychological and physiological needs (Berkman *et al.* 1997). Therefore, understanding scuba divers' motivations will enable the stakeholders to have strategies for their management and marketing activities in the target market and satisfy its minimum requirements and needs. Various researchers have examined the motivations among scuba divers (e.g. Burke 2002; Cottrell and Meisel 2004; Davis 1997; Davis *et al.* 1996; Davis and Tisdell 1995; Dearden *et al.* 2006; Ditton and Baker 1999; Edney 2012; Howard 1999; Meyer *et al.* 2002; Todd *et al.* 2002; Wilks 1992).

## Scuba divers' motivations

Understanding motivation is inherently difficult. Iso-Ahola (1999) states that the greatest challenge to understanding motivation is that it cannot be observed.

Researchers are therefore forced to rely upon individuals to report their motivation or to make inferences from observations of actual participation (Plummer 2009). Several perspectives of motivations have been suggested by researchers in the area of scuba diving. Each of the perspectives will be examined next.

### *Leisure motivation (intrinsic and extrinsic views)*

The understanding of scuba diving motivation can be examined from the perspective of leisure motivation. This consists of intrinsic and extrinsic motivations. Intrinsic motivation is derived from the inner self of an individual (Meisel and Cottrell, 2004, p.393) where self-satisfaction and enjoyable feeling (Ryan and Deci 2000a:56) are more important than the rewards obtained externally. In contrast, extrinsic motivation is derived from the reward or achievement obtained externally by an individual (Ryan and Deci 2000a:60).

Studies on leisure motivation (e.g. Iso-Ahola 1979, 1999; Iwasaki and Mannell 1999; Neulinger 1974; Shaw 1985) have largely focused on intrinsic motivation. The key aspect of intrinsic motivation is to identify individuals who derive intrinsic reward through participation and engagement in leisure activities (Weissinger and Bandalos 1995; Weissinger and Iso-Ahola 1984). These individuals have relatively strong self-determination, strong personality, and are capable of undertaking challenging leisure activities, such as rock climbing, sky diving, and scuba diving.

Even though intrinsic motivation is an important element of leisure activity (Graef *et al.* 1983; Iso-Ahola 1979; Neulinger 1974), the more recent motivational theories suggest that considering the presence of intrinsic motivation alone may not be sufficient (Ryan and Deci 2000b). A study on the motivation of leisure participation by Ryan and Deci (2000b) discovered that intrinsic motivation is indeed not the only feature in five out of seven types of activities. Several of these activities have both intrinsic and extrinsic motivations. In fact, the literature has shown that extrinsic motivation may exist exclusively in certain leisure activities (Graef *et al.* 1983; Mannell *et al.* 1988; Stebbins 1992). From the scuba diving perspective, examples of intrinsic motivation are to be adventurous and to learn something new. To socialize with other divers and to gain recognition from people are examples of extrinsic motivation.

### *Motivations by divers' profiles*

As scuba diving is a risky recreational activity (Ewert 1994), divers are generally perceived to have goal-driven behaviour. Scuba divers may pursue the activity with different individual goals. Stimulation (Ewert 1994) is required to satisfy the goal or to induce new goals. Divers may have several motivations for their individual goals and these may differ in their significance (Ewert 1994; Mannell and Kleiber 1997).

Rice (1987) categorizes divers' motivations into three: 'hard core', 'tourist', and 'potential'. While 'hard core' divers dive to admire underwater flora and fauna and the challenges of the various diving conditions, 'tourist' divers only dive as a part of the holiday itineraries. 'Potential' divers are the beginners who are eager to try scuba diving. Tabata (1992) classifies divers into 'adventure divers' who seek challenge and excitement in the marine environment and 'educational divers' whose primary intention in diving is 'to learn about marine environment'. In a PADI survey, Richardson (1995) reports that of all divers' taking part, 81 per cent were motivated 'to seek adventure', and 71 per cent 'to enjoy being with nature'.

Divers' motivations may also be viewed from the perspective of specific groups: 'certified', 'introductory', 'reef day trip', and 'liveaboard divers'. Burke (2002) reports similar motivations among these different groups of divers at the Great Barrier Reef, Australia. The most prominent motivations among all groups are 'to experience the beauty of nature', followed by 'to develop skill in diving', 'to experience something new and different', and 'to experience an undeveloped environment'. The study also discovers that 'getting physical exercise' and 'social interaction' are among the two least important motivations to the respondents.

### Motivations by dive site locations

Most scuba diving studies have been carried out on a specific scuba diving desti-nation, such as the Great Barrier Reef (Burke 2002; Wilks 1992), Vanuatu (Howard 1999), Texas offshore waters (Ditton and Baker 1999), New York State Great Lakes (Todd *et al.* 2002), Florida Keys (Cottrell and Meisel 2004), North Central Florida (Meyer *et al.* 2002), Phuket (Dearden *et al.* 2006), and Chuuk Lagoon (Edney 2012) (see Table 6.1).

Davis and Tisdell (1995) studied scuba divers' motivations in Australia and found that 'desire to experience wilderness', 'interest in marine ecology', 'under-water features', 'marine life', and 'underwater image' were among the reasons divers embarked on the activity. The authors report that divers are also motivated by 'the adventurous aspect of activity in nature' and 'underwater photography'. Some are motivated merely 'to experience the activity'. Davis *et al.* (1996) found that the two major scuba diving motivations in Australia were 'the variety and abundance of marine life and corals' and 'the underwater geological formations'. 'The attractive underwater flora and fauna' as well as 'the opportunity to experi-ence adventure' are also reported as major motivators to draw first time divers into Australia's dive sites (Davis and Tisdell 1995; Davis *et al.* 1996; Davis 1997; Wilks 1992). Wilks (1992) examined divers' reasons to start scuba diving in the Great Barrier Reef. Major reasons among them were 'the desire to see the reef up close' and 'the challenge of a unique experience'. Motivations of 'relaxation', 'social interaction', and 'image of scuba diving sport' were reported as least important among the first time divers in Australia (Davis 1997).

In Vanuatu, Howard (1999) discovered that most divers were motivated 'to view spectacular natural scenes', 'to relax', and 'to experience something new'. Similar to the study findings of Ditton and Baker (1999), 'physical fitness' and 'social interaction' were the least important motivations among divers in Vanuatu. Ditton and Baker (1999) examined the motivations and involvement of divers at the artificial reefs in Texas. The important motivations among divers, reported in sequence order, were 'to look at fish and other aquatic life', 'to experience tranquility underwater', 'to experience adventure and excitement', 'to relax', and 'to experience new and different things'. Other motivations that rated as moderately important were 'physical exercise' and 'social interaction' (being with friends, family recreation), which are similar findings to those of Burke (2002).

Cottrell and Meisel (2004) investigated scuba divers' motivations as part of understanding personal responsibility for the protection of the marine environment in the Florida Keys. They argue that motivations will influence the individual's commitment or personal interest towards an activity, which in turn will affect responsible environmental behaviour. There are 28 motivational items included in the study, of which 22 were adopted from Todd *et al.* (2002). From the total sample of 300 divers, factor analysis reveals motivation dimensions explaining 60 per cent of the variance. These are experience, skill, escape, interest, social, and personal challenge. Experience is reported as the most important motivational factor, followed by escape, social, and interest. Skill and personal challenge are the least important motivation among divers.

## *Motivations by development levels and specialization*

Todd *et al.* (2002) divided divers into five development levels. These are beginner, intermediate, advanced, expert, and post-expert. In her study on scuba divers in New York's Great Lakes, respondents were required to self-select their level of development. A total of seven indicators (23 items) were used to measure the level of development. These are commitment, skill, experience, participation, amateur/ professional development, knowledge, and equipment. One-way analysis of variance between groups (ANOVA) shows that the mean difference between the indicators and the level of development are significant ($p < 0.0001$). Similar results have been reported when these indicators were adopted in measuring the level of development in other leisure activities such as quilt makers, outdoor adventurists, and climbers, indicating good reliability and validity of the measures in defining each level of development.

At the beginner level, divers would have the least commitment, skill, experience, participation, amateur/professional development, knowledge, and equipment. These seven indicators increase gradually when divers move forward to the next three levels of development: intermediate, advanced, and expert. However, as the development stage moves from expert to post-expert, divers' scores on all the development measures fall below expert stage, almost equalling the advanced level. Participation of the divers in the activity at post-expert stage was found to be lower, as compared with the advanced stage. The exceptional case is in 'experience' where a gradual increase of concentration among the divers has been observed from expert to post-expert stage, due to the cumulative nature of the activity (Todd 2000).

Different levels of scuba divers' development possess different motivations. according to Todd *et al.* (2002). The authors studied the relationship between divers' level of development and diving motivation among New Yorkers, using a mixed-method of both qualitative and quantitative survey. The initial in-depth interview revealed 20 motivation items which were later quantitatively measured using the 5-point Likert scale. From factor analysis, six factors emerged which explain 60 per cent of the variance. The divers' motivation factors are 'adventure', 'learning', 'escape', 'personal challenge', 'social interaction', and 'stature'. The factor of stature is similar to the image factor earlier proposed by Ewert (1993) which is a form of extrinsic motivation. Todd *et al.* (2002) found the importance of adventure and learning (both intrinsic motivation) escalates from the beginners' level, all the way to the experts' level, but decreases when reaching the post-experts' level. In contrast, social interaction motives (extrinsic motivation) increase in dominance among less experienced divers. The personal challenge motive (intrinsic motivation) decreases while stature and escape motives (both extrinsic motivation) increase along the development curve.

When divers reach the post-expert level, they tend to share knowledge and teach others in order to remain involved in the leisure activity (Stebbins 1979, 1992). Todd *et al.* (2002) discovered that the thrill of activity itself is the most important motivation among divers, similar to the findings of Ditton and Baker (1999). The opportunities to 'admire the underwater flora and fauna', 'explore new things', 'be adventurous', 'be in exciting and stimulating environment', and 'learn about the underwater environment' make up significant items of diving motivations. Todd *et al.* (2002) add that societal pressures and norms ranked the lowest among divers' motivation.

In a study in Phuket, Thailand, Dearden *et al.* (2006) propose that divers' motivations vary with the degree of specialization. Divers with high and moderate specialization are more motivated to 'observe marine flora and fauna', 'expand knowledge', and 'develop diving skills'. The three motivations are also the motivation of divers with low specialization. Highly specialized divers are low in the motivation to develop diving skills, as compared with novice divers. Motivational factors of environment (good weather, warm water, water visibility, diving condition) and service features (information by dive master, good dive master, good dive buddy, and additional activities) are rated highly by low specialized divers, as compared with highly specialized divers. Highly specialized divers are also motivated by diving experiences with sharks, mantra rays, and turtles.

Edney (2012) investigated the motivations of wreck divers at Chuuk Lagoon in the Federated States of Micronesia. Similar to Todd *et al.* (2002), the author employed a mixed-method approach, namely survey questionnaires and in-depth interviews. The findings indicate that the top three motivations of wreck divers are 'to see historically significant shipwrecks, artifacts, and marine life', 'to penetrate wrecks', and 'to enjoy the peace and tranquility of the underwater environment'. Respondents emphasize the importance of the historical aspect in wreck diving.

### *Motivations by gender*

Meyer *et al.* (2002) explored the motivations of scuba divers in North Central Florida. The result is explained from the perspective of gender. Male divers are more extrinsically motivated, while female divers are more intrinsically motivated. Male divers are motivated 'to see historically significant shipwrecks', 'to collect interesting artifacts', 'to use dive equipment', and 'to experience risk'. On the other hand, female divers indicate the important motivations as being 'to prove to themselves that they can dive', 'to boost self-confidence', 'to do something creative and challenging', and 'to learn about underwater environment'.

In the study of wreck divers' motivations at Chuuk Lagoon (Edney 2012), male divers were found to give importance to technical aspects of diving such as 'appreciating artifacts', 'penetrating the wreck', and 'exploring and discovering machinery, fittings, complexity and size of the wreck'. On the other hand, female divers were more motivated 'to see marine life'.

*Table 6.1* Summary of scuba divers' motivation dimensions

| Source(s) | Research location | Research method | Dimensions |
|---|---|---|---|
| Edney (2012) | Chuuk Lagoon | Mixed of qualitative and quantitative | Seeing historically significant shipwrecks<br>Artifacts<br>Seeing marine life<br>Penetrate wrecks<br>Enjoy peace and tranquility of the underwater environment<br>Exploring and discovering machinery and fittings<br>Complexity and size of wreck |
| Dearden *et al.* (2006) | Phuket | Quantitative | Marine life<br>Expand knowledge<br>Develop diving skill<br>Environmental<br>Service features<br>Resources |
| Cottrell and Meisel (2004) | Florida Keys | Quantitative | Diver experience<br>Skill<br>Escape<br>Interest<br>Social<br>Personal challenge |
| Todd *et al.* (2002) | New York State divers | Mixed of qualitative and quantitative | Personal challenge<br>Stature<br>Escape<br>Learn<br>Adventure<br>Social interaction |
| Burke (2002) | Great Barrier Reef | Quantitative | Experience the beauty of nature<br>Skill development in diving or snorkelling<br>Experiencing something new and different<br>Experiencing an undeveloped environment<br>Physical exercise<br>Social interaction |

*Table 6.1* Continued

| Source(s) | Research location | Research method | Dimensions |
|---|---|---|---|
| Meyer *et al.* (2002) | North Central Florida | Quantitative | Adopted Todd *et al.* (2002) items, came out with 7 dimensions upon factor analysis but no name has been given to the 7 dimensions in the article |
| Ditton and Baker (1999) | Texas offshore waters | Quantitative | Look at fish and other aquatic life<br>Experience tranquility underwater<br>Experience adventure and excitement<br>Relaxation<br>Experience new and different things<br>Physical exercise<br>Social interaction<br>Spear fishing |
| Howard (1999) | Vanuatu | Quantitative | Viewing spectacular natural scenes<br>Relaxation<br>Experiencing something new<br>Physical fitness<br>Social interaction |
| Davis (1997) | Australia | Quantitative | Underwater attraction<br>Experience adventure<br>Relaxation<br>Social interaction<br>Image of the sport of diving |
| Davis *et al.* (1996) | Australia | Quantitative | Diving environment<br>Underwater attraction<br>Experience adventure |
| Davis and Tisdell (1995) | Australia | Quantitative | Experience wilderness<br>Interest in marine ecology<br>Underwater features<br>Marine life<br>Underwater image<br>Experience adventure<br>Hobbies |
| Wilks (1992) | Great Barrier Reef | Quantitative | See the reef up close<br>Challenge of a unique experience<br>Underwater attraction<br>Experience adventure |

## Implications of scuba diving motivation knowledge

The understanding of divers' motivations is pertinent for any country or scuba diving operators which aim to develop and promote a destination as a divers' paradise. The knowledge could guide in the provision of services and experiences which are sought after by divers. Also, effective marketing could then be targeted to the intended segment of divers. For example, both Meyer *et al.* (2002) and Edney (2012) reveal significant differences between genders and their motivations to scuba dive. The scuba diving industry may need to develop products and services which are more adventurous or extreme for male divers, while female divers may need a more leisured and relaxed experience. Additionally, different scuba diving packages could be offered to cater for different levels of development and specialization, as divers' motivations are different along the level of development (Todd *et al.* 2002) and the levels of specialization (Dearden *et al.* 2006). The potential harmful scuba diving motivations which could result in irresponsible behaviour underwater could also be detected. The discussion on divers' behaviour will be the focus of the next chapter (Chapter 7).

## References

Bennet, M. (2003) 'Scuba Diving Tourism in Phuket, Thailand, Pursuing Sustainability', PhD thesis, University of Victoria, Canada.

Berkman, H., Lindquist, J. and Sirgy, M. J. (1997) *Consumer Behavior: Concepts and Marketing Strategy*, Lincolnwood, IL: NTC Business Books.

Burke, A. (2002) *Understanding Great Barrier Reef Visitors: Profiles of Certified Divers, Introductory Divers, Reef Day Trip Divers, Live-aboard Divers – Data Summary Report*, Brisbane: University of Queensland. Online. Available HTTP: <http://www.reef.crc.org.au/research/sustainable_tourisim/pdf/B2.1.1Divers.pdf> (accessed 28 May 2012)

Cottrell, S. P. and Meisel, C. (2004) 'Predictors of Personal Responsibility to Protect the Marine Environment among Scuba Divers', in J. Murdy (ed.) *Proceedings of the 2003 Northeastern Recreation Research Symposium*, Gen. Tech. Rep., ME 317. Newton Square, PA: US Department of Agriculture, Forest Service, Northeastern Research Station: 252–261.

Davis, D. (1997) 'The Development and Nature of Recreational Scuba Diving in Australia: A Study in Economics, Environmental Management and Tourism', PhD thesis, University of Queensland.

Davis, D. and Tisdell, C. (1995) 'Recreational Scuba Diving and Carrying Capacity in Marine Protected Areas', *Ocean and Coastal Management*, 26(1):19–40.

Davis, D., Banks, S. A. and Davey, G. (1996) 'Aspects of Recreational Scuba Diving in Australia', in G. Prosser (ed.) *Proceedings from the Australian Tourism and Hospitality Research Conference*, Coffs Harbour: Bureau of Tourism Research Canberra, ACT.

Dearden, P., Bennett, M. and Rollins, R. (2006) 'Implications for Coral Reef Conservation of Diver Specialization', *Environmental Conservation*, 33(4):353–363.

Dignan, D. (1990) 'Scuba Gaining among Mainstream Travelers', *Tour and Travel News*, 1:44–45.

Ditton, R. B. and Baker, T. L. (1999) *Demographics, Attitudes, Management Preferences, and Economic Impacts of Sport Divers using Artificial Reefs in Offshore Texas Waters*, Department of Wildlife and Fisheries Sciences: Texas A and M University College Station.

Edney, J. (2012) 'Diver Characteristics, Motivations and Attitudes: Chuck Lagoon', *Tourism in Marine Environment*, 8(2):7–18.

Ewert, A. (1993) 'Differences in the Level of Motive Importance Based on Trip Outcome, Experience Level and Group Type', *Journal of Leisure Research*, 25(4):335–349.

Ewert, A. (1994) 'Playing the Edge: Motivation and Risk Taking in a High-altitude Wildernesslike Environment', *Environment and Behavior*, 26(1):3–24.

Ewert, A. (2001) 'Trends in Adventure Recreation: Programs, Experiences and Issues', in K. LuR and S. MacDonald (eds.) *Proceedings of the 5th International Outdoor Recreation and Tourism Trends Symposium*, East Lansing Michigan: Michigan State University: 327–335.

Graef, R., Gsikszentmihalyi, M. and Gianinno, S. M. (1983) 'Measuring Intrinsic Motivation in Everyday Life', *Insure Studies*, 2(2):155–168.

Howard, J. (1999) 'How do Scuba Diving Operators in Vanuatu Attempt to Minimize their Impact on the Environment?', *Pacific Tourism Review*, 3(1):61–69.

Iso-Ahola, S. E. (1979) 'Basic Dimensions of Definitions of Leisure', *Journal of Insure Research*, 11(1):28–39.

Iso-Ahola, S.E. (1999) 'Motivational Foundations of Leisure', in E. L. Jackson and T. L. Burton (eds.) *Leisure Studies: Prospects for the Twenty-first Century*, State Gollege, PA: Venture Publishing: 35–51.

Iwasaki, Y. and Mannell, R.C. (1999) 'Situational and Personality Influences on Intrinsically Motivated Leisure Behavior: Interaction Effects and Cognitive Processes', *Leisure Sciences*, 21(4):287–306.

Kassin, S. (1998) *Psychology* (2nd edn), Upper Saddle River, NJ: Prentice Hall.

Mannell, R. and Kleiber, D. (1997) *The Social Psychology of Leisure*, State College, PA: Venture Publishing.

Mannell, R. G., Zuzanek, J. and Larson, R. W. (1988) 'Leisure States and "Flow" Experiences: Testing Perceived Freedom and Intrinsic Motivation Hypotheses', *Journal of Leisure Research*, 20(4):289–304.

Meisel, C. and Cottrell, S. (2004) 'Differences in Motivations and Expectations of Divers in the Florida Keys', in J. Murdy (ed.) *Proceedings of the 2003 Northeastern Recreation Research Symposium*, Gen. Tech. Rep. NE-317, Newtown Square, PA: US Department of Agriculture, Forest Service, Northeastern Research Station: 393–401.

Meyer, L., Thapa, B. and Pennington-Gray, L. (2002) 'An Exploration of Motivations among Scuba Divers in North Central Florida', in R. Schuster (ed.) *Proceedings of the 14th Northeastern Recreation Research Symposium*, Gen. Tech. Rep. NE-302, Newton Square, PA: US Department of Agriculture, Forest Service, Northeastern Forest Experiment Station: 292–295.

Murray, E. J. (1964) *Motivation and Emotion*, Englewood Cliffs, NJ: Prentice Hall.

Neulinger, J. (1974) *Psychology of Leisure*, Springfield, IL: Charles G. Thomas.

Ngazy, Z., Jiddawi, N. and Cesar, H. (2001) 'Coral Bleaching and the Demand for Coral Reefs: A Marine Recreation Case in Zanzibar', paper presented at the International Consultative Workshop for Economic Valuation and Policy Priorities for Sustainable Management of Coral Reefs World Fish Center's Headquarters, Penang, Malaysia, December 8–10.

Ong, T. F. and Musa, G. (2012) 'Examining the Influences of Experience, Personality and Attitude on Scuba Divers Underwater Behaviour: A Structural Equation Model', *Tourism Management*, 33(6):1521–1534. Online. Available HTTP: <www.cabdirect.org/abstracts/20123268027.html;jsessionid=33BE4CCD4BCFAD8D572817B0EBC10AAD> (accessed 8 April 2013).

PADI (2012) 'Worldwide Corporate Statistic 2011'. Online. Available HTTP: <http://www.padi.com/scuba/about-padi/PADI-statistics/default.aspx> (accessed 28 March 2012).

Plummer, R. (2009) *Outdoor Recreation, An Introduction*, New York: Routledge.

Rice, K. (1987) 'Special Report: Scuba Diving: Dive Market requires Specialized Skill and Information', *Tour and Travel News*, (February 9):24–27.

Richardson, D. (1995) *The Business of Diving: A Guide to Success in Recreational Dive Industry*, Santa Ana, CA: PADI.

Ryan, R. M. and Deci, E. L. (2000a) 'Intrinsic and Extrinsic Motivations: Classic Definitions and New Directions', *Contemporary Educational Psychology*, 25:54–67.

Ryan, R. M. and Deci, E. L. (2000b) 'Self-determination Theory and the Facilitation of Intrinsic Motivation, Social Development, and Well-being', *American Psychologist*, 55(1):68–78.

Shaw, S. M. (1985) 'The Meaning of Leisure in Everyday Life', *Leisure Sciences*, 7:1–24.

Stebbins, R. A. (1979) *Amateurs – On the Margin between Work and Leisure*, Beverly Hills, CA: Sage.

Stebbins, R. A. (1992) *Amateurs, Professionals, and Serious Leisure*, Montreal: McGill-Queen's University Press.

Tabata, R. S. (1992) 'Scuba Diving Holidays', in C. M. Hall and B. Weiler (eds.) *Special Interest Tourism*, New York: Belhaven: 171–184.

Todd, S. L. (2000) 'Scuba Diving in New York's Great Lakes: From Novice to Professional' (New York Sea Grant Institute Completion Report), Cortland: Department of Recreation & Leisure Studies, SUNY, Cortland.

Todd, S., Graefe, A. and Mann, W. (2002) 'Differences in Scuba Diver Motivations Based on Level of Development', in S. Todd (ed.) *Proceedings of the 2001 Northeastern Recreation Research Symposium*, Gen. Tech. Rep. NE-289, Newton Square, PA: US Department of Agriculture, Forest Service, Northeastern Forest Experiment Station: 104–114.

Travel Industry Association of America (1998) *The Adventure Travel Report, 1997*, Washington, DC: Travel Industry Association of America.

Weissinger, E. and Bandalos, D. L. (1995) 'Development, Reliability, and Validity of a Scale to Measure Intrinsic Motivation in Leisure', *Journal of Leisure Research*, 27(4):379–400.

Weissinger, E. and Iso-Ahola, S. E. (1984) 'Intrinsic Leisure Motivation, Personality and Physical Health', *Loisir et Societé Society and Leisure*, 7(1):217–228.

Wilks, J. (1992) 'Introductory Scuba Diving on the Great Barrier Reef', *Australian Parks and Recreation*, 28(4):18–23.

# 7 Responsible underwater behaviour

*Tah Fatt Ong and Ghazali Musa*

## Introduction

For the past two decades, the rising popularity of scuba diving as a recreational activity has resulted in a tremendous growth in the dive tourism industry. Evidence of such popularity can be observed from the global leapfrog increase in numbers of certified divers from 2.5 million in 1988 to 17.8 million in 2008 (PADI Statistics 2011). The Professional Association of Diving Instructors (PADI) estimated that 600,000 new divers are certified yearly, representing an annual growth of 6 per cent. As reported by Mintel (2006), it was estimated that 2 to 3 million certified divers had taken some kind of scuba-diving related holiday in the Asia-Pacific region during 2005. In the Egyptian Red Sea, divers' visitation has increased by ten times, compared with the 1990s (Harriott 2002; Garrod 2008). In fact scuba diving tourism is now a multibillion dollar industry and is recognized by the World Tourism Organisation (UNWTO) as one of the fastest growing sectors of the tourism trade. Among factors which contribute to this rapid growth of scuba diving tourism, in a relatively short period of time, are the development of safer and affordable diving equipment (Davis and Tisdell 1996), coupled with the advances in technology that produce marine craft for easy access to remote diving areas (Parker 2001) and the increasing interest in nature, conservation, and environmental matters (Dimmock and Wilson, 2009; Harriott *et al.* 1997; Orams 1999).

However, the proliferation of dive tourism is not without costs to the marine environment. Globally, coral reefs are facing a wide range of anthropogenic stresses from human activities such as coastal development, pollution, anchor damage, destructive fishing, coral mining, over-fishing, and sedimentation (Bell 1992; Nemeth and Nowlis 2001; Negri *et al.* 2002; Burke *et al.* 2002; Saphier and Hoffmann 2005). The increasing popularity of scuba diving activity may be posing threats to the growth and reproduction of the coral reefs (Barker and Roberts 2004).

Concern over the detrimental effects of divers on the marine environment is evidenced through the numerous reports in scuba diving studies undertaken since the 1990s. The negative impacts of scuba divers on the coral reef are apparent in various studies conducted in different parts of the world, such as the Northern Red

Sea (Riegl and Velimirov 1991), Egypt (Hawkins and Roberts 1992), the Caribbean Island of Bonaire (Dixon *et al.* 1993), and Australia (Harriott *et al.* 1997), among others. The findings reveal alarming results concerning the impoverished condition of the marine environment caused by divers, and call for further attention regarding the issue of marine conservation.

Subsequently, studies about ways to mitigate these negative consequencs of diving have been conducted using four approaches. These include the examination of the carrying capacity of dive sites (Davis and Tisdell 1995; Harriott *et al.* 1997; Rouphael and Inglis 1997; Zakai and Chadwick-Furman 2002), the identification of divers' demographic and behavioural characteristics that may have greater negative results than others (Barker and Roberts 2004; Rouphael and Inglis 2001), types of intervention that may influence divers' underwater behaviour (Barker and Roberts 2004; Medio *et al.* 1997), and the positive impacts of recreational divers' involvement in the marine environmental monitoring programme (Goffredo *et al.* 2010; Goffredo *et al.* 2004; Hodgson 1999; Pattengill-Semmens and Semmens 2003).

## Codes of conduct in diving activity

The growing awareness of the impacts of dive tourism activities on the marine environment has led a number of management regimes and organizations to establish and adopt codes of conduct or practice for the diving industry. Codes of conduct are written sets of behavioural expectation, which are also known as guidelines or codes of practice (Garrod 2008). Often, codes of conduct are formed based on an informal code of ethics. They are recognized as a formal adoption of codes of ethics by the industry. Codes of conduct may be written by governments, non-governmental organizations, academics, industry operators, local communities, or through collaboration of the related stakeholders. These codes of conduct may be meant for the industry operators, tourists, local communities, or a combination of the stakeholders. Usually, the codes of conduct are implemented as a set of rules according to which the activity concerned should be pursued. These codes may or may not be monitored, and there may be formal sanctions imposed on those breaking the codes, such as the removal of an industry licence to operate. The codes may also be sanctioned informally, involving a mixture of social pressures and peer-group expectation.

Codes of conduct and guidelines for scuba diving are intended to help tour operators to improve their environmental management and minimize divers' impacts on the marine environment. Guidelines for environmental management are crucial, due to the fragility of the coral reef and marine environment. Minimal impact techniques, such as Low Impact Diving (LID), are necessary for environmental protection as well as a diver's safety and enjoyment. Such guidelines suggest that divers should follow the standard rules for environmentally-aware diving while underwater. In relation to this, several guidelines for recreational diving are put forward by marine conservation organisations. According to standard requirements for recreational scuba diving proposed by ICRAN–MAR (International Coral Reef Action Network–Mesoamerican Reef 2006), divers must obey all applicable local and national laws and regulations on diving activity. These guidelines include: avoiding interactions with marine life, maintaining an awareness of fins, use of equipment and handling of underwater cameras, adjusting buoyancy, and securing equipment to avoid contacting corals or stirring up sediments while diving. Divers are expected to dive safely, both for their health and for the protection of the marine environment. Divers are not allowed to touch or contact corals or other reef dwelling organisms. They are not to stand and rest on coral reefs. Spear fishing, chasing, harassing, riding, and feeding fish are strictly prohibited. Collecting shells and corals as souvenirs is not allowed. In addition, the International Ecotourism Society (2001) advocated that the codes of conduct for responsible divers include regular review and update of diving skills such as buoyancy control, finning, and underwater positioning. This would promote divers' safety and minimise negative impacts on the marine environment.

In the safety aspect of diving, relevant guidelines and codes of conduct would include the following:

1   Make sure that all divers are trained and certified by a recognized international training agency and are physically fit to dive. Every diver (or, in the case of minors, a parent or legal guardian) must sign a liability release form before being allowed to dive.
2   Every diver is required to show proof of insurance covering medical evacuation and treatment for decompression sickness, barotrauma, or other dive-related injuries.
3   Ensure that divers check that their dive gear and equipment are in good working order and appropriate condition before the dive.
4   Make sure that safety rules, as well as any special instructions or emergency procedures, are explained to the divers by the dive leader.
5   Ensure that divers attend dive briefings before every dive and comply with depth limits, time limits, and other instructions from the dive leader.
6   All divers are required to carry the following safety item on every dive: a surface marker buoy (SMB), such as a sausage, lift bag, emergency flag, or other appropriate visual and auditory signalling device.

## What constitutes responsible diving behaviour?

Responsible diving behaviour refers to specific responsible behaviour exhibited by divers towards their own safety/health and the protection of marine environment, while diving underwater (Ong and Musa 2012). It is concerned with what divers do when diving underwater.

Thapa *et al.* (2006) attempted to understand the marine based environmental behaviours among scuba divers based on surveys utilizing divers' self-reported behaviour. They found that there are three dimensions: 'contact behaviour' (related to physical contact with aquatic marine life), 'general diving behaviour', and 'general educational behaviour' (related to education).

However, Ong and Musa (2012) provide a greater understanding of the various aspects of underwater responsible behaviour with three distinct self–reported behaviours of divers, namely 'safety diving behaviour', 'buoyancy control diving behaviour', and 'non-contact diving behaviour'. This safety diving behaviour involves practices such as checking underwater position/orientation regularly, bringing a safety sausage/signalling device, inspecting regulator readings from time to time, practising good finning technique, and monitoring diving depth while diving. The buoyancy control diving behaviour relates to diving skills which include keeping neutrally buoyant at all times, maintaining a safe distance from the reef, and staying off the bottom while diving underwater. The non-contact diving behaviour is concerned with avoiding actions such as holding onto coral, touching coral, and standing or resting on coral. This categorization is more differentiating compared with that of *Thapa et al.* (2006), and covers the two main aspects of scuba diving which are the safety and the protection of marine environment.

## Factors influencing environmental responsible behaviour

In explaining responsible environmental behaviour, among the psycho-social variables commonly identified by researchers are attitude, locus of control (LOC), knowledge, responsibility, social norm, sexual role, sensitivity, and intention to act (Boerschig and DeYoung 1993; Hines *et al.* 1987; Hungerford and Volk 1990; Sia *et al.* 1985). In the meta-analysis of research on responsible environmental behaviour (Hines *et al.* 1987), the four prominent psycho-social variables associated with the formation of responsible environmental behaviour are attitude, behavioural intention, LOC/self-efficacy, and moral responsibility. Another study on determinants of responsible environmental behaviour by Bamberg and Möser (2007) revealed that, besides behavioural intention, attitude, and behavioural control, another prominent predictor of responsible environmental behaviour is personal moral norms. Other related determinants which have indirect influences include problem awareness, moral and social norms, guilt, and attribution processes.

## Factors influencing underwater responsible behaviours

In the context of scuba diving, psycho-social variables related to underwater responsible behaviour were examined by Ong and Musa (2011, 2012). It was found that five prominent psycho-social antecedents are experience level, diving attitude, personality, personal norms, and subjective norms, and they govern how responsible is divers' underwater behaviour. The influences of these factors on underwater responsible behaviour are illustrated in Figure 7.1. The related factors are described in detail in the following section.

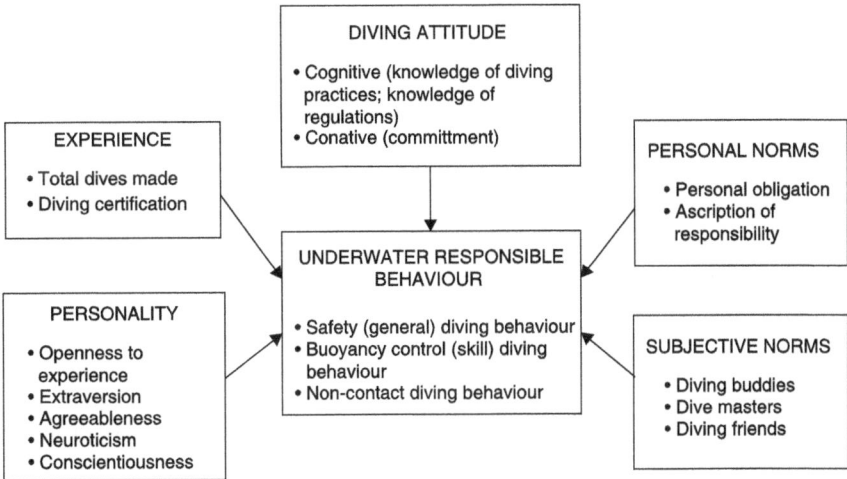

*Figure 7.1* Factors influencing underwater responsible behaviour.

## Experience

Several researchers have contended that an individual's past experiences do influence future leisure behaviour (Williams *et al.* 1990; Shinew 1993). The influence of past experience on an individual is reflected in the skill level of the individual, as well as how he/she feels, behaves, and makes decisions. Experience in scuba diving is recognized as the sum of accumulated life experiences a diver has in performing scuba diving activity. It can be identified through the total number of dives made and the level of diving certification (Todd 2000; Todd *et al.* 2000; Musa *et al.* 2011; Ong and Musa 2012).

Findings in scuba diving literature indicate that the level of divers' experience directly influences underwater behaviour (Rouphael and Inglis 1997; Todd 2000; Musa *et al.* 2011; Ong and Musa 2012). Several studies revealed that more experienced divers made significantly less contact with the reef than less experienced divers (Talge 1992; Davis and Tisdell 1995; Rouphael and Inglis 1997, Barker and Roberts 2004). Roberts and Harriott (1994) defined inexperienced divers as those who have logged fewer than 100 dives. In Walters and Samways's (2001) study, novice divers were found to make one damaging contact per 6 dives, while moderately experienced and experienced divers made contact about once every 14 dives and once every 23 dives, respectively.

Thapa *et al.* (2006) found that there is a positive relationship between levels of specialization and marine based environmental behaviours among divers. This was further confirmed by Ong and Musa (2012) who recorded that more experienced divers are more responsible in underwater behaviour. Experience involves behaviour related to skill and knowledge. More experienced divers are more exposed to the underwater environment and acquire a higher level of training, which improves their diving competency and skill. Advanced divers tend to have better underwater buoyancy control and finning techniques which subsequently inflict less impact on the marine environment (Davis and Tisdell 1995; Roberts and Harriott 1994). They also have greater capabilities to adapt to various challenging diving situations, such as strong currents, poor visibility, and different diving environments (Harriott *et al.* 1997; Newhouse 1990; Rouphael and Inglis 1997).

Among the mentioned factors, Ong and Musa (2012) found that the experience construct has the most influence on the prediction of underwater behaviour among divers. To enhance divers' underwater responsible behaviour, endeavours to improve the skills and knowledge of the less experienced divers need to be emphasized. It is important for dive masters to give additional attention and guidance to less experienced divers when diving underwater. Furthermore, dive masters and instructors should ensure that the skills among divers, not only the less experienced but even the experienced ones, are appropriate for the dive sites. As experience level can be easily and readily gauged through numbers of dives made (dive logbook) and diving certification, these could be used as benchmarks or guidelines to manage divers' visitation to 'fragile' islands such as Sipadan Island in Malaysia (Musa 2002). For example, the relevant authority could impose 50 logged dives as the minimum requirement for eligibility to visit the island, because divers are likely to face strong currents and differing underwater topography, which require them to have sufficient skills and experience.

## Diving attitude

In the process of environmental behaviour formation, attitude is recognized as one of the most important influences on behaviour (Newhouse 1990). Attitude is generally understood as a psychological state that predisposes a person to act favourably or unfavourably to an event or situation (Eagly and Chaiken 1993). Thus, diving attitude is described as an individual's favourable or unfavourable feelings with regard to scuba diving in the marine environment (Ong and Musa 2012). It represents specific attitudes toward ecology and environmental actions regarding the marine environment.

Based on general environmental dispositions, McCawley and Teaff (1995) noted that divers who are concerned about negative environmental impacts have a tendency to be more concerned with preservation and demonstrate more support and understanding for rules and regulations. In the diving literature, advanced divers are more inclined to be responsible for their own actions (Thapa *et al.* 2005). Ong and Musa (2012) further explored and explained the components that constitute diving attitude. They discovered that diving attitude can be represented by three components which are knowledge of dive practice and knowledge of regulations (cognitive component), awareness of diving behaviour consequences (belief/affective component), and personal commitment to marine issue resolution (conative component).

Thus, the concept of diving attitude can be explained as follows: for an individual to act responsibly towards an object or situation, certain information or knowledge about the object needs to be acquired. For example, divers need to know the marine environment, and the skills needed to perform the activity, so that they will not cause danger to themselves as well as the marine environment. Additionally, they also need to have knowledge of marine park regulations on how to mitigate destructive impacts on the marine environment. Past occasions or experience in divers who have been involved in marine conservation activity (conative/behavioural dimension) is of substantial importance in influencing diving attitude. Thus, the previous experience or involvement of divers in marine conservation activities could be taken into consideration by authorities or governing bodies, as a prerequisite for divers to engage in diving activity in 'fragile' dive sites.

Among these components, the cognitive domain (knowledge of diving practice, and knowledge of regulations) and the conative domain (commitment) demonstrate stronger influences in the formation of positive diving attitudes. The importance of the cognitive domain indicates that knowledge plays a crucial role in the positive influence on attitude, which in turn affects behaviour. The conative domain, which involves behavioural commitment, demonstrates that, in situations where individuals feel committed to resolving impact problems, they are more likely to engage in responsible behaviour.

Thus the basic scuba diving knowledge and skill required to be mastered for the certification of scuba divers play an important role in the cultivation of positive diving attitudes. Knowledge of the marine environment and regulations should not be neglected. Integrated programmes and continuous education about marine conservation could enhance divers' awareness of behaviour consequences and a personal commitment to environmental responsibility. To enhance the commitment of divers, the involvement of divers in the conservation of aquatic resources should be encouraged, with the support and sponsorship of various stakeholders such as marine conservation organizations, governmental agencies, and the diving industry. With substantial sponsorship from the stakeholders, divers could be offered the chance to be involved, at preferably no cost, in marine conservation activities such as underwater clean-ups and reef monitoring programmes. As individuals possess a vested interest and a positive attitude towards diving, combined with knowledge, commitment, and awareness about marine conservation, they are more likely to demonstrate responsible underwater diving behaviour.

## Personality

According to Ryckman (2007), personality is a dynamic and organized set of characteristics possessed by a person that uniquely influences his/her cognitions, motivations, and behaviours in various situations. The literature finds that people with different personality profiles show distinct environmental behaviour (Ramanaiah *et al.* 2000). The influence of personality on responsible underwater behaviour may be explained by the nature of diving activity itself. While diving underwater, behaviours such as inspection of regulator readings, underwater positioning, and avoiding touching coral reef, are repeated often, and have the potential to become routine or habitual in nature. Kassin (2003) explained that personality traits are related to the habitual pattern of behaviour and thoughts. As such, personality traits may capture routine or habitual aspects of behaviour that eventually influence behaviour.

Based on the Five Factor Model (FFM), Ong and Musa (2012) identified that the personality traits of openness to experience, extraversion, and agreeableness are characteristics of divers who are more likely to be responsible underwater. Openness to experience in individuals is associated with a higher order personal value of self-transcendence, reflecting an expanded sense of self and a greater concern for others (Mayer and Frantz 2004). Hence, they are more empathic and likely to develop a personal connection with nature, which in turn tends to result in responsible scuba diving behaviour underwater. Extraversion possesses sociable and affectionate characteristics which are concurrent with the tendency to act in a responsible manner while diving underwater. Agreeableness results in individuals who are generally altruistic, considerate, caring, and responsible: it is generally expected that these divers will exhibit underwater responsible behaviour. This underlies the relationship between the three personality traits and responsible underwater behaviour.

However, highly neurotic divers were found to be more irresponsible underwater (Musa *et al.* 2011). Diving operators should be aware that divers with high level of neuroticism, who possess nervous, insecure, and worried characteristics, are more likely to display irresponsible underwater behaviour. This group of divers may require closer supervision from dive leaders while diving underwater. They can also be paired with buddies having personality traits of extroversion, openness to experience, and agreeableness. Active intervention might be needed to avoid any unnecessary detrimental impact caused by these divers to the marine environment, as well as any behaviour that is unsafe for them underwater. Thus, awareness and comprehension of the individual diver's personality is an important element in the duties of dive masters/instructors in enabling them to understand and monitor the diver's underwater behaviour more effectively.

## Personal norms

The moral Norm-Activation Theory (NAT) of altruism (Schwartz 1973) explained that personal norms are a direct determinant of altruistic behaviour. Personal norms represent 'the beliefs held by the individual with regard to how he or she should behave' (Oom Do Valle *et al.* 2005: 381). In the context of scuba diving, personal norms are referred to as an individual's conviction or belief towards the conservation of the marine environment. It is primarily internalized. Ong and Musa (2012) described the term as referring to a personal obligation to marine conservation, responsible behaviour underwater, and participation in marine conservation activities.

In relation to underwater responsible behaviour dimensions, personal norms have the strongest correlation with non-contact diving behaviour, followed by buoyancy control diving behaviour, and safety diving behaviour (Ong and Musa 2011). The positive correlation between personal norms and non-contact diving behaviour indicates that, as awareness of consequences and ascription of responsibility towards marine environment increases, divers are less likely to engage in diving behaviour such as holding onto, or resting on, coral and disturbing marine life.

Scuba diving is an appreciative activity that involves attempts to enjoy the natural environment without altering its natural state (Dunlap and Heffernan 1975). The internalization feature of personal norms (Schwartz 1977) plays an important role in minimizing non-contact diving behaviour among divers. To develop positive personal norms among divers, education and personal involvement/experience (in marine conservation) could provide better understanding and interpretation of marine conservation among divers. Several scholars have indicated that exposure to real life experience in nature helps develop emotional affinity and protective behaviour towards nature (Millar and Millar 1996; Pooley and O'Conner 2000). As reported by Dearden *et al.* (2007), divers who witnessed negative impacts of diving activity, such as anchor damage, garbage disposal, and divers' impact on coral reef, are significantly more likely to indicate interest in participating in reef conservation projects. Recognizing that direct experience is often the most powerful teacher (Manfredo and Bright 1991; Orams 1995), informal education through direct experience should be encouraged and guided by dive instructors. Among popular marine conservation programmes are underwater garbage and Crown of Thorns cleaning and reef checking surveys. All these activities enhance divers' personal norms towards marine environment and influence their underwater responsible behaviours.

## Subjective norms

According to Norm-Activation Theory (Schwartz 1973), another factor which influences altruistic behaviour is social or subjective norms. Subjective norms are described as a person's 'perception that most people who are important to him think he should or should not perform the behaviour in question' (Fishbein and Ajzen 1975: 302). An individual tends to take into account the normative expectations of important others when he/she intends to perform a certain behaviour. Thus, subjective norms refer to the specific referents that dictate or influence individuals in terms of how they should behave. In the case of scuba diving, the specific referents refer to diving buddies/partners, dive masters/instructors, and family members of the divers. Dive masters/instructors are found to have the greatest influence on divers' responsible behaviour while diving underwater, followed by the influence of diving buddies/partners and other diving friends (Ong and Musa 2012). Thus, ongoing training programmes for dive instructors to continuously upgrade their diving skills and knowledge on marine environmental conservation ought to be provided. Such programmes could improve the effectiveness with which environmental dive briefings are given to all dive groups.

In relation to responsible underwater behaviour, subjective norms are found to significantly correlate to skill (buoyancy control) in diving behaviour (Ong and Musa 2011). This association indicates that certain specific referent individuals (i.e. diving buddies/partners, dive masters/instructors, other diving friends and family members) have positive influences on divers behaving responsibly under-water. The skill (buoyancy control) in diving behaviour relates to activity such as good finning techniques as well as good buoyancy control. This implies that prac-tices such as pre-dive briefings by dive masters and discussion sessions among diving communities are useful in promoting divers' skill (buoyancy control) diving behaviour.

However, Schwartz (1973) also highlighted that the influence of subjective norms on individual behaviour is not direct, but mediated by personal norms of altruistic behaviour. In the context of scuba diving, this indirect relationship was supported by Ong and Musa (2012). As explained by Kallgren *et al.* (2000) the influence of social norms in the formation of personal norms seems to be based on easily accessible sources of information as to how others validate specific envi-ronmental behaviours. Often our personal understanding is influenced by dialogue with other people who interpret and frame rules within a personal context. The internalization of personal norms is a social construction process in which a shared meaning of a situation is created (Vygotsky 1981). Therefore, specific referents within the diving community and environment positively influence divers' personal norms, which in turn affect responsible diving behaviour. Common activities, such as communication and interaction among the diving community and pre-dive briefings, have a significant role in influencing personal norms of divers towards environmental and safety diving behaviour. In addition, the role of buddy divers also should be extended beyond the concern of safety so as to include the responsibility of safeguarding the marine environment.

## Management strategies for divers' responsible underwater behaviour

There are many strategies and methods to manage the impacts of divers on the marine environment. Very often, different strategies are applied with reference to a number of factors, such as the causes, location, the extent of the impact, the cost, and the ease and effectiveness of the implementation. Basically, these strategies can be viewed from two perspectives: direct and indirect management strategies. The direct management approach is concerned with managing the visitor/diver by providing information and education, enforcing regulations, and regulating numbers, group size, and length of stay of divers. The indirect approach deals with managing dive sites, whereby destination infrastructure and the natural environ-ment are manipulated to influence divers on where to go and what to do. As an example, designation of Marine Protected Areas (MPA) is among one of the well-known strategies commonly used in this approach.

From the previous discussion, it is beyond doubt that education plays a vital role in the formation of divers' positive diving attitude and responsible behaviour under-water. Other than the cognitive aspect, the conative dimension is also important to take into account when working to change diving attitudes and divers' underwater responsible behaviour (Ong and Musa 2012). Many researchers have emphasized environmental education and interpretation programmes as important channels to enhance the awareness of environmental problems as well as establish the basis for conserving the environment (Sia *et al.* 1985; Sivek and Hungerford 1989). Hence, more complex considerations may be needed to support an environmental education programme for divers to promote underwater responsible behaviour.

Education and dissemination of information concerning marine environmental conservation to divers are accomplished in various ways. Among them are the diving certification process, pre-dive and post-dive briefing, environmental education programmes, brochures, and signage. To enhance the conative component, dive professionals should encourage divers to be involved and enrol in environmental conservation organizations and participate in related conservation programmes. Such social activities enhance relationships among divers, and lead to higher involvement and personal identification with the sport, which in turn may increase environmentally responsible behaviours. In order to improve the effectiveness of the information on regulations, the approach to the presentation of information may need to be revised. Rather than emphasizing what divers should not do, perhaps it would be more effective to communicate the reasons for not so doing, and convey the message positively by emphasizing what they should do. In this context, messages need to be designed in such a way as to provide information with practical and technical advice on how to practise 'eco-friendly' dives, rather than just warning divers not to damage the reef. This detailed informative approach and redirection in communicating the message is more likely to stimulate personal norms and steer them to performing responsible diving behaviour. This reorientation of the communication mode would probably be more effective in instilling positive environmental behaviour among divers.

Other than education, formal enforcement of regulations is another management strategy that is commonly implemented by governments. This includes imposing penalties and fines on divers who have behaved irresponsibly and violated the regulations set forth by the local authority/governing body. In addition, the governing body could control the numbers of divers visiting a particular site, and regulate the group size and length of stay of divers in 'fragile' dive destinations.

In the indirect approach, the designation of marine parks and marine reserves will enhance better management of dive sites and monitoring of diving activities. Strategies such as zoning, carrying capacity, restoration, construction of artificial dive sites, permit requirement, and user-payments could also be considered where appropriate.

Zoning involves identifying smaller units or zones within the protected area, each with prescribed levels of environmental protection and certain levels and types of public use. Zoning of protected areas could benefit and protect the natural environment as well as provide a range of recreation opportunities that suit the capabilities of divers. Carrying a capacity strategy involves limiting the number of scuba divers at a dive site, so that overcrowding and resource depletion can be avoided. Restoration is concerned with lessening the pressure on a high-use dive site by resting it for a period of time.

Another management approach is the voluntary involvement of dive operators in promoting codes of conduct and diving guidelines in their operations. Accreditation of dive operators as eco-dive centres can benefit both the operators and the natural environment (Dowling 1996). Accredited companies are said to gain a competitive advantage over other competitors as they are recognised for operating in a sustainable manner. Key elements emphasized in the accreditation process include education and interpretation, application of sustainable minimal impact techniques, operations, and awareness. Besides, in providing specific certification courses, the participants should be required to educate and train eco-divers who are committed and willing to contribute to marine conservation programmes. This provides additional impetus in marine conservation efforts and potentially reduces the negative impacts of divers on the aquatic environment.

In terms of monitoring divers' responsible behaviour, both dive operators and dive guides/leaders play critical roles in overseeing the behaviour of divers while diving. Intervention by dive guides on irresponsible divers underwater would reduce damage to the coral reef. Giving an in-depth briefing before diving could decrease damaging contact with the reef (Medio *et al.* 1997). During briefing sessions, there should be equal emphasis put on the security and the fragility of marine environment. Besides, as earlier stated, dive operators should ensure that the skills among divers are appropriate for the dive sites. In addition, several recommendations have been proposed for the dive operators to assist in monitoring divers' responsible behaviour while diving. Among these recommendations is included the requirement that divers sign a responsible code of diving ethics during the pre-dive briefing. This may emphasize to the diver the awareness and importance of being responsible. There is also a suggestion that a certification renewal programme should be imposed on inactive divers who have lapsed from diving activity for more than five years (Thapa *et al.* 2006). Introducing certification for underwater camera users is another useful suggestion which can be considered.

## Sustainability in scuba diving

Scuba diving is often referred to as a marine ecotourism activity, due to its nature-based characteristics. The recreational activity relies heavily on the pristine nature of the underwater environment, in order to support the sustainability of scuba diving. Divers thus have responsibility to actively preserve the favourable condition of the marine environment, which enables the continuation of the activity for current and future generations of scuba divers.

As mentioned by Jennings (2007), the future and sustainability of scuba diving is strongly related to attitudes, behaviours, and practices; knowledge and education; and management practices. Education and knowledge affect the behaviour, practices and attitudes of divers, which in turn promote sustainable scuba diving activity, whereas, management practices and support from related stakeholders provide impetus in the preservation of a healthy marine ecosystem which eventually ensures the sustainability of scuba diving industry.

In relation to education, it is recommended that the present curricula of scuba diving certification programmes should be enhanced by the inclusion of education

(Pepe 2010) in sustainable scuba diving. Information concerning environmental issues, including the impacts and importance of the role of the individual diver on the sustainability of the marine environment, could create awareness among them of their responsibility for attitudes and behaviour while diving.

To enhance the learning effect of certification, divers should be encouraged to participate in more diving activities or achieve higher skill and experience through certification programmes. The involvement of divers in regularly organized marine environmental campaigns/activities would reinforce their knowledge and commitment towards preserving the marine environment. These engagements could provide divers with updates on important environmental issues and best practices for sustainable scuba diving activity. In relation to this, well-planned and coordinated conservation activities/programmes are vital. Such programmes could include the formation of online diver communities, the promotion of eco-diver projects, the organisation of sponsored underwater cleaning activities, and the recruitment of membership in marine conservation organizations. Recent studies on the involvement of recreational divers as volunteers in marine conservation monitoring programmes (Goffredo *et al.* 2010; Goffredo *et al.* 2004; Pattengill-Semmens and Semmens 2003) indicate encouraging results in enhancing divers' stewardship towards marine conservation activities. This type of programme presents an excellent avenue to foster both the cognitive and conative domains of diving attitude in the development of responsible diving behaviour among divers.

The importance of diving environment sustainability could be further promoted through numerous marketing efforts. Such efforts could include the provision of easily accessible information and the promotion of sustainable scuba diving through relevant websites. Tangible items such as brochures, stickers, postcards, and collectible posters can be used as promotional tools in the dissemination of sustainable scuba diving. These items can also be distributed to divers via mailing lists maintained by non-profit organizations or dive operators. Distributing and displaying informational signage concerning sustainable diving practices that meet local environmental regulations in marinas, scuba shops, and popular scuba diving sites is another feasible marketing approach.

However, the effectiveness of such a strategy depends upon the collaboration of all the stakeholders in the diving industry. This includes scuba divers, dive operators, diving associations, dive certification agencies, marine conservation organizations, and governmental agencies, among others. The assistance and support of educational institutions and related interest groups could boost the success in the implementation of relevant programmes.

## Conclusion

This chapter has presented an overview of the dive tourism industry and divers' impacts on the aquatic environment. Concern for the sustainability of the marine environment has led to the imperative and critical need to comprehend the underwater behaviours among scuba divers. As well as the codes of conduct, the important elements which need to be kept in mind among scuba diving industry players are experience, diving attitude, personality, personal norms, and subjective norms. The management of scuba diving behaviour requires both direct (on divers) and indirect (on dive sites) approaches, which have been discussed in detail in this chapter. The future and the sustainability of the scuba diving industry depend on the attitudes, behaviours, and practices of divers, the management of scuba diving operations, and the policies and regulations instituted by the authorities; of which, the dissemination and the application of the knowledge of, and education in, sustainable scuba diving practices will be the most crucial. In short, the accomplishment of preserving the fragile and delicate aquatic environment critical to the recreational scuba diving industry will require a collective effort of all stakeholders in the industry; this includes divers, dive operators, diving associations, marine conservation organizations, and governmental agencies.

# References

Bamberg, S. and Möser, G. (2007) 'Twenty Years after Hines, Hungerford, and Tomera: A New Meta-analysis of Psycho-social Determinants of Pro-environmental Behaviour', *Journal of Environmental Psychology*, 27(1):14–25.

Barker, N. H. L. and Roberts, C. M. (2004) 'Scuba Diver Behaviour and the Management of Diving Impacts on Coral Reefs', *Biological Conservation*, 120(4):481–489.

Bell, P. R. F. (1992) 'Eutrophication and Coral Reefs – Some Examples in the Great Barrier Reef Lagoon', *Water Research*, 26:553–568.

Belknap, J. (2008) 'A Study of the Relationship between Conservation Education and Scuba Diver Behavior in the Flower Garden Banks National Marine Sanctuary', PhD Thesis, A & M University, Texas.

Boerschig, S. and De Young, R. (1993) 'Evaluation of Selected Recycling Curricula: Educating the Green Citizen', *Journal of Environmental Education*, 24(3):17–22.

Burke, L., Selig, L. and Spalding, M. (2002) *Reefs at Risk in Southeast Asia*, Washington DC: World Resource Institute.

Davis, D. and Tisdell, C. (1995) 'Recreational Scuba-diving and Carrying Capacity in Marine Protected Areas', *Ocean and Coastal Management*, 26(1):19–40.

Davis, D. and Tisdell, C. (1996) 'Economic Management of Recreational Scuba Diving and the Environment', *Journal of Environmental Management*, 48(3):229–248.

Dearden, P., Bennett, M. and Rollins, R. (2007) 'Perceptions of Diving Impacts and Implications for Reef Conservation', *Coastal Management*, 35(2):305–317.

Dimmock, K. and Wilson, E. (2009) 'Risking Comfort? The Impact of In-water Constraints on Recreational Scuba Diving', *Annals of Leisure Research*, 12(2):173–194.

Dixon, J. A., Scura, L. F. and van't Hof, T. (1993) 'Meeting Ecological and Economic Goals: Marine Parks in the Caribbean', *Ambio*, 22:117–125.

Dowling, R. K. (1996) 'The Implementation of Ecotourism in Australia', paper presented at The Second International Conference: The Implementation of Ecotourism: Planning, Developing and Managing for Sustainability, Bangkok, Thailand.

Dunlap, R. E. and Heffernan, R. B. (1975) 'Outdoor Recreation and Environmental Concern: An Empirical Examination', *Rural Sociology*, 40(1):18–29.

Eagly, A. H. and Chaiken, S. (1993) *The Psychology of Attitudes*, Orlando, FL: Harcourt Brace Jovanovich College Publishers.

Fishbein, M. and Ajzen, I. (1975) *Belief, Attitude, Intention and Behavior: An Introduction to Theory and Research*, Reading, MA: Addison-Wesley.

Garrod, B. (2008) 'Market Segments and Tourist Typologies for Diving Tourism', in B. Garrod and S. Gössling (eds.) *New Frontiers in Marine Tourism: Diving Experiences, Sustainability, Management*, Amsterdam: Elsevier: 31–49.

Garrod, B. and Gössling, S. (2008) *New Frontiers in Marine Tourism: Diving Experiences, Sustainability, Management*, Amsterdam: Elsevier.

Goffredo, S., Piccinetti, C. and Zaccanti, F. (2004) 'Volunteers in Marine Conservation Monitoring: A Study on the Distribution of Seahorses carried out in Collaboration with Recreational Scuba Divers', *Conservation Biology*, 18:1492–1503.

Goffredo, S., Pensa, F., Neri, P., Orlandi, A., Gagliardi, M., Velardi, A. and Zaccanti, F. (2010) 'Unite Research with what Citizens do for Fun: "Recreational Monitoring" of Marine Biodiversity', *Ecological Applications*, 20(8):2170–2187.

Harriott, V. J. (2002) *Marine Tourism Impacts and their Management on the Great Barrier Reef*, CRC Reef Research Centre Technical Report No. 46, Townsville, Queensland: CRC Reef Research Centre.

Harriott, V. J., Davis, D. C. and Banks, S. A. (1997) 'Recreational Diving and its Impact in Marine Protected Areas in Eastern Australia', *Ambio*, 26(3):173–179.

Hawkins, J. P. and Roberts, C. M. (1992) 'Effects of Recreational Scuba Diving on Fore-reef Slope Communities of Coral Reefs', *Biological Conservation*, 62(3):171–178.

Hines, J. M., Hungerford, H. R. and Tomera, A. N. (1987) 'Analysis and Synthesis of Research on Responsible Environment Behavior: A Meta-analysis', *Journal of Environmental Education*, 18(2):1–8.

Hodgson, G. (1999) 'A Global Coral Reef Assessment', *Marine Pollution Bulletin*, 38:345–355.

Hungerford, H. R. and Volk, T. L. (1990) 'Changing Learner Behavior through Environmental Education', *Journal of Environmental Education*, 21(3):8–21.

ICRAN MAR 1 (2006) 'Standard Requirements for Recreational Scuba Diving Services in the Mesoamerican Reef System', ICRAN MAR Standards and Code Taskforce, San Francisco, CA: ICRAN–MAR. Online. Available HTTP: <http://www.icran.org/pdf/MAR-Pages/tourism/Docs/Std%20requirements%20for%20recreational%20scuba%20diving%20services%20in%20the%20MAR%20(eng).pdf> (accessed 20 February 2009).

Jennings, G. (2007) *Water-based Tourism, Sport, Leisure, and Recreation Experiences*, Boston: Butterworth-Heinemann.

Kallgren, C. A., Reno, R. R. and Cialdini, R. B. (2000) 'A Focus Theory of Normative Conduct: When Norms Do and Do Not Affect Behavior', *Personality and Social Psychology Bulletin*, 26(8):1002.

Kassin, S. (2003) *Psychology*, Saddle River, NJ: Prentice-Hall.

Manfredo, M. J. and Bright, A. D. (1991) 'A Model for Assessing the Effects of Communication on Recreationists', *Journal of Leisure Research*, 23(1):1–20.

McCawley, R. and Teaff, J. (1995) 'Characteristics and Environmental Attitudes of Coral Reef Divers in Florida Keys', in F. Stephen McCool and A. E. Watson (eds.) *Linking Tourism, the Environment, and Sustainability*, Ogden, UT: US Forest Service, Intermountain Research Station: 63–68.

Mayer, F. S. and Frantz, C. M. (2004) 'The Connectedness to Nature Scale: A Measure of Individuals' Feeling in Community with Nature', *Journal of Environmental Psychology*, 24(4):503–515.

Medio, D., Ormond, R. and Pearson, M. (1997) 'Effect of Briefings on Rates of Damage to Corals by Scuba Divers', *Biological Conservation*, 79(1):91–95.

Millar, M. G. and Millar, K. U. (1996) 'The Effects of Direct and Indirect Experience on Affective and Cognitive Responses and the Attitude–Behavior Relation', *Journal of Experimental Social Psychology Quarterly*, 32:561–579.

Mintel (2006) *Niche Market Tourism – International*. Online. Available HTTP: <http://www.mintel.com> (accessed 17 November 2012).

Musa, G. (2002) 'Sipadan: A Scuba Diving Paradise: An Analysis of Tourism Impact, Diver Satisfaction and Tourism Management', *Tourism Geographies*, 4(2):195–209.

Musa, G., Seng, W. T., Thirumoorthi, T. and Abessi, M. (2011) 'The Influence of Scuba Divers' Personality, Experience, and Demographic Profile on their Underwater Behavior', *Tourism in Marine Environments*, 7(1):1–14.

Negri, A. P., Smith, L. D., Webster, N. S. and Heyward, A. J. (2002) 'Understanding Ship Grounding Impacts on a Coral Reef: Potential Effects of Anti-foulant Paint Contamination on Coral Recruitment', *Marine Pollution Bulletin*, 44:111–117.

Nemeth, R. S. and Nowlis, J. S. (2001) 'Monitoring the Effects of Land Development on the Near-shore Reef Environment of St Thomas, USVI', *Bulletin of Marine Science*, 69(2):759–775.

Newhouse, N. (1990) 'Implication of Attitude and Behaviour Research for Environmental Conservation', *The Journal of Environmental Education*, 22(1):26–32.

Ong, T. F. and Musa, G. (2011) 'An Examination of Recreational Divers' Underwater Behaviour by Attitude-behaviour Theories', *Current Issues in Tourism*, 14(8):779–795.

Ong, T. F. and Musa, G. (2012) 'Examining the Influences of Experience, Personality and Attitude on Scuba Divers' Underwater Behaviour: A Structural Equation Model', *Tourism Management*, 33:1521–1534.

Oom Do Valle, P., Rebelo, E., Reis, E. and Menezes, J. (2005) 'Combining Behavioral Theories to Predict Recycling Involvement', *Environment and Behavior*, 37(3):364–396.

Orams, M. B. (1995) 'Towards a more Desirable Form of Ecotourism', *Tourism Management*, 16(1):3–8.

Orams, M. (1999) *Marine Tourism: Development, Impacts and Management*, London: Routledge.

PADI (2011) 'Statistics'. Online. Available HTTP: <http://www.padi.com/scuba/about-padi/PADIstatistics/default. aspx> (accessed 20 February 2009).

Parker, S. (2001) 'Marine Tourism and Environmental Management on the Great Barrier Reef', in V. Smith and M. Brent (eds.) *Hosts and Guests Revisited:Tourism Issues in the 21st Century*, New York: Cognizant Communication Corporation: 232–241.

Pattengill-Semmens, C. V. and Semmens, B. X. (2003) 'Conservation and Management Applications of the Reef Volunteer Fish Monitoring Program', *Environmental Monitoring and Assessment*, 81(1–3):43–50.

Pepe, S. L. (2010) 'Caution Diver Below! A Case for Enhanced Environmental Education and Policies to Raise Awareness of Sustainable Scuba Diving', New York, State University of New York Empire State College.

Pooley, J. A. and O'Connor, M. (2000) 'Environmental Education and Attitudes: Emotions and Beliefs Are What is Needed', *Environment and Behavior*, 32(5):711–713.

Ramanaiah, N. V., Clump, M. and Sharpe, J. (2000) 'Personality Profiles of Environmentally Responsible Groups', *Psychological Reports*, 87(1):176–178.

Riegl, B. and Velimirov, B. (1991) 'How Many Damaged Corals in Red Sea Reef Systems? A Quantitative Survey', *Hydrobiologia*, 216/217:249–256.

Roberts, L. and Harriott, V. J. (1994) 'Recreational Scuba Diving and its Potential for Environmental Impact in a Marine Reserve', in O. Bellwood, H. Choat and N. Saxena (eds.) *Recent Advances in Marine Science and Technology*, Townsville, Australia: James Cook University of North Queensland: 95–704.

Rouphael, A. B. and Inglis, G. J. (1997) 'Impacts of Recreational Scuba Diving at Sites with Different Reef Topographies', *Biological Conservation*, 82(3):329–336.

Rouphael, A. B. and Inglis, G. J. (2001) 'Take Only Photographs and Leave Only Foot-prints? An Experimental Study of the Impacts of Underwater Photographers on Coral Reef Dive Sites', *Biological Conservation*, 100(3):281–287.

Ryckman, R. M. (2007) *Theories of Personality*, Belmont, CA: Wadsworth Pub Co.

Saphier, A. D. and Hoffmann, T. C. (2005) 'Forecasting Models to Quantify Three Anthropogenic Stresses on Coral Reefs from Marine Recreation: Anchor Damage, Diver Contact and Copper Emission from Antifouling Paint', *Marine Pollution Bulletin*, 51(5–7):590–598.

Schwartz, S. H. (1973) 'Normative Explanations of Helping Behavior: A Critique, Proposal, and Empirical Test 1', *Journal of Experimental Social Psychology*, 9(4):349–364.

Schwartz, S. H. (1977) 'Normative Influences on Altruism', *Advances in Experimental Social Psychology*, 10:221–279.

Shinew, K. J. (1993) 'The Attractiveness and Effectiveness of Organizational Reward Options', unpublished doctoral dissertation, Clemson University, Clemson, SC.

Sia, A., Hungerford, H. and Tomera, A. (1985) 'Selected Predictors of Responsible Environmental Behaviour', *The Journal of Environmental Education*, 17(2):31–40.

Sivek, D. L. and Hungerford, H. R. (1989) 'Predictors of Responsible Environmental Behavior: An Analysis', *Journal of Environmental Education*, 21(2):35–40.

Talge, H. (1992) 'Impact of Recreational Divers on Scleractinian Corals at Looe Key, Florida', paper presented at the Seventh International Coral Reef Symposium, Guam.

Thapa, B., Graefe, A. R. and Meyer, L. A. (2005) 'Moderator and Mediator Effects of Scuba Diving Specialization on Marine-based Environmental Knowledge-behavior Contingency', *The Journal of Environmental Education*, 37(1):53–67.

Thapa, B., Graefe, A. and Meyer, L. A. (2006). 'Specialization and Marine based Environmental Behaviours among Scuba Divers', *Journal of Leisure Research*, 38(4):601–615.

Todd, S. (2000) *Scuba Diving in New York's Great Lakes: From Novice to Professional* (New York Sea Grant Institute Completion Report). Cortland: Department of Recreation and Leisure Studies, SUNY Cortland.

Todd, S., Cooper, T. and Graefe, A. (2000) 'Scuba Diving and Underwater Cultural Resources, Differences in Environmental Beliefs, Ascriptions of Responsibility, and Management Preferences Based on Level of Development', paper presented at the 2000 Northeastern Research Symposium, Radnor, PA.

Vygotsky, L. S. (1981) 'The Genesis of Higher Mental Functions', in J. V. Wertsch (ed.) *The Concept of Activity in Soviet Psychology*, White Plains, NY: Sharpe: 144–188.

Walters, R. and Samways, M. (2001) 'Sustainable Dive Ecotourism on a South African Coral Reef', *Biodiversity and Conservation*, 10(12):2167–2179.

Williams, D. R., Schreyer, R. and Knopf, R. C. (1990) 'The Effect of the Experience Use History on the Multidimensional Structure of Motivations to Participate in Leisure Activities', *Journal of Leisure Research*, 22(1):36–54.

Zakai, D. and Chadwick-Furman, N. E. (2002) 'Impacts of Intensive Recreational Diving on Reef Corals at Eilat, Northern Red Sea', *Biological Conservation*, 105(2):179–187.

# 8 Experience, interpretation and meanings

*Balvinder Kler and Emily Moskwa*

## Introduction

Within the scuba diving tourism context, this chapter explores one of the most longstanding topics in tourism research: the tourist experience. Because the tourist experience relates directly to the feelings of people, and dive experiences are unique among leisure pursuits, an in-depth understanding of scuba diving experiences and perceptions about being underwater are critical for the success of the industry. Dive experiences are often intense and meaningful. Committed divers invest time and energy into diving, and, through their willingness to travel near and far, acquire experiences that enrich their lives. Ask a diver about favourite dive sites and the response is vivid, detailed, and often unravels an emotional connection to *place*. There is now an increasing appreciation of the role of the human involvement with the environment in both land and marine management, and an improved understanding of the connections people have with their environment can help bridge the gap between behavioural and ecological science and tourism management.

## Journeys of experience

Although much research has been undertaken on the tourist experience (e.g. Turner 1969; Urry 1990; Mossberg 2007), scholars are only now beginning to fully understand and conceptualise the notion (Rickly-Boyd 2010). Tourism is a leisure activity; visitors are drawn by the unusual and seek to escape from the minutiae of everyday reality (Smith 1977). Accordingly, tourism is often reported as an opportunity to rejuvenate us and facilitate a 'get-away-from-it-all' experience. A wide base of tourism scholarship cites the construction of self as fundamental to this experience (e.g. Davidson 2005; Desforges 2000), referring to self essentially as the way in which we understand who we are and what we are about (Gergen 1991). It is from within this context that this chapter considers the unique underwater experience of scuba diving, and the way in which people form bonds with the sites they visit. We begin with an explanation of the underwater experience, as well as the importance of interpretation in guiding positive experiences.

## Underwater experiences

Close underwater encounters are thought to produce positive feelings of excitement, adventure, freedom and relaxation. Traditionally, scuba diving has been considered an activity which revolves around thrill and adventure seeking, falling into the same category of sensation seeking as parachute jumping, rock climbing or speeding in a car (Zucherman and Neeb 1979). It is associated with challenge and danger, with participants often said to possess a desire to engage in activities which involve some physical risk. Scuba divers require specialised technical equipment to survive their recreational pursuit – probably adding to the excitement and adventure; and, as suggested by Cater and Cater (2007), their reliance on this equipment may also help create a sense of respect for the unfamiliar of the underwater encounter. Additionally, research into the psychological and behavioural effects of leisure participation also places high importance on the impact of interpretation as another component that cannot be overlooked when considering the human dimension of the environment and the relationship people have with places.

## Interpretation

At the same time as wanting to gain psychological benefits through contact with nature, outdoor leisure participants are said to be motivated to interact with, and interpret, what they see during their experiences. The biophilia hypothesis (Wilson 1984) suggests an instinctive bond between humans and other living systems. Humans subconsciously seek connections with nature, and this interaction (and the associated benefits) is thought to lead to greater respect for, enjoyment, and valuing of nature (Zajonic 1968). Interpretation is considered an essential tool for tourism managers, allowing them to deepen the intellectual and emotional connections between leisure participants and the environment they are visiting (Ham 1992). Although not extensively tested in the marine tourism sphere, there is widespread belief in the links between leisure participation, environmental interpretation, and positive changes in behaviour (Weiler and Ham 2001).

Based on theory from the field of communications psychology, the strongest intellectual and emotional connections between people and places arise from interpretation which is thought-provoking rather than fact-oriented. Thematic interpretation is hence often proposed as a suitable method for helping people form stronger connections with places. Through the strategic delivery of themes (sometimes referred to as central or take-home messages), thematic interpretation recognises that the most powerful impressions people take away with them from a site are the conclusions or meanings they have drawn from the facts presented. This is based on the fundamental premise that, once people attach meanings to a place being interpreted, the place matters more to them. From a marketing perspective, higher levels of satisfaction, word-of-mouth promotion and repeat visitation would be expected as a result. From a management perspective, more environmentally friendly behaviour would be anticipated. While the provision of factual information is important, the information itself could be tailored to assist visitors in understanding a place in a way which is relevant to, and informs, their own lives and influences their attachment. As these journeys of experience unfold, varying underwater experiences guided by interpretation are undertaken. Research in this field continues to build a base to enhance our understanding of the dive tourist experience.

## Worldwide research on diver sub-aquatic interactions

Human–nature relationships have gained much academic attention in recent years. In a broad tourism context, social studies have reported on the increased support for conservation and the increased values visitors place on nature after greater contact with it through participation in marine tourism activities. However, as far as dive tourism is concerned, researchers need to increase knowledge on the different ways in which scuba divers interact with the marine environment (Ormsby *et al.* 2004).

Currently, environmental education has been shown to play a positive role in reducing negative impacts, as demonstrated in the success of pre-dive briefings in influencing the behaviour of divers under water (Halpenny 2002; Medio *at al.* 1997; Townsend 2003). Madin and Fenton (2004) evaluated the usefulness of interpretative programmes on a liveaboard, and found significant changes in visitors' self-reported knowledge of the reef environment as a result of the trip. Mayes *et al.* (2004) found tourists had stronger feelings about conservation and the state of marine environments, and an increased desire to help conservation programmes after participating in educational dolphin-feeding tours; this is a concept also supported by Orams (1999) and Higginbottom and Tribe (2004).

Elsewhere, Cheng *et al.* (2005) concluded that examining reef tourists' environmental attitudes and behaviour can help managers design educational materials and management plans to protect marine resources and enhance visitor experiences. Thapa *et al.* (2006) identified a positive association between recreation specialisation and marine based environmental behaviours amongst 370 scuba divers in south-west Florida. As specialisation increased, environmentally responsible behaviours improved, with the affective dimension of specialisation providing the strongest predictive power for environmental behaviour. Subsequently, Dinsdale and Fenton (2006) used photographic survey and personal construct theory to identify how people ascribe meanings to a coral reef environment. Results suggested participants with a broad range of experience of coral reefs have similar value systems, as they prescribed similar meanings to the coral reef environment. Such results are useful to build an understanding between different stakeholders in the community, and support collaborative resource management.

Using mixed qualitative and quantitative methods, Belknap's (2008) research described how environmental interpretation programmes have the ability to arouse divers' curiosity, engage their emotions, and motivate them to minimise impacts while visiting reef systems. Divers were reported to be largely open to learning, as well as to changing their behaviour, and it was concluded that their participation in on-board education helped engender a sense of stewardship for the marine environment. Informal learning and interpretation that involves divers' emotions was seen as an essential component for the development of positive environmental values (rather than just increasing knowledge). MacCarthy *et al.* (2006) explored the concept of customer satisfaction in relation to the scuba diving consumption experience and suggest the experience involves both tangible (e.g. skills development, encounters with marine life) and intangible (e.g. deep emotions) aspects, and both are used to derive satisfaction. Cater (2009) also focused on the experiential component of scuba diving, suggesting there are a wide range of sensations and feelings involved which deserve inquiry.

## Comfort, constraints and negotiation (CCN)

Dimmock's (2010) conceptual model of the underwater experience revolves around comfort, constraint and negotiation (CCN), found to be the three prevailing features of underwater encounters (Figure 8.1). The CCN model offers a visual depiction of the general process divers' move through during a dive. It recognises every dive is a different experience, with the circular shape of the model emphasising the unique and dynamic features of scuba diving, illustrating how events are not experienced in a linear order.

The CCN model (Dimmock 2010) describes how a diver descends and passes preliminary negotiation to ease into the dive at the inner circle. This in-water 'comfort' is described in either the physical, social, psychological or visual context. Comfort is transitory (broken line at outer boundary). Arrows pointing into the comfort layer acknowledge each of the different contexts, and reflect diminishing comfort from disruption (the introduction of constraints). Correspondingly, arrows point out of the comfort layer to the middle circle, 'constraints', also a temporary state (outer boundary line is also broken, but where disruption has occurred and risks are presented). The outer circle, 'negotiation', reflects how divers may be required to adjust to being within the ocean, both upon descent and ascent of a dive. Minor constraints may be resolved using a 'consolidate' strategy, whereas more complex constraints may involve a 'cooperate' strategy, namely, working with a dive buddy to negotiate the challenge. If a diver experiences substantial constraint, the negotiation strategy may be to 'cancel' a dive, also represented by an arrow from the negotiation circle towards the exit (Dimmock 2010).

Dimmock's (2010) CCN model places positive experiences of comfort at the heart of an adventure experience, but also recognises that some divers choose to trade the comfort of staying within their limitations for the thrill and challenge of negotiating constraints. With its emphasis on comfort (as opposed to risk and challenge, as has traditionally been the case), the model highlights the importance of a comfortable 'place' within an adventure activity and the interrelated physical and social aspects of the dive experience. The CCN model has potential application in a wide range of management considerations. In other work, Musa *et al.* (2011) explored the influence of a scuba diver's personality on their underwater behaviour and found that divers with higher neuroticism

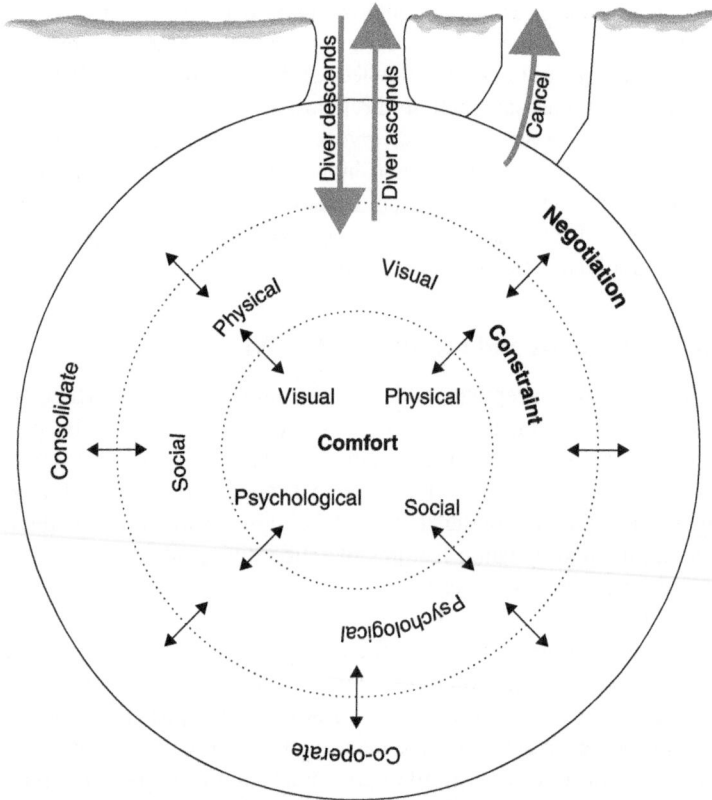

*Figure 8.1* CCN: a model of in-water comfort, constraint and negotiation.

Source: Used with kind permission Cognizant Communications Corporation: DOI 10–3727/1544273 10X12764412618966. Dimmock, K. (2010) 'CCN: a model of in-water comfort, constraint, and negotiation', *Tourism in Marine Environments* 6 (4), p.154.

(depressed, tense, worried or nervous characteristics) demonstrated higher levels of irresponsible underwater behaviour. They suggest dive operators should be more sensitive with divers who appear unstable, anxious or worried – divers who may encounter more constraints requiring negotiation to ensure a comfortable dive experience.

This broad but fragmented literature in the human-environment field of scuba diving tourism reveals a call to better understand the interface between people and the underwater environment for sustainable tourism outcomes. Adaptive management needs to respond to human–nature relationships, including the meanings and values divers give to places resulting from place attachments, interpretation, and the unique underwater experience of scuba diving itself. Recent work has turned to focusing on attachments to *place* through recreational diving which can be utilised to plan and manage dive sites and destinations.

## The sub-aquatic as place

*Place* is an important component of any outdoor recreation experience, and dive tourism activities are intimately tied to particular underwater settings, be they specific reefscapes or dive destinations. Such self-selected activity-place inter-actions often occur in rather special and unique recreation settings (Kruger and Jakes 2003) which become important to the user, evolving into a special or favourite place. Imagine regular trips to the site of your first dive; imagine a sense of ownership over a reef because you descend regularly to greet the resident turtles; remember the site where you dived with your dad? How is this attachment possible and what influences it? Almost 40 years ago, Tuan (1977) suggested that *space* becomes *place* through the transforming powers of meaning, value and familiarity. This was supported by Fishwick and Vining (1992), who suggested places take on an identity of their own due to the repeated exposures and social-psychological processes of people–place interactions. Similarly, Schroeder discovered that attachment occurred over time 'when people have highly valued aesthetic and emotional experiences in specific places or types of settings' (2002:8). Why have such attachments become important?

First, relationships to place are worthy of inquiry to study the benefits people gain through contact with nature in leisure-based settings, such as satisfaction or enjoyment with their visit, self-fulfilment perhaps. Second, these bonds may influ-ence subsequent decisions for motivation and destination choice, repeat visitation, and word-of-mouth recommendation. Finally, as dive tourism continues to flourish, reefs and other dive sites face overcrowding, and the congestion underwater affects the quality of the dive experience. The solution is often to limit the number of divers, or create artificial reefs which may solve one problem, but create another. Divers who travel great distances to experience a particular reef might feel short-changed. Marine tourism management needs an awareness of the dynamic and emergent processes by which attachments are formed (Eisenhauer *et al.* 2000).

Although such emotional bonds have been documented within popular literature (Cousteau and Dumas 2004; Harrigan 1992; Love 2000; Ecott 2001), the academic literature on dive tourism has only recently begun to examine the meaning of place for divers as an essential consideration for marine tourism management. This chapter introduces two concepts that examine people–place relationships, through two distinct pathways. Sense of place aims to elucidate meanings of lived experi-ences, therefore, it follows a qualitative approach. Place attachment is a positive, emotional bond that forms between people and special places (Low and Altman 1992; Moore and Graefe 1994), and follows a quantitative approach to inquiry. Both concepts are closely related, but often these inquiry approaches produce different but complementary outcomes. Here, we elaborate on each approach.

### Sense of place

Sense of place is defined as the extent to which an individual values or identifies with a particular natural setting (Williams and Roggenbuck 1989). It is also an integration of the knowledge, values, emotions and actions associated with a place (Jorgensen and Stedman 2001). Patterson and Williams (2005) add that a sense of place is multi-faceted, and a useful framework for exploring the relationship between humans and the environment. Three influential components to the formation of an attachment include the characteristics of the physical environment (the resource), human use and experience of the environment (the activity), and the social and psychological processes (meanings and affect) rooted in the setting (Brandenburg and Carroll 1995; Hammitt *et al.* 2006; Stedman 2003). The components of sense of place are often referred to as place meanings, or the feelings and subjective perceptions an individual ascribes to a specific place, which, coupled with the importance of a setting, produces the formation of a bond between person and place.

Sense of place is located within a 'meanings-based approach' which attempts to understand the quality of wilderness experiences mainly in terms of the role that these play in the broader context of the participant's life (Arnould and Price 1993; Andereck *et al.* 2006; Borrie and Birzell 2001). Experiences are seen as dynamic and emergent, not static and discrete. The approach focuses on understanding personal connections through stories about the recreational experience which produce fulfilling narratives consistent with the recreationist's life (Patterson *et al.* 1998; Borrie and Birzell 2001). Although descriptions might include the physical attributes of a place, it is the stories conveyed that makes the place meaningful, emphasising the relationship between the person, the setting and the experience (Williams 2008). According to Farnum *et al.* (2005), place meanings represent both symbolic and evaluative beliefs which structure the way an individual understands the world. At an individual level, meanings might focus on personal connections to place (e.g. location of first dive); whereas at a group level, focus might be on the symbolic meanings of place that are shared amongst members (e.g. dive buddy or dive club).

The evidence from related fields is convincing. Recreational settings are meaningful places, and the meanings recreationists attach to places are diverse and complex (Bricker and Kerstetter 2002; Hammitt *et al.* 2006; Schroeder 1996). Researchers exploring how recreationists relate to places as whole entities (as opposed to specific attributes) confirmed that recreationists have emotional and symbolic ties to the setting (Bricker and Kerstetter 2002; Kyle *et al.* 2003; Moore and Graefe 1994; Williams *et al.* 1992). How is this understanding useful for dive tourism management?

As a framework, sense of place allows managers to access, assess, inventory and monitor socio-cultural meanings of places, and incorporate these into planning and management processes (Brandenburg and Carroll 1995; Mitchell *et al.* 1993). Sense of place has been used to assess how people evaluate natural environments; improve the provision of optimal recreation experiences; and, plan and encourage the use of public spaces (Farnum *et al.* 2005; Warzecha and Lime 2001; Williams and Stewart 1998). Growing evidence links sense of place to environmentally responsible behaviour amongst recreationists (Halpenny 2006; Kaltenborn and Williams 2002; Mitchell *et al.* 1993; Stedman 2002; Vaske and

Kobrin 2001). In sum, an understanding of the multiple meanings that divers have for the reefscape may foster an 'identification of the activities, benefits, and experiences that managers should aim to provide' (Borrie and Birzell 2001:36). Sense of place captures, documents and interprets the experiences of dive tourists for the benefit of people, place and industry. Recently, Wynveen *et al.* (2010) examined place-related meanings of recreational visitors (residents and tourists) as ascribed to Australia's Great Barrier Reef Marine Park. This chapter presents findings of a study on scuba divers' sense of place towards the sub-aquatic which illuminates experiences through which place becomes meaningful (see Sub-Aquatic Meanings Model, page 142).

## Place attachment

Sense of place is also referred to in the literature as *place attachment*, which denotes the positive attachments individuals have with places which help people form a sense of belonging or purpose (Relph 1976; Tuan 1980). These are widely reported to generate responses to environmental practices and a sense of stewardship. In the broader environmental management context, emotions and values are indeed argued to be strongly related to appreciation for, and consequent protection of, the environment, playing an important part in shaping an individual's behaviour (Fishbein and Ajzen 1975; Iozzi 1989).

Two dimensions within the construct of place attachment are *place identity* and *place dependence*. These dimensions examine two different sources of meaning for the relationship between humans and places (Kyle *et al.* 2004). Place identity concerns the significance of places within the context of how the human psyche connects to certain places and helps create a sense of belonging through a collection of interpretations, ideas and related feelings about physical settings (Proshansky *et al.* 1983). Knowing that recreationists have high levels of place identity, as opposed to place dependence, would be valuable knowledge for managers because it would suggest that there is potential for repeat visitation, providing that the place meanings and attachment are preserved (Stedman 2002). Recreationists with place identity would also be more willing to accommodate rises in fees and fund conservation measures (Kyle *et al.* 2003; Vaske and Kobrin 2001).

In contrast, place dependence is described in terms of how people perceive themselves to be practically associated with a place or places (Stokols and Shumaker 1981), and is theorised as a function of how well a space facilitates a user's chosen activity (Moore and Graefe 1994). It considers how places compare to one another, and the quality of a place in reference to the availability of social and physical resources (Pretty *et al.* 2003).

Place attachment essentially argues that people have more than a functional attachment to landscapes; they have a deep and complex attachment that relates to their emotions. Different places and settings will accordingly either facilitate or hinder the quality of the scuba diving experience. It is proposed that these experiences might be influenced by both the CCN model presented earlier and place attachment (see Place attachment – the quantitative perspective, page 144).

## Sub-Aquatic Meanings (SAM) model – the qualitative perspective

In an attempt to identify place meanings for reef environments, findings from a qualitative study are presented to elucidate the experience of sub-aquatic recreation. Semi-structured interviews (Schroeder 1996) requested 16 British divers to describe places (dive sites and/or destinations) that were special, and to explain what thoughts, feeling, memories and associations came to mind. Four major themes and nine sub-themes associated with place experience emerged from the analysis. These indicators of place-based meanings formed the basis of the *Sub-Aquatic Meanings (SAM)* model which conveys an understanding about experiences through which place becomes meaningful. In order to illustrate the hierarchical relationships between themes and sub-themes, the SAM model is represented in Figure 8.2.

The SAM model demonstrates a clear contribution of both physical and social aspects of the dive experience to the formation of place meanings (Kler 2007; Kler *et al.* 2006). The model depicts place meanings as consisting of a sense of wonderment, being in a different world, splendid isolation and fellowship, which are the outcomes of diver and sub-aquatic interactions. SAM suggests that meanings are formed through an interaction of the diver, the setting and other people (i.e. dive buddy, or the dive group). The forté of the physical environment is that the experience of beauty, encounters with marine life, adventure, are different to the terrestrial environment. The opportunity to discover and learn is encouraging, not only because skill is involved, but also because it is in a unique environment. The thrill of being underwater accentuates the experience, and adds to the significance of place. SAM suggests meaningful places offer remoteness (small dive groups), and the opportunity to dive with like-minded divers (advanced

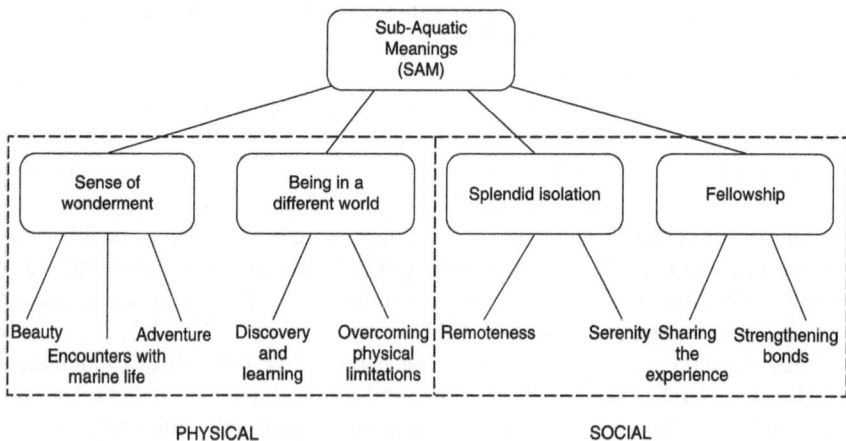

*Figure 8.2* Sub-Aquatic Meanings (SAM) model.

Source: Kler, unpublished PhD thesis (2007)

versus novice divers). Places that presented serenity enhance the meaning of place. Importantly, the social nature of scuba diving contributes to the formation of meanings, and other divers may influence how participants value a place.

Although the model is purely contextual, it emphasises the relationship between a person and a place (Williams 2008) and answers the question, 'what kind of place is this?' (Stedman 2008: 64). The following interview data demonstrate the significance of these attributes and experiences towards the formation of sub-aquatic meanings (Table 8.1).

*Table 8.1* The sub-aquatic experience

| Theme | Examples of diver descriptions |
|---|---|
| Beauty | 'Animals underwater are *really*, really spectacular and you don't expect them to be. It's amazing that . . . nudibranches . . . the little sea slugs are far more beautiful underwater than the slugs we have on land.' |
| Encounters with marine life | 'That was where I met my first 12 metre whale shark. *[chuckles]* We've got video footage . . . You can see the person in it and the width of the mouth is longer than the person who's next to it. It's that big and that just puts it into perspective. And that kind of memory *[pauses]* is just awesome, that's it!' |
| Adventure | 'There's something quite fascinating about wrecks . . . when something's been underwater for a long time, and you go inside, I suppose part of it is the mystery of it. . . the sort of feeling of exploring something, you know? . . . So you get some nice stuff on the ships, and a lot of marine life around, you know, so it's nice, nice diving.' |
| Discovery and learning | 'A shrimp gobi . . . this idea that you've got a shrimp that digs out a hole and you've got the gobi that lives in the hole with it. When the gobi gets worried because there's a predator coming, the shrimp goes into the hole as does the gobi – and so you've got this sort of, wonderful symbiotic relationship'. |
| Overcoming physical limitations | 'I really enjoy having that freedom in the water . . . you feel weightless so . . . it's actually very relaxing and it's a really nice experience in that . . . no best way to describe it really . . . you have this weightlessness, so it's very freeing.' |
| Remoteness | 'I learnt there and then I've also dived lots of places since. Nowhere's really come close to it. So I've ended up going back even though it takes 32 hours to get there. I like it because, the first thing it's remote. I hate diving in big groups you know? Four, six, maximum! So, it's quite exclusive, but small. It's quite adventurous, it takes a certain kind of diver to go there, as in they really want, they really want to be diving.' |

(*continued overleaf*)

*Table 8.1* Continued

| Theme | Examples of diver descriptions |
| --- | --- |
| *Serenity* | 'There's specifically a reef called Stringer which is two small little islands of coral in the middle of the ocean. It's just . . . somewhere where I can be away from everything . . . I think because there's so much life there, it's just like a completely other world and it just fascinates me. Personally . . . when I'm underwater, it gives me an opportunity to completely clear my head. . . . it's definitely a release, it's therapeutic.' |
| *Sharing the experience* | 'I just feel really happy . . . we talk about what we saw and "I didn't see this last time" and have a joke with some people who completely missed the wreck or . . . just didn't see what we saw. It's just . . . with a group of friends . . . we'll just chat about it and have a laugh about what we just did.' |
| *Strengthening bonds* | 'And it's great when you're underneath . . . it's something you do together you know? And . . . the kids getting older ? they still like to do it. So it's a nice kind of family activity; it's exciting; it's a little bit different you know? Over the years, it's nice as your relationships change in the family . . . it's nice to feel that you can do things with them that are still relevant.' |

Source: Kler, unpublished PhD thesis (2007)

## Place attachment – the quantitative perspective

Quantitative research specifically relating scuba divers and sense of place is limited. In a recent study, Moskwa (2012) examined the emotional relationship Australian divers have with their underwater surroundings by comparing the place attachments between local divers and visitors to a dive site, using a place attachment scale where participants indicated their level of agreement with a series of statements relating either to place identity or place dependence (Table 8.2).

*Table 8.2* Place identity and place dependence statements

**Place identity**
    I am very attached to this place
    This place means a lot to me
    I feel this place is a part of me
    I identify strongly with this place
    I feel happiest when I am at this place
    I feel a sense of pride for this place
    I really miss this place when I am away from it for too long
    I like to introduce this place to my family and/or friends

**Place dependence**
    No other place can compare to this one
    This place is the best for what I like to do
    I get more satisfaction diving at this place than any other
    I wouldn't substitute other activities for diving here

Source: Moskwa (2012)

Her survey revealed very high place attachment, and a difference between the place attachments of visitors and local residents (Table 8.3). While local residents recorded significantly higher place identity values than tourists, it was the tourists who recorded the strongest feelings related to the instrumental qualities of dive sites (the way the social and physical resources of a place facilitate their desired leisure experiences). Accordingly for tourists in particular, the instrumental qualities of dive sites have an important role in forming place attachments.

While it may not be surprising that divers form close attachments with underwater environments if one contemplates their acceptance of the challenges of diving and their literal immersion in a new environment, it is of value to explore. The study also indicated that, as levels of place attachment increased, diver (self-reported) behaviour became more environmentally friendly. Considering the recent and fast growth of the dive tourism industry and the potential negative impacts of inappropriately managed dive sites, sense of place research clearly has important implications for marine management.

## Implications

The SAM model and findings of the place attachment study indicate the divers do form connections with the places where they recreate. Marine park managers need to understand the full range of meanings attached to recreational settings to help identify the activities, benefits and experiences that could be provided (Borrie and Birzell 2001). The SAM model provides a description of such meanings and could be used to develop marketing and management strategies. Properties of the sub-aquatic environment which make place meaningful, as described in the model, should be preserved to ensure the experiences divers seek are available. This may motivate repeat visitation. Moreover, interpretation strategies could focus on retaining and enhancing Sub-Aquatic Meanings and encourage the formation of place attachment.

It makes sense that if divers are highly place attached, managers should devote more resources to understanding these attachments. Integration of environmental psychology theory, where attitudes and values can be used to predict environmental behaviours (Bechtel 1997; Fishbein and Ajzen 1975), may be one useful method employed to assist in the development of successful policies and initiatives for marine tourism management. Tourism managers should consider how dive sites facilitate intimate connections with particular geographical areas. They should remember that tourism is often typified as the experience of place, and in a scuba diving context, this experience will be influenced by CCN, interpretation and the emotional bonds one forms with a dive site.

Diving for its own sake is not usually the primary motivation for divers. It is the discovery opportunities that each place and each new experience offers that often dominate the motivation to scuba dive. Settings are not only facilitative ingredients, but are primary considerations and drawcards for recreational participants. This is important to recognise because, as marine tourism pursuits increase, greater management challenges may be encountered in finding the best balance in

*Table 8.3* Comparison between place attachments of local residents and tourists

| Place attachment dimensions | Local residents (n=84) | | | Tourists (n=87) | | | All divers (n=171) | | |
|---|---|---|---|---|---|---|---|---|---|
| | *Internal consist.** | *Mean*** | *SD* | *Internal consist.** | *Mean*** | *SD* | *Internal consist.** | *Mean*** | *SD* |
| Place identity | α = 0.94 | 5.36 | 1.29 | α = 0.93 | 5.07 | 1.5 | α = 0.93 | 5.21 | 1.41 |
| Place dependence | α = 0.9 | 3.86 | 1.57 | α = 0.87 | 4.94 | 1.36 | α = 0.9 | 4.42 | 1.55 |

Notes:

* Chronbach's alpha (a) was used to assess internal consistency.

** On a scale from 1 (= very low) to 7 (= very high).

accommodating both people and places. While carrying capacity frameworks enable managers to evaluate and monitor environmental impacts, they may not incorporate what a place really means to its users, and how environmental attitudes arising from thematic interpretation, CCN, SAM and place attachment relate to behaviour.

If a scuba diver's affective domain is better engaged, opportunities and incentives for environmentally friendly behaviour are increased. By understanding the human dimension of the environment, tourism managers may be better equipped to aim policies and programmes at changing divers' personal attitudes and values, as a means of limiting long-term damage to dive sites. In line with Ham (2007), this may involve incorporating interpretation into the recreational diving experience to focus more on users' environmental beliefs and helping them connect to the places they visit.

Tourism management is likely to be unsuccessful if there is a disconnection with people or a lack of understanding of the people it is trying to influence. If the knowledge derived from academic studies is not connected to the social context, incorporating the attitudes and perspectives of all scuba divers, managers will not be fully able to work towards the long-term sustainability of marine tourism.

## Conclusion

Places are entrenched with meanings. People assign meanings to, and derive meanings in their lives from, places. This chapter has introduced the reader to how journeys of experience – the uniqueness of being underwater, forming an emotional attachment to a place, and experiencing environmental interpretation – should be considered in the management of scuba diving tourism. The bonds divers have with places, the way they interact with and interpret what they see, and the comfort, constraint and negotiations they experience, help transform a space to a place through the power of meaning, consequently helping generate environmental practices and a sense of stewardship for dive sites that will lead to more sustainable diving tourism operations.

## References

Andereck, K., Bricker, K S., Kerstetter, D. and Nickerson, N. P. (2006) 'Connecting Experiences to Quality: Understanding the Meanings Behind Visitors' Experiences', in G. Jennings and N. P. Nickerson (eds.) *Quality Tourism Experiences*, Oxford: Elsevier Butterworth-Heinemann: 81–98.

Arnould, E. J. and Price, L. L. (1993) 'River Magic: Extraordinary Experience and the Extended Service Encounter', *Journal of Consumer Research*, 20(June):24–45.

Bechtel, R. B. (1997) *Environment & Behavior: An Introduction*, Thousand Oaks, CA: Sage Publications.

Belknap, J. (2008) *A Study of the Relationship between Conservation Education and Scuba Diver Behavior in the Flower Garden Banks National Marine Sanctuary*. Texas A&M University. Online. Available HTTP: <//hdl.handle.net/1969.1/ETD-TAMU-3244> (accessed 14 December 2010).

Borrie, W. T. and Birzell, R. M. (2001) 'Approaches to Measuring Quality of Wilderness Experience', in W. A. Friedmund and D. N. Cole (eds.) *Visitor Use Density and Wilderness Experience: Proceedings*, RMRS-P-20, Missoula, MT, Ogden, Utah: USDA Forest Service, Rocky Moutain Research Station: 29–38.

Brandenburg, A. M. and Carroll, M. S. (1995) 'Your Place or Mine? The Effect of Place Creation on Environmental Values and Landscape Meaning', *Society and Natural Resources*, 8:381–398.

Bricker, K. S. and Kerstetter, D. L. (2002) 'An Interpretation of Special Places: Meanings Whitewater Recreationists Attach to the South Fork of the American River', *Tourism Geographies*, 4(4):396–425.

Cater, C. I. (2009) 'The Life Aquatic: Scuba Diving and the Experiential Imperative', *Tourism in Marine Environments*, 5(4):233–244.

Cater, C. and Cater, E. (2007) *Marine Ecotourism: Between the Devil and the Deep Blue Sea*, Oxfordshire, UK: CAB International.

Cheng, J., Thapa, B. and Confer J. J. (2005) 'Environmental Concern and Behaviors Among Coral Reef Tourists at Green Island, Taiwan', *Tourism in Marine Environments*, 2(1):39–43.

Cousteau, J.-Y. and Dumas, F. (2004) *The Silent World*, Washington, DC: National Geographic Adventure Classics.

Davidson, K. (2005) 'Alternative India: Transgressive Spaces', in A. Jaworski and A. Pritchard (eds.) *Discourse, Communication and Tourism*, Clevedon, UK: Channel View Publications: 28–52.

Desforges, L. (2000) 'Travelling the World – Identity and Travel Biography', *Annals of Tourism Research*, 27(4):926–945.

Dimmock, K. (2010) 'CCN: Towards a Model of Comfort, Constraints and Negotiation in Recreational Scuba Diving', *Tourism in Marine Environments*, 6(4):145–160.

Dinsdale, E. A. and Fenton, D. M. (2006) 'Assessing Coral Reef Condition: Eliciting Community Meanings', *Society and Natural Resources*, 19:239–258.

Ecott, T. (2001) *Neutral Buoyancy: Adventures in a Liquid World*, New York: Grove Press.

Eisenhauer, B. W., Krannich, R. S. and Blahna, D. J. (2000) 'Attachments to Special Places on Public Lands: An Analysis of Activities, Reasons for Attachments, and Community Connections', *Society and Natural Resources*, 13:421–441.

Farnum, J., Hall, T. and Kruger, L. E. (2005) *Sense of Place in Natural Resource Recreation and Tourism: An Evaluation and Assessment of Research Findings*, Gen. Tech. Rep. PNW-GTR-660. Portland, OR: USDA, Forest Service, Pacific Northwest Research Station.

Fishbein, M. and Ajzen, I. (1975) *Belief, Attitude, Intention, and Behavior: An Introduction to Theory and Research*, Reading, MA: Addison-Wesley.

Fishwick, L. and Vining, J. (1992) 'Toward a Phenomenology of Recreation Place', *Journal of Environmental Psychology*, 12:57–63.

Gergen, K. J. (1991) *The Saturated Self: Dilemmas of Identity in Contemporary Life*, New York: BasicBooks.

Halpenny, E. A. (2002) 'Tourism in Marine Protected Areas', in P. F. J. Eagles and S. F. McCool (eds.) *Tourism in National Parks and Protected Areas. Planning and Management*, Wallingford: CABI Publishing: 211–234.

Halpenny, E. A. (2006) 'Environmental Behaviour, Place Attachment and Park Visitation: A Case Study of Visitors to Point Pelee National Park', unpublished PhD thesis, University of Waterloo, Canada.

Ham, S. (1992) *Environmental Interpretation: A Practical Guide for People with Big Ideas and Small Budgets*, Golden, CO: Fulcrum/North American Press.

Ham, S. (2007) 'Can Interpretation Really Make a Difference? Answers to Four Questions from Cognitive and Behavioral Psychology', in *Proceedings of the Interpreting World Heritage Conference*, Vancouver, Canada: 42–52.

Hammitt, W. E., Backlund, E. A. and Bixler, R. D. (2006) 'Place Bonding for Recreation Places: Conceptual and Empirical Development', *Leisure Studies*, 25(1):17–41.

Harrigan, S. (1992) *Water and Light. A Diver's Journey to a Coral Reef*, Austin: University of Texas Press.

Higginbottom, K. and Tribe, A. (2004) 'Contributions of Wildlife Tourism to Conservation', in K. Higginbottom (ed.) *Wildlife Tourism: Impacts, Management and Planning*, Altona, Victoria: Common Ground/Sustainable Tourism CRC: 99–123.

Iozzi, L. A. (1989) 'What Research Says to the Educator. Part One: Environmental Education and the Affective Domain', *Journal of Environmental Education*, 20(3):3–9.

Jorgensen, B. S. and Stedman, R. C. (2001) 'Sense of Place as an Attitude: Lakeshore Owners' Attitudes Towards their Properties', *Journal of Environmental Psychology*, 21:233–248.

Kaltenborn, B. P. and Williams, D. R. (2002) 'The Meaning of Place: Attachments to Femundsmarka National Park, Norway, Among Tourists and Locals', *Norwegian Journal of Geography*, 56:189–198.

Kler, B. K. (2007) 'Sub-Aquatic Meanings: A Phenomenological Study of Scuba Divers' Experience of Place', unpublished PhD thesis, University of Surrey, UK.

Kler, B. K., Tribe, J. and Miller, G. (2006) 'Discover Scuba: Experiencing Dive Destinations', paper presented at RC50 (International Tourism), International Sociological Association XVI World Congress of Sociology, July 2006.

Kruger, L. E. and Jakes, P. J. (2003) 'The Importance of Place: Advances in Science and Application', *Forest Science*, 49(6):819–821.

Kyle, G., Absher, J. D. and Graefe, A. R. (2003) 'The Moderating Role of Place Attachment on the Relationship Between Attitudes Towards Fees and Spending Preferences', *Leisure Sciences*, 25:33–50.

Kyle, G., Graefe, A., Manning, R. and Bacon, J. (2004) 'Effects of Place Attachment on Users' Perceptions of Social and Environmental Conditions in a Natural Setting', *Journal of Environmental Psychology*, 24(2):213–225.

Love, R. (2000) *Reefscape: Reflections on the Great Barrier Reef*, St Leonards, UK: Allen and Unwin.

Low, S. M. and Altman, I. (1992) 'Place Attachment: A Conceptual Inquiry', in I. Altman and S. M. Low. (eds.) *Place Attachment*, New York and London: Plenum Press: 1–12.

MacCarthy, M., O'Neill, M. and Williams, P. (2006) 'Customer Satisfaction and Scuba-Diving: Some Insights from the Deep', *The Services Industries Journal*, 26(5):537–555.

Madin, E. M. P. and Fenton, D. M. (2004) 'Environmental Interpretation in the Great Barrier Reef Marine Park: An Assessment of Programme Effectiveness', *Journal of Sustainable Tourism*, 12(2):121–137.

Mayes, G., Dyer, P. and Richins, H. (2004) 'Dolphin–Human Interaction: Pro-environmental Attitudes, Beliefs and Intended Behaviours and Actions of Participants in Interpretation Programs: A Pilot Study', *Annals of Leisure Research*, 7(1):34–53.

Medio, D., Ormond, R. F. G. and Pearson, M. (1997) 'Effect of Briefings on Rates of Damage to Corals by Scuba Divers', *Biological Conservation*, 79:91–95.

Mitchell, M. Y., Force, J., Carroll, M. S. and McLaughlin, W. J. (1993) 'Forest Places of the Heart', *Journal of Forestry*, 91(4):32–37.

Moore, R. L. and Graefe, A. R. (1994) 'Attachments to Recreation Settings: The Case of Rail-trail Users', *Leisure Sciences*, 16(1):17–31.

Moskwa, E. (2012) 'Exploring Place Attachment: An Underwater Perspective', *Tourism in Marine Environments*, 8(1/2):33–46.

Mossberg, L. (2007) 'A Marketing Approach to the Tourist Experience', *Scandinavian Journal of Hospitality and Tourism*, 7(1):59–74.

Musa, G., Wong, T. S., Thirumoorthi, T. and Abessi, M. (2011) 'The Influence of Scuba Divers' Personality, Experience, and Demographic Profile on their Underwater Behavior', *Tourism in Marine Environments*, 7(1):1–14.

Orams, M. (1999) *Marine Tourism: Development, Impacts and Management*, London: Routledge.

Ormsby, J., Moscardo, G., Pearce, P. and Foxlee, J. (2004) *A Review of Research into Tourist and Recreational Uses of Protected Natural Areas*, Research Report No. 79. Townsville: Great Barrier Reef Marine Park Authority.

Patterson, M. E., Watson, A. E., Williams, D. R. and Roggenbuck, J. R. (1998) 'An Hermeneutic Approach to Studying the Nature of Wilderness Experiences', *Journal of Leisure Research*, 30(4):423–452.

Patterson, M. E. and Williams, D. R. (2005) 'Maintaining Research Traditions on Place: Diversity of Thought and Scientific Progress', *Journal of Environmental Psychology*, 25:361–380.

Pretty, G., Chipuer, H. and Bramston, P. (2003) 'Sense of Place amongst Adolescents and Adults in Two Rural Australian Towns: The Discriminating Features of Place Attachment, Sense of Community and Place Dependence in Relation to Place Identity', *Journal of Environmental Psychology*, 23(3):273–287.

Proshansky, H. M., Fabian, A. K. and Kaminoff, R. (1983) 'Place-identity: Physical World Socialization of the Self', *Journal of Environmental Psychology*, 3(1):57–83.

Relph, F. (1976) *Place and Placedness*, London: Pion Limited.

Rickly-Boyd, J. M. (2010) 'The Tourist Narrative', *Tourist Studies*, 9(3):259–280.

Schroeder, H. W. (1996) *Voices from Michigan's Black River: Obtaining Information on 'Special Places' for Natural Resource Planning*, Gen. Tech. Rep. NC-184, St Paul, MN: US Department of Agriculture, Forest Service, North Central Forest Experimentation Station.

Smith, V. L. (1977) *Hosts and Guests: The Anthropology of Tourism*, Philadelphia: University of Pennsylvania Press.

Stedman, R. C. (2002) 'Toward a Social Psychology of Place. Predicting Behavior from Place-based Cognitions, Attitude, and Identity', *Environment and Behavior*, 34(5):561–581.

Stedman, R. C. (2003) 'Sense of Place and Forest Science: Toward a Program of Quantitative Research', *Forest Science*, 49(6):822–829.

Stedman, R. C. (2008) 'What Do we "Mean" by Place Meanings? Implications of Place Meanings for Managers and Practitioners', in L. E. Kruger, T. E. Hall and M. C. Stiefel (eds.) *Understanding Concepts of Place in Recreation Research and Management*, Portland, OR: US Department of Agriculture, Forest Service, Pacific Northwest Research Station.

Stokols, D. and Shumaker, S. A. (1981) 'People in Places: A Transactional View of Settings', in J. H. Harvey (ed.) *Cognition, Social Behavior, and the Environment*, Hillsdale, NJ: Erlbaum: 441–488.

Thapa, B., Graefe, A. and Meyer, L. A. (2006) 'Specialisation and Marine based Environmental Behaviours among Scuba Divers', *Journal of Leisure Research*, 38(4):601–615.

Townsend, C. (2003) 'Marine Ecotourism through Education: A Case Study of Divers in the British Virgin Islands', in B. Garrod and J. C. Wilson. (eds) *Marine Ecotourism: Issues and Experiences*, Clevedon, UK: Channel View Publications: 138–154.

Tuan, Y. F. (1977) *Space and Place. The Perspective of Experience*, Minneapolis: University of Minnesota Press.

Tuan, Y. F. (1980) 'Rootedness versus Sense of Places', *Landscape*, 24(1):3–8.

Turner, V. (1969) *The Ritual Process*, Chicago: Aldine.

Urry, J. (1990) *The Tourist Gaze. Leisure and Travel in Contemporary Societies*, London: Sage Publications.

Vaske, J. J. and Kobrin, K. C. (2001) 'Place Attachment and Environmentally Responsible Behaviour', *The Journal of Environmental Education*, 32(4):16–21.

Warzecha, C. A. and Lime, D. W. (2001) 'Place Attachment in Canyonlands National Park: Visitors' Assessment of Setting Attributes on the Colarado and Green Rivers', *Journal of Park and Recreation Administration*, 19(1):59–78.

Weiler, B. and Ham, S. (2001) 'Tour Guides and Interpretation in Ecotourism', in D. Weaver (ed.) *Encyclopedia of Ecotourism*, Wallingford, UK: CAB International: 549–563.

Williams, D. R. (2008) 'Pluralities of Place: A User's Guide to Place Concepts, Theories, and Philosophies in Natural Resource Management', in L. Kruger, T. Hall and M. Steifel (eds.) *Understanding Concepts of Place in Recreation Research and Management*, Portland, OR: USDA Forest Service, Pacific Northwest Research Station.

Williams, D. R. and Roggenbuck, J. W. (1989) 'Measuring Place Attachment: Some Preliminary Results', in L. H. McAvoy and D. Howard (eds) *Abstracts of the 1989 Leisure Research Symposium*, Arlington, VA: National Recreation and Park Association: 32.

Williams, D. R. and Stewart, S. I. (1998) 'Sense of Place. An Elusive Concept that is Finding a Home in Ecosystem Management', *Journal of Forestry*, 96(5):18–23.

Williams, D. R., Patterson, M. E., Roggenbuck, J. W. and Watson, A. E. (1992) 'Beyond the Commodity Metaphor: Examining Emotional and Symbolic Attachment to Place', *Leisure Sciences*, 14:29–46.

Wilson, E. O. (1984) *Biophilia*, Cambridge, MA: Harvard University Press.

Wynveen, C. J., Kyle, G. and Sutton, S. (2010) 'Place Meanings Ascribed to Marine Settings: The Case of the Great Barrier Reef Marine Park', *Leisure Sciences*, 32(3):270–287.

Zajonic, R. B. (1968) 'Attitudinal Effects of Mere Exposure', *Journal of Personality and Psychology*, 9(2):1–29.

Zucherman, M. and Neeb, M. (1979) 'Sensation Seeking and Psychopathology', *Psychiatry Research*, 1(3):255–264.

# 9  Scuba diving satisfaction

*Thinaranjeney Thirumoorthi, Kee Mun Wong and*
*Ghazali Musa*

## Introduction

Recreational scuba diving is among the benefits that can be experienced in the marine environment (Ngazy *et al.* 2001: 118) and divers travel from distant parts of the world to view beauty underwater (Tabata 1992). However, the escalating trend of the scuba diving industry is of concern, as the activity is carried out in a fragile marine environment. In addition, the threats of global warming (Hoegh-Guldberg 1999) risk many negative effects on coral reef and marine life. Thus, the sustainability of scuba diving tourism is, at best, questionable.

The concept of tourism sustainability was initially established because of the need to account for the interrelationships between tourism and the environment (Farsari and Prastacos 2000). Sustainable development became the buzzword, out of concern for conservation and the preservation of natural resources (Choi and Sirakaya 2006). The sustainability concept in relation to tourists' activity requires balance in the management of the types and frequency of activity in the marine environment. If this is done, the activity can be carried out in the area without compromising environmental quality (Vinals *et al.* 2003:82).

The detrimental impact on coral reefs needs serious attention, as it will affect the ecological system in the long run and the affected destination will become less attractive for scuba divers in the near future. The sustainability of the scuba diving business, however, requires not only the minimization of environmental impact, but also the provision of satisfactory scuba diving experiences. Indeed, visitor satisfaction is a crucial indicator to measure the sustainability of tourism development (Miller 2001; Blackstock *et al.* 2006).

Satisfaction is defined as the result of comparing experience with the diver's expectation of the destination visited (Pizam *et al.* 1978:315). It is vital to measure divers' satisfaction, as its fulfillment may lead to both increased loyalty and positive word of mouth. Positive attributes are required for the design of attractive promotional messages in the marketing of scuba diving, together with serving as differential factors when compared with competitors. On the other hand, negative attributes provide the opportunity for further improvement in the provision of scuba diving services to divers.

## Scuba divers' satisfactions

Customer satisfaction often determines the potential viability of a business. Its measurement requires the identification of which product or service attributes contribute to satisfaction (Fuller and Matzler 2007). Destination management should emphasize the need to keep customers satisfied with all aspects of attractions, facilities and services within the area (Kozak and Rimmington 2000). With the proliferation of tourist destinations and attractions, researchers continue to explore the preference or conditions which are likely to influence tourists' satisfaction.

In reference to scuba diving, several satisfaction studies have been carried out (e.g. Davis and Tisdell 1996; Graham *et al.* 2001; MacCarthy *et al.* 2006; Musa 2002; Musa *et al.* 2006; O'Neill *et al.* 2000; O'Reilly 1982; Paterson *et al.* 2012; Tabata 1992), as presented in Table 9.1. Marine life and coral reefs are among the main contributors to diving satisfaction (Paterson *et al.* 2012; MacCarthy *et al.* 2006; Musa 2002; Graham *et al.* 2001; Davis and Tisdell 1996; O'Reilly 1982).

O'Neill *et al.* (2000) introduce DIVEPERF to measure the service quality of scuba diving in Western Australia. A quantitative survey instrument was employed to validate the findings of qualitative surveys. The study reports that divers are happy with services provided by the dive operators, as all the five dimensions of service quality scored above average. In general, the assurance dimension is rated the highest in terms of overall performance and importance, and this is followed by responsiveness, empathy, reliability and tangibles. Divers indicate their preferences for operators who are friendly, professional and place firm emphasis on security. The results provide evidence that the service providers have successfully instilled trust and confidence in the divers who patronized their services. In this study, assurance refers to the various aspects of safety and security in scuba diving.

Even during the in-depth interviews, divers indicated that the safety aspect is the most important attribute in choosing scuba diving operators. The importance of this aspect is further validated in the quantitative survey finding. However, the study by O'Neill *et al.* only examined the satisfaction from the perspective of services delivered by staff. It is also necessary to measure satisfaction in the scuba diving environmental dimensions, as well as the social aspects experienced by divers with other divers during their holiday.

O'Reilly (1982) points out that divers expect clarity, underwater scenery, marine life, accessibility and low costs for their dive trips. In Hawaii, Tabata (1992) discovered that other conditions – such as boat facilities and the availability of beautiful underwater geological formations – are among the sought after conditions for a satisfactory diving experience. The demand for a particular dive site, according to Davis and Tisdell (1996), is a function of many variables. Two of the more important variables are price and environmental quality. Quality refers to aesthetic appeal, interesting marine life and visibility. Additionally, important utilities for recreational scuba diving include ease of access, the

*Table 9.1* Satisfaction dimensions and items

| Source(s) | Research location | Research method | Dimensions/items |
|---|---|---|---|
| Paterson *et al.* (2012) | Florida Keys, US | Quantitative | Experiencing easy diving conditions<br>Experiencing good underwater visibility<br>Relaxing<br>Seeing unique underwater features<br>Experiencing natural surroundings<br>Seeing large fish<br>Seeing live coral<br>Seeing a healthy reef<br>Seeing undamaged reef sites<br>Seeing marine life |
| Musa *et al.* (2006) | Layang-Layang Island, Malaysia | Quantitative | Underwater nature<br>Comfort and ease of access to dive sites |
| MacCarthy *et al.* (2006) | South West and Queensland, Australia | Qualitative | Water clarity<br>Underwater landscapes<br>Marine life<br>Diving buddies |
| | Thailand | | The camaraderie of fellow divers<br>Encounters with total strangers during the dive<br>Equipment reliability<br>Safety and operator efficiency |
| Musa (2002) | Sipadan Island, Malaysia | Quantitative | Marine life<br>Friendly/helpful<br>Staff<br>Good buddies<br>Water temperature<br>Easy dive access |
| Graham *et al.* (2001) | Palau, Micronesia | Qualitative | Corals/reef<br>Fishes<br>Sharks<br>Value |
| O'Neill *et al.* (2000) | Western Australia | Mix of qualitative and quantitative | Assurance<br>Tangibles<br>Empathy<br>Reliability |
| Davis and Tisdell (1996) | – | Conceptual paper | Price<br>Aesthetic appeal<br>Interesting marine life visibility<br>Ease of access<br>Condition of the site<br>The quality of the diving<br>The availability of substitutes |
| Tabata (1992) | – | – | Boat facilities<br>Availability of natural geological formations |
| O'Reilly (1982) | – | – | Clarity<br>Underwater scenery<br>Marine life<br>Accessibility<br>Cost |

condition of the site, the quality of diving and the availability of substitutes. Some divers avoid crowded dive sites.

Knowledge of reasons for an unsatisfactory experience is equally important, as addressing these would be a matter of greater urgency. Graham *et al.* (2001) calculate that the net value of a dive visit is the total utility or valued enjoyed minus the price paid. Using 13 attributes to measure divers' satisfaction, they conclude that the dramatic biophysical impacts of coral bleaching are among factors which caused the difference in the satisfaction scores for the attribute of corals/reef and fish species.

MacCarthy *et al.* (2006) state satisfaction can be achieved from the dive which has water clarity, beautiful underwater landscapes and marine life. Satisfaction may also be derived from diving buddies, the camaraderie of fellow divers and even the serendipitous encounters with total strangers during the dive. The results of the MacCarthy *et al.* (2006) quantitative survey reveal that factors of equipment reliability, safety and operator efficiency (functional service) are important criteria in determining divers' satisfaction. Their qualitative research results discover a multitude of issues, some functional, some technical, but many experiential and certainly subjective elements, which may determine satisfaction. Some of the criteria in measuring divers' satisfaction fall outside the immediate control of the dive operator. Weather is a perfect example. Nevertheless, MacCarthy *et al.* (2006) point out that in situations where divers experience both technical and functional dissatisfaction, they may still offset this dissatisfaction with enough experiential satisfaction, so that their overall experience remains positive.

Musa (2002) examined divers' satisfaction when visiting Sipadan Island by measuring 24 items which represent diving environment, services and impacts. The findings indicate that 97.8 per cent of divers were satisfied with their experience on the island. The top five satisfaction attributes were marine life, friendly/helpful staff, good buddies, water temperature and easy dive access. Concerns were raised pertaining to haphazard tourism development, crowding and the worsening of underwater visibility. In 2006, Musa *et al.* measured the satisfaction of scuba divers in Layang-Layang Island using 16 satisfaction items. Five satisfaction factors revealed were services, lodging and food, environment, safety facilities and underwater nature. They reported that only the underwater nature dimension significantly influences overall satisfaction among divers. This signifies the intensity of dependency of the scuba diving industry on this single dimension which is represented by marine life, coral reefs, the underwater landscape and water temperature.

Paterson *et al.* (2012) examined how diving environmental characteristics (physical and biological) influence non-resident divers' satisfaction in Florida Keys. The respondents were asked to indicate their degree of satisfaction with 10 items, namely, seeing a healthy reef; experiencing easy diving conditions; experiencing good underwater visibility; seeing undamaged reef sites; seeing marine life; seeing large fish; seeing unique underwater formations; seeing live coral; experiencing natural surroundings; and relaxing. The authors report that the discrepancies between expectations and perception (experience) and the specialization level of divers influence their level of satisfaction. The findings indicate that seeing large fish contributes to divers' overall satisfaction across all specialization levels. Divers are also found to have realistic expectations, as generally they are satisfied with their diving experience.

Within the studies of preference and satisfaction of divers, emphasis is generally placed on the rating of individual scuba diving satisfaction attributes (e.g. O'Reilly 1982; Tabata 1992; Davis and Tisdell 1996; Musa 2002; Graham *et al.* 2001; MacCarthy *et al.* 2006; Paterson et al. 2012). Only few researchers group these attributes into specific factors or dimensions (e.g. O'Neill *et al.* 2000; Musa *et al.* 2006). In general, the studies that measure divers' satisfaction could be summarized in three main dimensions: destination characteristics, dive operator service and social interaction (see Table 9.2). Destination characteristics refer to underwater visibility, marine life, underwater scenery, water temperature, and so on. The second dimension – dive operator services – is concerned with the service quality and satisfaction with services such as boat facilities, safety, dive equipment and staff. The third dimension – social interaction – emphasizes the quality of social experience with other fellow divers. In Table 9.2, with the exception of O'Neill *et al.* (2000) who only studied the service quality of the staff, all other studies agrees that destination characteristics are a crucial dimension in measuring scuba divers' satisfaction. This clearly indicates the importance of this aspect in measuring satisfaction. Therefore, it is vital to maintain the ecological balance of the marine life and coral reefs, as these attributes are the most important contributing factor to divers' satisfaction.

## Managerial and marketing implications of divers' satisfaction

Scuba diving satisfaction is an important element for both environmental and commercial sustainability of the scuba diving industry. This knowledge is

*Table 9.2* Summary of satisfaction dimensions

| Researcher studies of scuba diving satisfaction | Scuba diving dimensions | | |
|---|---|---|---|
| | Destination characteristic | Dive operator service | Social interaction |
| O'Neill *et al.* (2000) | | X | |
| O'Reilly (1982) | X | | |
| Tabata (1992) | X | X | |
| Davis and Tisdell (1996) | X | | |
| MacCarthy *et al.* (2006) | X | X | X |
| Musa (2002) | X | X | X |
| Musa *et al.* (2006) | X | | |
| Paterson *et al.* (2012) | X | | |

beneficial for the management of experiences and services which divers expect to be delivered by dive operators. Scuba diving operators will be mindful of the marine environment preferred and valued by divers. Satisfied divers are likely to return to experience the holiday destination again. They are also more likely to recommend their positive experience to others.

Diver satisfaction provides pertinent pointers to divers' needs and preferences in the marine environment. Empirical results can elicit both the highly and poorly rated attributes of the scuba diving experience. The highly rated attributes can facilitate the design of effective promotional messages which reflect the reality of the destination and at the same time can potentially differentiate divers' experiences compared with other destinations. On the other hand, dive operators could also enhance their services by improving the poorly rated attributes of scuba divers' experience.

Feedback from divers in satisfaction surveys may also point to the opportunity for new products and services development to be offered to scuba divers. In conclusion, the knowledge of divers' satisfaction is important for the industry's sustainability in terms of both the development and the operation of the scuba diving industry.

## References

Blackstock, K., McCrum, G., Scott, A. and White, V. (2006) *A Framework for Developing Indicators of Sustainable Tourism*, The Cairngorms National Park Authority (CNPA) and Macaulay Institute Sustainable Tourism Indicator Framework Project, The Macaulay Institute.

Choi, H. C. and Sirakaya, E. (2006) 'Sustainability Indicators for Managing Community Tourism', *Tourism Management*, 27(6):1274–1289.

Davis, D. and Tisdell, C. (1996) 'Economic Management of Recreational Scuba Diving and the Environment', *Journal of Environmental Management*, 48(3):229–248.

Farsari, Y. and Prastacos, P. (2000) 'Sustainable Tourism Indicators: Pilot Estimation for Municipality of Hersonissos, Crete', Municipality of Hersonissos, Hersonissos.

Fuller, J. and Matzler, K. (2000) 'Customer Delight and Market Segmentation: An Application of the Three-factor Theory of Customer Satisfaction on Life Style Groups', *Tourism Management*, 29(1):116–126.

Graham, T., Idechong, N. and Sherwood, K. (2001) 'The Value of Dive-tourism and the Impacts of Coral Bleaching on Diving in Palau', in *Coral Bleaching: Causes, Consequences and Responses*, selected papers presented at the 9th International Coral Reef Symposium on 'Coral bleaching: assessing and linking ecological and socio-economic impacts, future trends and mitigation planning'. Coastal Management Report No. 2230, H. Z. Schuttenberg (ed.) Coastal Resources Center, University of Rhode Island, Kingston, US.

Hoegh-Guldberg, O. (1999) 'Climate Change, Coral Bleaching and the Future of the World's Coral Reefs', *Marine and Freshwater Research*, 50(8):839–866.

Kozak, M. and Rimmington, M. (2000) 'Tourist Satisfaction with Mallorca, Spain, as an Off-season Holiday Destination', *Journal of Travel Research*, 38(3):260–269.

MacCarthy, M., O'Neill, M. and Williams, P. (2006) 'Customer Satisfaction and Scuba Diving: Some Insights from the Deep', *The Service Industries Journal*, 26(5):537–555.

Miller, G. (2001) 'The Development of Indicators for Sustainable Tourism: Results of a Delphi Survey of Tourism Researchers', *Tourism Management*, 22(4):351–362.

Musa, G. (2002) 'Sipadan: A Scuba Diving Paradise: An Analysis of Tourism Impact, Diver Satisfaction and Tourism Management', *Tourism Geographies*, 4(2):195–209.

Musa, G. Kadir, S. L. S. A. and Lee, L. (2006) 'Layang Layang: An Empirical Study on Scuba Divers' Satisfaction', *Tourism in Marine Environments*, 2(2):89–102.

Ngazy, Z., Jiddawi, N. and Cesar, H. (2001) 'Coral Bleaching and the Demand for Coral Reefs: A Marine Recreation Case in Zanzibar', paper presented at the International Consultative Workshop for Economic Valuation and Policy Priorities for Sustainable Management of Coral Reefs WorldFish Center's Headquarters, Penang, Malaysia, December 8–10.

O'Neill, M. A., Williams, P., MacCarthy, M. and Groves, R. (2000) 'Diving into Service Quality – the Dive Tour Operator Perspective', *Managing Service Quality*, 10(3):131–140.

O'Reilly, M. B. (1982) 'Sport Diving in Texas: A Study of Participants, their Activity and Means of Introduction', MS thesis, Texas A & M University, College Station, US.

Paterson, S., Young, S., Loomis, D. K. and Obenour, W. (2012) 'Resource Attributes that Contribute to Nonresident Diver Satisfaction in the Florida Keys, US', *Tourism in Marine Environments*, 8(2):47–60.

Pizam, A., Neumann, Y. and Reichel, A. (1978) 'Dimensions of Tourist Satisfaction with a Destination Area', *Annals of Tourism Research*, 5(3):314–322.

Tabata, R. S. (1992) 'Scuba Diving Holidays', in *Special Interest Tourism*, C. M. Hall and B. Weiler (eds.) Belhaven, New York, NY: 171–184.

Vinals, M. J., Morant, M., Ayadi, E. L., Teruel, L., Herrera, S., Flores, S. and Iroldi, O. (2003) 'A Methodology for Determining the Recreational Carrying Capacity of Wetlands', in *Marine Ecotourism: Issues and Experiences*, B. Garrod and J. C. Wilson (eds.) Channel View Publications, Clevedon, UK: 79–106.

# Part IV

# Scuba diving sustainability

# 10 The business of scuba diving

*Kay Dimmock, Terry Cummins and
Ghazali Musa*

## Introduction

This chapter examines the scuba diving industry from a business and management perspective. The global growth in scuba diving demand experienced from the late twentieth into the twenty-first century has created the need and interest to better understand factors surrounding the management of scuba diving tourism, to achieve economic and environmentally sustainable outcomes. In the scuba diving industry, the three main business foci are service delivery, the management of divers' experience and the minimization of environmental impacts.

Critical to scuba diving business is successful relationships with scuba divers and other sectors of the industry in the provision of dive training, equipment, travel packages and the scuba diving experience itself. The challenges confronting the scuba diving industry are complex. Managers seek business success while managing individuals who are at leisure in marine environments; both activities have the potential to create environmental harm. This chapter draws insights from knowledge of management, customer service and marketing in examining aspects of business in scuba diving tourism.

## Background of scuba diving tourism

The attraction of a seaside holiday to escape the demands of working life is one of the main contributors to the development of the tourism industry (Page and Connell 2009). Tourists have long visited coastal areas to enjoy the quality and natural beauty of the outdoor environment (Cater and Cater 2007). Some tourists also seek encounters with marine life. Scuba diving is one of the most attractive of such encounters, as divers can be immersed underwater and experience close encounters with marine flora and fauna. The chance to witness rare or endangered marine species is one of the most important reasons motivating people to scuba dive (Cummins 2008). Dobson (2008) adds that divers are attracted to the opportunity to be underwater with marine wildlife such as dolphins, sharks and turtles.

The increasing demand for and interest in being active in natural environments has encouraged entrepreneurs to venture into providing scuba diving tourism businesses, especially in light of the potential economic rewards (Cummins 2008;

Dikou and Troumbis 2006; Gössling *et al.* 2008). Locations with attractive and high quality marine resources may wish to offer scuba diving and, in doing so, create greater diversity in the provision of tourism products and services in the area. This business opens access to new tourist markets, along with building collaborations with other sectors in the tourism industry (Dikou and Troumbis 2006).

The success of scuba diving tourism businesses in recent decades reflects the appeal of the activity to a bigger tourism market as a form of soft adventure tourism (Dimmock 2009; Trauer 2006). This attraction has been supported by technological advances, with a range of scuba diving equipment and other related products made available. These products together with related services allow divers different levels of contact with marine environments. The minimal communication and the highly physical and sensory nature of being underwater affects divers differently (Cater 2008). Perceived risk experienced by divers is managed by ensuring that adequate levels of training have been achieved before allowing them to scuba dive, and the diving operation is managed with a minimum requirement for safety standards (Morgan and Fluker 2002). These efforts have resulted in an increase in divers' in-water comfort and satisfaction (Williams *et al.* 2001) and broadened the appeal of scuba diving activity to the public (Cater 2006; Morgan and Dimmock 2006; Wilks 1992).

## Dive tourism business

Historically, scuba diving was considered a high risk activity pursued by hardy adventurers, and it generated much less commercial activity than it does today (Sylvester *et al,* 1987). Formerly, some scuba diving providers may have been lifestyle entrepreneurs, motivated to start their business in order to generate an income stream allowing them to pursue a particular lifestyle. However, contemporary factors, indeed, the cost of providing services expected by divers, have led to a new breed of managers entering the scuba diving industry. Globally, small business operations are a distinctive feature of scuba diving businesses which face considerable challenges operating within the current volatile marketplace. The need to provide access to high quality dive sites along with efficient safety and risk management processes (Coxon *et al.* 2008; McKercher 1998; Williams and Soutar 2005) are the two crucial tasks to be delivered by the operators (Williams and Soutar 2005; Quinn *et al.* 2011). This is echoed by Dimmock (2003) who notes that, in Australia, regional dive tourism operators identify access to quality dive sites which accommodate variation in ocean conditions, and providing satisfactory divers' experiences as two of the challenges facing businesses.

From the outset, scuba diving has been equipment intensive, demanding financial resources to establish a retail dive centre. There is need for a compressor and air bank, an equipment inventory for sale and hire, and adequate marine craft and motor vehicles to transport divers to the dive sites. There must be close scrutiny of return on investment (ROI) from this financial outlay. Scuba diving tourism managers today must work with international training standards and apply responsible codes of practice which emphasize safety in scuba diving (Coxon *et al.* 2008). The existence of medical support services, such as the Divers Alert Network (DAN) and the greater number of decompression chambers throughout the world has helped increase the safety standards of the industry. The availability of this additional infrastructure allows scuba divers to be more confident with the service and safety standards available in new and remote dive locations.

## Services and the scuba diving business

The escalating growth in scuba diving tourism activity warrants the need for the industry's operation to be managed with sustainable principles (Garrod and Wilson 2004; McCool and Moisey 2001; Pickering and Weaver 2003). This is crucial if the resources on which business success is dependent are to be protected (Cater and Cater 2007; Orams 1996).

The size and scope of the scuba diving tourism industry is difficult to estimate. At the end of 2011, PADI worldwide (the largest scuba training provider) had recorded 6100 registered retailers and resort operators providing PADI training services (PADI n.d.). There are also other scuba training providers and the total number must be considerably greater. Moreover, any total does not take into account the fact that there are operators who register in one location, and yet deliver their diving services in multiple jurisdictions. For example, some operators with boats in several locations in the Asian Pacific and Maldives registered only once (personal communication) but operate several elements of their business, some of which are in different locations.

The business of scuba diving involves the provision of both tangible and intangible goods and services. Examples of tangible components are scuba diving equipment, the diving C-card and related souvenirs. The intangible components include education and skill development, dive charter services and dive guides. Scuba diving operators occupy a critical space in the interaction between divers and the marine environment. Williams *et al.* (2001) stress the importance of intangible elements in providing satisfaction to scuba divers. The quality of scuba diving services delivered has substantial influence on the level of satisfaction experienced by divers (Williams *et al.* 2001). The service quality experienced at a diving destination could also serve to differentiate operators or destinations, and stimulate repeat business or positive recommendations (Coghlan 2012; O'Neill *et al.* 2000).

The services involved with scuba diving are an excellent illustration of the services categories proposed by Lovelock *et al.* (2009). This is depicted in Table 10.1. As stated earlier, scuba diving services have both tangible and intangible actions. Within each action, the service is directed either to people or to their possessions. For people-processing, an example of tangible action is when divers are transported to the dive site using buses or boats. For possession-processing, the operators need to be vigilant in the safe-keeping of divers' belongings such as luggage and scuba diving equipment. While at the destination divers can engage in mental-stimulus-processing, some of which may be in the form of pre-dive

*Table 10.1* Tangible and intangible actions in services

| Nature of service act | People | Possessions |
|---|---|---|
| Tangible actions | *People-processing* (services directed at people) e.g. transport, boats, etc. | *Possession-processing* (services directed at physical possessions) e.g. luggage, diving equipment, etc. |
| Intangible actions | *Mental-stimulus-processing* (services directed at people's mind) e.g. dive briefing, video shows, etc. | *Information-processing* (services directed at intangible assets) e.g. diving C-card, travel insurance, etc. |

Source: Lovelock *et al.* (2009)

briefings and video shows to highlight the marine life in the area. Information-processing may include the diving C-card, travel insurance and credit card information which facilitate the business operation and commercial transactions involved. Being mindful of these categorizations points clearly to a need to deliver seamless service encompassing all four categories of scuba diving services.

O'Neill *et al.* (2000) state that customer satisfaction with standards of service quality is important for both scuba divers and dive tourism operators. Operators need to create positive awareness of their business operations, while divers need to ensure the holiday provides value for money. Dimmock (2003) states that experiences at dive sites are critical elements which influence their satisfaction. O'Neill *et al.* (2000), who studied the service quality delivered to divers, emphasize the importance of intangible experience derived from the staff in the form of responsiveness, assurance, empathy and reliability. Within these criteria, divers acknowledged their support for operators who incorporated professionalism in their service through customer welcome, attention to detail, safety measures, coordination of operations handled by staff, and interpretation and environmental education. Williams *et al.* (2001) add that these features provide a sense of trust and professionalism for the scuba diving operators. The discerning nature of scuba divers and their expectation for service quality has seen the industry respond positively and create a more sophisticated and effective business delivery.

Scuba diving operators often need to juggle the adventurous need of divers and the need to ensure safety and security. Williams and Soutar (2005:255) note that 'the ability to plan (and control) when and where participants can experience stress and arousal is vital to the successful management of an adventure operation'. On the other hand, Morgan (2000) confirms that high levels of safety precaution help secure divers' trust in scuba diving operators, which ultimately influences divers' decision making. The safety aspect of service quality, which is within the dimension of assurance, is mandatory, regardless of the size of scuba diving operations. Backpackers, for example, regularly use social media to search for the safest and best dive sites, and for operators with a good customer service reputation (personal communication). In social media, such as Facebook, Tripadvisor and Travel Blogs, divers review the ratings and comments from other divers related to specific destinations, and this greatly enhances the speed of their decision making process (Tuten and Solomon 2013).

We propose that the scuba diving industry could be made up of four Es. These are (1) Equipment, (2) Education, (3) Experience and (4) Environment. Table 10.2 outlines the roles each E can play within the industry. The industry's survival is mutually dependent on the health of each component. The four Es outline important areas of responsibility in the industry and the complexity inherent for scuba diving managers.

The services of dive tourism organisations are typically delivered to scuba divers via a range of distribution channels, adding to the special nature of the service delivery for this industry. Lovelock *et al.* (2009) further suggest that services can be distributed to customers in three ways. These are (A) when the

*Table 10.2* The 4Es of scuba diving tourism services

---

*Education:* Diving skill and competence development is established by training agencies (e.g. PADI, Scuba Schools International [SSI], National Association of Underwater Instructors [NAUI], Scuba Diving International [SDI]), of which many are represented at the retail and resort level of the industry. Cater and Cater (2007) point out that education through interpretative experiences is how individuals come to learn more about marine environments. Scuba diving involves a standardized and formalized approach to achieving competence standards through demonstrated skill development and training to become a licensed diver.

*Equipment:* A critical component necessary to enable time to be spent safely underwater is scuba diving equipment. There is a high degree of competition in the diving equipment manufacturing sector. As a result, some manufacturers build their own networks of distribution channels through which exclusive trading conditions are established and targeted at retail dive centres.

*Experience:* Retail dive centres provide dive charters, dive guides and other services as part of the experience at local dive sites. Dive operators are required to provide not only excellent experiences in the delivery of core products – scuba diving and the marine life – but also the supplementary products such as transport, accommodation and camaraderie experience.

*Environment:* Cater and Cater (2007) state that the tourism industry is a major stakeholder in marine ecotourism because of the symbiotic relationship between the industry and resources which constitute the marine tourism attraction. Indeed, there has been increasing attention given to the need for improvements to marine environments through conservation and management (Bell *et al.* 2011; Pearce and Kirk 1986). In response, the dive industry has become an active leader in promoting awareness of and engagement with marine resource protection through support for marine conservation projects, awareness campaigns and marine wildlife protection (Townsend 2008). The establishment of the Project Aware Foundation has been valuable to inform and involve divers and other marine supporters to participate actively in marine conservation practices. Steps have been taken in the greening of the industry through conservation efforts as part of localized initiatives at an individual destination level. The role of volunteer diving groups established at identified destinations has also been important for marine conservation (Hammerton *et al.* 2012).

---

customer visits the organization, (B) when the organization visits the customer, or (C) when the customer and organization transact remotely.

Scuba divers visit the organization (Option A) when they are present at the organizations' establishment to purchase equipment, taking scuba diving education and training, booking a scuba diving trip or even scuba diving at the destination itself. Examples of Option B can be observed when the operators organize a pick-up service for divers from home or hotel. The increased role of technology in service delivery and consumption means the customer and organisation can also transact remotely (Option C). The preliminary theory involved with scuba diving education and training certification can now be carried out online at home. This leaves scuba diving training at the destination being completed in less time. More time can then be spent on leisure dives with whatever time is left after completing the certification.

## Networks and collaborations in the scuba diving tourism business

The scuba diving business is comprised of various organizations which offer goods and services to divers. Constructive relationships encourage growth in the current competitive environment (Wilson 2011). Challenges can be particularly great for small to medium enterprises (SMEs) in regional areas or developing locations where there is limited tourism infrastructure. In today's business environments, networks have become important to business because they provide a platform for partnerships and network structure, an example of which is the development of scuba diving e-commerce services (Valentina and Passiante 2009).

Knowledge sharing and relationship building have the potential to create competitive advantage (Braun 2002). Novelli *et al.* (2006) state that network relations have potential to unleash dynamic and innovative services. Business relationships, according to Freytag and Ritter (2005), are the basis of an organization's approach to operations which will have impacts on their business decisions and actions. One such partnership is the implementation of greater environmental awareness and eco-action which promotes green business operations and can benefit stakeholders in scuba diving tourism. For example, a dive centre in partnership with a local restaurant which uses only seafood fished sustainably can generate a powerful message as well as build customer interest and support (Denny 2011). The initiative is aimed at building green business profiles and developing collaborative business relations which will benefit the business, environment and divers.

For scuba diving operators, there are also potential network relationships with other tourism sectors. These collaboration opportunities could occur at the business level as well as the destination level. The opportunities can be derived, for example, from the practical and physical limits which are placed on a diver (see Table 10.3). While these practical features restrict the time spent on scuba diving, collaboration could be extended to non-diving activities so that other tourism sectors can benefit economically from scuba divers. In Association of Southeast Asian Nations (ASEAN) countries, it is common to package a dive holiday with visits to other cultural and natural attractions.

*Table 10.3* Practical features of scuba diving

| *Features of scuba diving* |
| --- |
| Cannot scuba dive all day |
| Average dive is approx. 40 minutes |
| Many divers only want 2 or 3 dives per day |
| Modern dive consumers have mixed interests and are open to a range of add-ons in their travel mix |
| Travelling divers must wait 24 hours after diving before flying or driving to altitude |

Furthermore as part of the travel industry supply chain, scuba divers may also patronize other tourism products and services in the form of transport, accommodation, shopping, restaurants, cultural sites, wildlife attractions and activities involving non-diving companions. All these features provide multiple avenues for business partnership and collaboration at the destination.

The benefits from network collaborations for small and medium sized tourism enterprises (Tinsley and Lynch 2001) include knowledge which may be otherwise difficult to access. The knowledge can build competitive advantage and be shared at the destination level, as well as throughout business channels (McLeod *et al.* 2010). Studies of network relationships have revealed advantages (Freytag and Ritter 2005) including the establishment of future value (Möller and Halinen 1999). Networks help identify capabilities necessary for coordinating inter-organization cooperation (Lemmetyinen and Go 2009) which can also strengthen the trust in the inter-organizational relationship (Petrou *et al.* 2007).

Trust in network relationships is invaluable in the scuba diving industry as retail dive centres choose to become affiliated with particular dive training agencies (e.g. PADI, SSI, NAUI, SDI). The retail dive centre must meet the training and service standards of the agency to become an affiliated representative. When asked what influences the decision to adopt a particular training brand for their retail centres, the common response given is the recognition the brand carries and the marketing power behind it (personal communication).

Firms in networks, according to Möller and Hallinen (1999), are analysed according to which among them assume leadership roles within a network, and set the benchmark from which to gauge the health and success of the network. Ultimately, the combination of organizations and their combined output, supply and demand within the network will establish the network and enhance opportunities and advantages for all involved at the destination level (Petrou *et al.* 2007).

## The marketing of scuba diving tourism

Marketing the dive industry can be carried out through several communication avenues including traditional channels (advertising, billboards, public relations and trade shows), and Internet marketing (Lovelock *et al.* 2009). Scuba diving expos have been a popular form of communication for the industry, with exhibitions held in large metropolitan centres (e.g. the US, Australia, Singapore and Malaysia). The largest (DEMA – Diving Equipment Manufacturers Association) is held annually in the US and attracts an international audience of dive industry personnel. International expos enable the convergence of industry sectors including equipment manufacturers (such as Aqua Lung, Cressi, Oceanic, Mares, Scuba Pro), education developers (PADI, SSI, NAUI), travel intermediaries (e.g. Dive Adventures, Allways Dive Expeditions) and scuba diving destinations and resorts, to showcase the latest offerings direct to the public. In recent years, there has been a positive impact in newly emerging markets such as Asia which has witnessed growth in the number of dive expos compared with mature markets such as Australia and the US.

While a range of communication channels for promoting scuba diving exist, industry surveys find that word-of-mouth (WOM) remains the most successful form of communication – this is when people tell one another about diving, whether this occurs via the telephone, face-to-face or social media. Such communication exchange among divers shows the importance of satisfying scuba divers' needs and wants from the first point of contact, so that satisfaction is achieved and the intention for repeat visitation and recommendation to others can be activated. In the event of dissatisfaction being experienced, industry players should institute efficient and fair service recovery which stimulates positive WOM and future loyalty intentions.

Generating awareness of scuba diving tourism requires effective communication about the activity, to create awareness, knowledge, interest and action. The communication preferably includes critical experiential elements involved, such as excitement, adventure and safety. When communicating a message which attracts divers to a particular destination, Musa *et al.* (2005) confirm a need for the most satisfactory elements of the experience to be part of the communication message. For example, the promise of sighting a particular form of wildlife can be disappointing if none are sighted, as occurred with one group of dive tourists to Southeast Africa's 'sardine run' (Dicken 2010). To counter disappointment, divers' expectation of the experience must be positioned appropriately.

On a similar note, researchers report that diving on Queensland's Great Barrier Reef (GBR) holds appeal for less experienced divers, with the environmental quality of the reef not as attractive to experienced divers (Pabel and Coghlan 2011). The heterogeneity across the scuba diving market suggests the GBR can be marketed to select target groups which is consistent with divers needs and wants (Pabel and Coghlan 2011). Inbound scuba divers have been targeted in response to Australian divers' preference for offshore exotic less expensive diving destinations. The strategy used to attract international divers includes quoting prices in US dollars. Collaboration between state governments, airlines and tourism promotion companies has informed inbound scuba divers there are choices to be made beyond one destination in their diving itineraries.

## Twenty-first century divers

The Internet age and twenty-first century technology has been advantageous for the industry and scuba diving tourism. Web-based technology has allowed more scuba divers to discover new dive sites and locations quickly and more easily. Social media have been phenomenal in their communication role regarding scuba diving tourism, particularly as an effective way to share the latest information and updated pictures and stories of dive tourism experiences. Examples of commonly used social media are Tripadvisor, Facebook, travel blogs and YouTube. Divers can find the most popular dive sites at what price, in real time.

Social media, to Tuten and Solomon (2013), is the fifth P for marketing. For scuba business operators, website and social media offer a direct and immediate communication link between the scuba diving industry and the public. For example, PADI and SSI have recently launched information apps which provide the public with information on dive centre locations using Google maps. Cummins (2008) notes that e-learning has had an impact on the way people learn scuba diving, with more divers completing the 'study' component of dive certification online before travel to the dive destination to complete the training course. Divers certified with PADI can receive a copy of their diver C-Card on their smartphone, avoiding the need to carry the card.

From an equipment perspective, technology has facilitated dive planning and decompression calculations. These tasks are now carried out efficiently by dive computers which provide greater reliability and increase safety, as decisions on diving depth, duration of surface interval and bottom time are handled by the accurate computer algorithms. Divers can also access marine identification information with Marine ID apps available for smartphones. Even e-books on marine flora and fauna are available for purchase and download. Their use in aquatic environments is enhanced by providing waterproof protective devices for smartphones and tablets.

## Sustaining the business of scuba diving tourism

For twenty-first century dive tourism operators, business decisions are influenced by multiple factors, as depicted in Table 10.4. The table outlines the range of management issues which demand attention. The interplay of scuba divers, government policies and regulations, ICT and the business environment highlights the complexity and competing values within which scuba diving tourism operates.

Weaver (2004) writes there is discrepancy between intent and implementation of sustainable practices in tourism. Additionally Lane (2009) states that progress towards sustainability within tourism has been slow. In the management of sustainable scuba diving business, there are three distinct areas that require attention. These are: (1) marine environmental awareness and conservation management, (2) service delivery and customer satisfaction management, and (3) sustainable business management.

*Table 10.4* Twenty-first century scuba diving tourism business challenges

| Divers | Government policies and regulations | Technology and ICTs | Business environment |
|---|---|---|---|
| Diversity in market segments | Public concerns for marine conservation | Rise in e-travel and e-distribution channels | Competitive sector |
| More flexibility demanded as time poor/income rich | Safety standards and regulation | Rapid pace of change to new technology and e-learning | Declining profits per unit sold |
| More niche products with shorter attention cycle | Focus on economic growth | Wider use of the Internet to support consumer adaptation of new technology | New market and product and services opportunities in new destinations |
| Increased use of ICTs acceptance of e-products and services | | Increased usage of social media to engage with divers | |

Source: Adopted from Page and Connell (2009)

Over recent decades, commentators have called for effective management on the detrimental impacts of scuba diving tourism to the environment. These impacts can result from, for example, crowding, over-development, poor diving skill and irresponsible behaviour (Musa and Dimmock 2012; Rouphael and Hanafy 2007). Townsend (2008) notes that, for some years, these issues have been recognized. Among scuba diving tourism stakeholders, there is now greater awareness and commitment to marine conservation and protection.

For scuba diving operators, to manage their businesses sustainably involves dealing with a competitive business environment and, at the same time, taking a long-term view. Williams and Soutar (2005) argue that many operators adopt a short-term approach to running a business. They add that there should be a better understanding of business practices which cater for a long-term and sustained business operation. As stated earlier, industry and business networks have the potential to support and offer direction in tourist destination management through information generation and sharing, as well as relationship exchange.

## Conclusion

Scuba diving business balances the need for economic viability, divers' satisfaction and environmental protection. Scuba diving requires the industry to deliver flawless services, which include both tangible and intangible experience for divers themselves and their possessions. Networks and collaborations among industry players, together with related sectors, could benefit considerably from the exchange of knowledge, management and business practices. The importance of word-of-mouth communication to reach divers is accentuated further by the increasing use of social media in decision making among divers. Yet, scuba diving industry sustainability continues to be uncertain in the future, with the difficulty in finding a balance between the needs of divers, businesses and environment. Scuba diving business demands an holistic appreciation of all the factors involved, and outcomes should balance the needs of 'people, planet and profit' (Cater and Cater 2007:179).

# References

Bell, C. M., Needham, M. D. and Szuster, B. W. (2011) 'Congruence among Encounters, Norms, Crowding, and Management in a Marine Protected Area', *Environmental Management*, 48(3):499–513.

Braun, P. (2002) 'Networking Tourism SMEs: e-Commerce and e-Marketing Issues in Regional Australia', *Information Technology and Tourism*, 5:13–23.

Cater, C. (2006) 'Playing with Risk? Participant Perceptions of Risk and Management Implications in Adventure Tourism', *Tourism Management*, 27:317–325.

Cater, C. (2008) 'Perceptions of and Interactions with Marine Environments: Diving Attractions from Great Whites to Pygmy Seahorses', in B. Garrod and S. Gössling (eds.) *New Frontiers in Marine Tourism: Diving Experiences, Sustainability, Management*, Amsterdam: Elsevier: 49–66.

Cater, C. and Cater, E. (2007) *Marine Ecotourism: Between the Devil and the Deep Blue Sea*, Wallingford: CABI.

Coghlan, A. (2012) 'Facilitating Reef Tourism Management through an Innovative Importance–Performance Analysis Method', *Tourism Management*, 33:767–775.

Coxon, C., Dimmock, K. and Wilks, J. (2008) 'Managing Risk in Tourist Diving: A Safety-Management Approach', in B. Garrod and S. Gössling (eds.) *New Frontiers in Marine Tourism: Diving Experiences, Sustainability, Management*, Amsterdam: Elsevier: 201–220.

Cummins, T. L. (2008) 'Recreational Scuba Diving and the Travel Experience', paper presented at 1st Commonwealth Conference on Sport Tourism, Kota Kinabalu, Malaysia.

Denny, M. (2011) 'Why Conservation?', *The Undersea Journal*, Third Quarter:54–61.

Dicken, M. (2010) 'Socio-economic Aspects of Boat-based Ecotourism during the Sardine Run within the Pondoland Marine Protected Area, South Africa', *African Journal of Marine Science*, 32(2):405–411.

Dikou, A. and Troumbis, A. (2006) 'Dive Tourism in North Aegean, Greece: Potential and Prospect', *Tourism in Marine Environments*, 3(2):131–143.

Dimmock, K. (2003) 'Managing Recreational Scuba Experiences: Exploring Business Challenges for New South Wales Dive Tourism Managers', *Tourism Review International*, 7(2):67–80.

Dimmock, K. (2009) 'Finding Comfort in Adventure: Experiences of Recreational Scuba Divers', *Leisure Studies*, 28(3):279–295.

Dobson, J. (2008) 'Shark! A New Frontier in Tourist Demand for Marine Wildlife', in J. Higham and M. Lück (eds.) *Marine Wildlife and Tourism Management: Insights from the Natural and Social Sciences*, Wallingford, UK: CABI: 49–65.

Freytag, P. and Ritter, T. (2005) 'Dynamics of Relationships and Networks – Creation, Maintenance and Destruction as Managerial Challenges', *Industrial Marketing Management*, 34:644–647.

Garrod, B. and Wilson, J. (2004) 'Nature on the Edge? Marine Ecotourism in Peripheral Coastal Areas', *Journal of Sustainable Tourism*, 12(2):95–120.

Gössling, S., Linden, O., Helmersson, J., Liljenberg, J. and Quarm, S. (2008) 'Diving and Global Environmental Change: A Mauritius Case Study', in B. Garrod and S. Gössling (eds.) *New Frontiers in Marine Tourism: Diving Experiences, Sustainability, Management*, Amsterdam, Elsevier: 67–92.

Hammerton, Z., Dimmock, K., Hahn, C., Dalton, S. and Smith, S. (2012) 'Scuba Diving and Marine Conservation: Collaboration at Two Australian Sub-tropical Destinations', *Tourism in Marine Environments*, 8(1/2):77–90.

Lane, B. (2009) 'Thirty Years of Sustainable Tourism: Drivers, Progress, Problems – and the Future', in S. Gössling, C. M. Hall and D. B. Weaver (eds.) *Sustainable Tourism Futures: Perspectives on Systems*, Hoboken: Routledge: 19–32.

Lemmetyinen, A. and Go, F. (2009) 'The Key Capabilities Required for Managing Tourism Business Networks', *Tourism Management*, 30(1):31–40.

Lovelock, C., Wirtz, J. and Chew, P. (2009) *Essentials of Services Marketing*, Singapore: Prentice Hall.

McKercher, B. (1998) *The Business of Nature-based Tourism*, Melbourne: Hospitality Press.

McLeod, M. T., Vaughan, D. R. and Edwards, J. (2010) 'Knowledge Networks in the Tourism Sector of the Bournemouth, Poole, and Christchurch Conurbation: Preliminary Analysis', *The Service Industries Journal*, 30(10):1651–1667.

McCool, S. F. and Moisey, R. N. (2001) 'Introduction: Pathways and Pitfalls in the Search for Sustainable Tourism', in S. F. McCool and R. N. Moisey (eds.) *Tourism, Recreation and Sustainability: Linking Culture and the Environment*, New York: CABI: 1–16.

Möller, K. and Halinen, A., (1999) 'Business Relationships and Networks: Managerial Challenge of Network Era', *Industrial Marketing Management*, 28:413–427.

Morgan, D. (2000) 'Adventure Tourism Activities in New Zealand: Perceptions and Management of Client Risk', *Tourism Recreation Research*, 25(3):1–12.

Morgan, D. and Dimmock, K. (2006) 'Risk Management in Outdoor Adventure Tourism', in J. P. Wilks, D. Pendergast and P. Leggat (eds.) *Tourism in Turbulent Times: Towards Safe Experiences for Visitors*, Amsterdam: Elsevier: 171–184.

Morgan, D. and Fluker, M. (2002) 'Risk Management Considerations in Australian Commercial Adventure Tourism', paper presented at the Council of Australian University Tourism and Hospitality Education conference, Tourism and Hospitality on the Edge, Fremantle, February.

Musa, G. and Dimmock, K. (2012) 'Introduction to Scuba Diving Tourism', *Tourism in Marine Environments*, 8(1/2):1–5

Musa, G., Kyed A., Kadir, S. and Lee, L. (2005) 'Layang Layang: An Empirical Study on Scuba Divers' Satisfaction', *Tourism in Marine Environments*, 2(2):89–102.

Novelli, M., Schmitz, B. and Spencer, T. (2006) 'Networks, Clusters and Innovation in Tourism: A UK Experience', *Tourism Management*, 27(6):1141–1152.

O'Neill, M., Williams, P., MacCarthy, M. and Groves, R. (2000) 'Diving into Service Quality: The Dive Tour Operator Perspective', *Managing Service Quality*, 10(3):131–138.

Orams, M. (1996) 'Using Interpretation to Manage Nature-based Tourism', *Journal of Sustainable Tourism*, 4(2):81–94.

Pabel, A. and Coghlan, A. (2011) 'Dive Market Segments and Destination Competitiveness: A Case Study of the Great Barrier Reef in View of Changing Reef Ecosystem Health', *Tourism in Marine Environments*, 7(2):55–66.

PADI (n.d.) 'The Way the World Learns to Dive', Professional Association of Diving Instructors. Online. Available HTTP: <http://www.padi.com/scuba/> (accessed 25 March 2012).

Page, S. and Connell, J. (2009) *Tourism: A Modern Synthesis* (3rd edn), Andover, Hampshire: Cengage Learning.

Pearce, D. G. and Kirk, R. M. (1986) 'Carrying Capacities for Coastal Tourism', *Industry and Environment*, 9(1):3–7.

Petrou, A., Pantziou, E., Dimara, E. and Skuras, D. (2007) 'Resources and Activities Complementarities: The Role of Business Networks in the Provision of Integrated Rural Tourism', *Tourism Geographies*, 9(4):421–440.

Pickering, C. and Weaver, D. B. (2003) 'Nature-based Tourism and Sustainability: Issues and Approaches', in R. Buckley, C. Pickering and D. B. Weaver (eds.) *Nature-based Tourism, Environment and Land Management*, Wallingford, UK: CABI: 7–10

Quinn, R. E., Faerman, S. R., Thompson, M. P., McGrath, M. R. and St Clair, L. S. (2011) *Becoming a Master Manager: A Competing Values Approach* (5th edn), Danvers, MA: Wiley.

Rouphael, A. and Hanafy, M. (2007) 'An Alternative Management Framework to Limit the Impact of Scuba Divers on Coral Assemblages', *Journal of Sustainable Tourism*, 15(1):91–103.

Sylvester, B. with Perry, D. and Blackburn, G. (1987) *The Magic of Scuba: A Complete Introductional Guide for the Australian Diver*, Dingley: Wednell.

Tinsley, R. and Lynch, P. (2001) 'Small Tourism Business Networks and Destination Development', *Hospitality Management*, 20:367–378.

Townsend, C. (2008) 'Dive Tourism, Sustainable Tourism and Social Responsibility: A Growing Agenda', in B. Garrod and S. Gössling (eds.) *New Frontiers in Marine Tourism: Diving Experiences, Sustainability, Management*, Amsterdam: Elsevier: 189–200.

Trauer, B. (2006) 'Conceptualizing Special Interest Tourism – Frameworks for Analysis', *Tourism Management*, 27:183–200.

Tuten, T. and Solomon, M. (2013) *Social Media Marketing*, Saddle River, NJ: Pearson.

Valentina, N. and Passiante, G. (2009) 'Impacts of Absorptive Capacity on Value Creation', *Anatolia*, 20(2):269–287.

Weaver, D. B. (2004) 'Tourism and the Elusive Paradigm of Sustainable Development', in A. Lew, C. M. Hall and A. Williams (eds.) *A Companion to Tourism*, Malden, MA: Blackwell: 510–522.

Wilks, J. (1992) 'Introductory Scuba Diving on the Great Barrier Reef', *Australian Parks and Recreation*, (Summer):18–23.

Williams, P. and Soutar, G. (2005) 'Close to the Edge: Critical Issues for Adventure Tourism Operators', *Asia Pacific Journal of Tourism Research*, 10(3):247–261.

Williams, P., O'Neill, M. and MacCarthy, M. (2001) 'Consumption Issues in Dive Tourism: An Exploratory Study', paper presented at the Asia Pacific Tourism Association Sixth Annual Conference, Phuket, Thailand.

Wilson, D. (2011) 'The Importance of Relationships in the Wine Sector', *Wine & Viticulture Journal*, March/April:82–83.

# 11 Scuba diving, environmental change and sustainability

*C. Michael Hall*

## Environmental change

Global change refers to planetary-scale biophysical and societal changes in the Earth system (Hall 2013). The global environment is always changing, although change is never uniform across time and space. Yet 'all changes are ultimately connected with one another through physical and social processes alike' (Meyer and Turner 1995: 304). However, what is most significant with respect to contemporary global environmental change is that it is not primarily due to natural processes. Instead, the scale and rates of change have increased dramatically as a direct result of human action related to the consumption of natural resources, the creation of new habitat for human activities (including tourism) which have in turned altered the habitats of other species, and the waste products of human consumption and production. Human impacts on the environment may have a global character in two ways. First, 'global refers to the spatial scale or functioning of a system' (Turner *et al.* 1990:15); the climate and the oceans have the characteristic of a global system. Second, global environmental change occurs if a change 'occurs on a worldwide scale, or represents a significant fraction of the total environmental phenomenon or global resource' (Turner *et al.* 1990:15–16); an example is coral bleaching. Tourism is significant for both types of change (Gössling 2002; Gössling *et al.* 2002; Gössling and Hall 2006a; Hall and Lew 2009).

The potentially negative impacts of tourism on the bio-physical environment at a local scale have been recognised since the late 1960s, including with respect to the results of marine activities such as scuba diving (Hall 2001). However, that tourism can have environmental impacts at a global scale is a much more recent conceptualisation that arguably developed from two primary influences (Hall and Lew 2009). The first was the emergence in the 1980s of the concept of sustainable development. The second influence was the application of systems approaches to the study of tourism which emphasised not only the destination but also the importance of generating areas and transit zones in assessing the wider impacts of tourism on the environment. The latter approach helped increase awareness of system-wide effects of tourism consumption at different scales, such as transport related greenhouse gas emissions that may be significant over the entire course of a tourist trip. Such an approach is also significant for seeking to assess the environmental impacts of scuba diving tourism, as the setting of different system boundaries will provide different outcomes. For example, many accounts of scuba diving impact are restricted to environments at specific dive locations or destinations (e.g. Rouphael and Inglis 1997; Hawkins *et al.* 1999; Musa 2002). However, such boundary setting may serve to ignore the provision of tourism infrastructure that scuba divers may use, including hotel and resort developments, as well as the environmental effects of actually getting to and from dive destinations from home environments. For example, the growth of coastal tourism in the Red Sea in the 1990s had immediate substantial impacts on coral reefs, in terms of both the effects of construction and infrastructure development as well as the direct effects of snorkelling and diving (Hawkins and Roberts 1994). In the longer term, the effects of such tourist developments have also included increased demands on scarce local water supplies (Gössling *et al.* 2012a).

The relationship between tourism and environmental change is not unidimensional. Tourism is simultaneously affected by and contributing to environmental change. Figure 11.1 illustrates some of these aspects by noting the

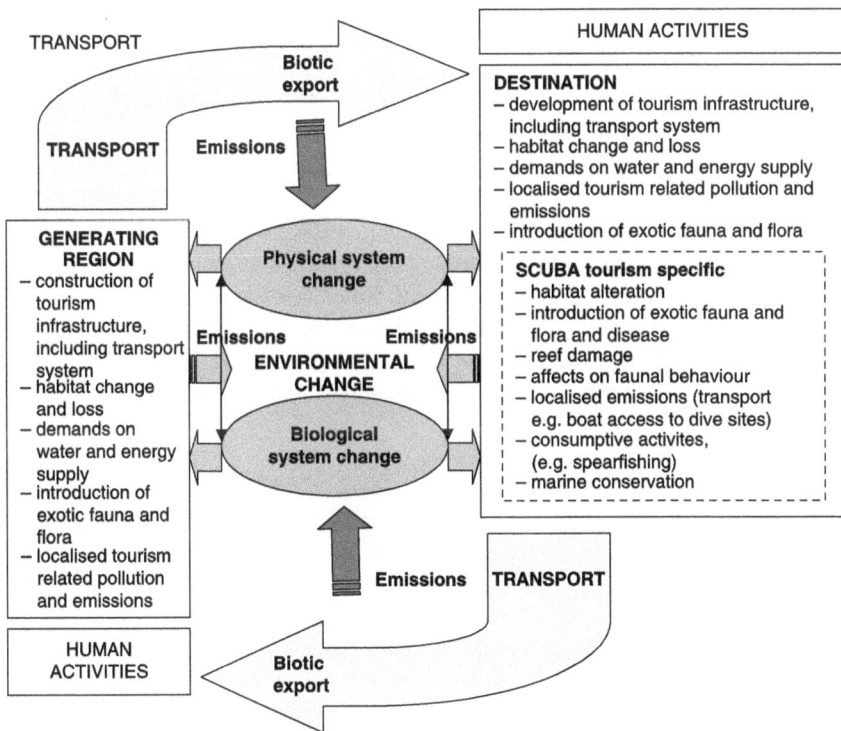

*Figure 11.1* The contribution of scuba diving tourism to environmental change (after Hall 2010b).

ongoing circulation of scuba tourists within the tourist system and the subsequent effects on the environment at various scales. The figure utilises Gössling's (2002) identification of key elements of global environmental change to which tourism contributes: changes in land cover and land use; energy use; biotic exchange and extinction of wild species; exchange and dispersal of diseases; and changes in the perception and understanding of the environment. The various elements of global environmental change can then be assessed both qualitatively and quantitatively where possible.

Gössling's (2002) estimates for 2001 with respect to tourism's contribution to Global Environmental Change (GEC), updated in Gössling and Hall (2006), have been more recently examined in Hall and Lew (2009) and Hall (2009) (Table 11.1); these suggest that the contribution of tourism to GEC continues to grow, not only as a result of increasing numbers of domestic and international tourist trips but also because of increases in distance travelled (Hall 2005, 2008; Gössling *et al.* 2009; Scott *et al.* 2012). The analysis of scuba tourists by Lew (Chapter 2, this volume) would tend to support the suggestion that a similar growth has occurred in the patterns of scuba diving tourism. Nevertheless, it is extremely difficult to apply Lew's estimates of scuba tourists because of the high degree of uncertainty as to the relative frequency of travel.

Tourism has historically been presented as more of a victim of environmental change than a contributor (e.g. Gable and Aubrey 1990), but during the 1990s, increased attention began to be given to tourism's role in environmental change at a global scale (e.g. Wilson 1997; Schafer and Victor 1999). In the 2000s, this focused especially on tourism's growing contribution to climate change with the scale of the contribution becoming recognised by lead organisations such as the United Nations World Tourism Organization (UNWTO 2007). However, within the scuba diving world, the emphasis appears clearly on the impacts of environmental change on scuba diving rather than scuba's contribution. For example, an analysis of the UK Scuba News (http://news.scubatravel.co.uk/), found that nearly all of the 140 plus stories that related to emissions focused on the effects of climate change on marine life, coral reefs and ocean acidification. Over a six-year period, not one news story focused specifically on the emissions contribution of scuba diving tourism.

## Emissions

In the case of $CO_2$, emissions resulting from tourism represent an increasing proportion of global greenhouse gas emissions (Scott *et al.* 2012). The United Nations World Tourism Organization, United Nations Environmental Programme and World Meteorological Organization (UNWTO, UNEP and WMO) (2008) estimate that, in 2005, approximately 40 per cent of these come from air transport, 32 per cent from car transport and 21 per cent from accommodation, with growth continuing to occur in all areas (Gössling *et al.* 2010). If tourism were a country, its emissions would come after the US, China, the European Union and Russia, although if the upper estimate of radiative forcing effects were used, tourism would rank only behind the US and China in terms of its contribution to climate change (Hall 2010b).

*Table 11.1* Tourism's contribution to global environmental change

| Dimension | 2001 estimates | 2007 estimates |
| --- | --- | --- |
| Number of international tourist arrivals | 682 million[1] | 898 million[1] |
| Number of domestic tourist arrivals | 3,580.5 million[2] | 4,714.5 million[2] |
| Total number of tourist arrivals | 4,262.5 million[2] | 5,612.5 million[2] |
| Change of land cover – alteration of biologically productive lands | 0.5% contribution[3] | 0.6–0.66% contribution[4] |
| Energy consumption | 14,080 PJ[3] | 18,585.6 PJ[4] |
| Emissions | 1400 Mt of $CO_2$-e[3] | 1848 Mt of $CO_2$-e[4] (1461.6 Mt of $CO_2$)[5] |
| Biotic exchange | Difficult to assess[3] | Difficult to assess, however rate of exchange is increasing[4] |
| Extinction of wild species | Difficult to assess[3] | Difficult to assess, particularly because of time between initial tourism effects and extinction events, but increasing. One estimate is 3.5–5.5% of species loss, with future higher figure being likely if climate change factors are considered[6] |
| Health | Difficult to assess[3] | Difficult to assess in host populations, but sickness in tourists in tropical destinations assessed at 50% by WHO[7] |
| World population[8] | 6,169.8 million | 6,632.2 million |
| Total number of tourist arrivals as % of world population | 69.1% | 84.6% |
| Number of international tourist arrivals as % of world population | 11.1% | 13.5% |

Notes:
1. United Nations World Tourism Organization (UNWTO) figures
2. Hall and Lew (2009) estimates, based on UNWTO data
3. Gössling (2002) estimate
4. Hall and Lew (2009) extrapolation, based on Gössling's estimates and other research
5. UNWTO, United Nations Environmental Programme (UNEP) and World Meteorological Organization (WMO) (2008) estimate for 2005
6. In Hall (2010a)
7. World Health Organisation (2003)
8. Mid-year world population estimate by US Census Bureau (2009)

Using Lew's (Chapter 3) estimates of scuba diving tourism, market size could provide a variation emissions contribution in 2007 ranging from 61.74 Mt of $CO_2$-e (million tons of carbon equivalent emissions) for a total scuba diving market of thirty million, and 6.17 Mt of $CO_2$-e for a scuba diving market of three million people; this utilises Gössling's (2002) estimates for emissions and assumes that the scuba diving market is tourism active. Such wide variations are not that helpful in themselves in providing an accurate account of emissions from scuba diving tourism, but perhaps it is just as important to recognise that scuba tourism – which often focuses on its environmental benefits – is also a contributor to emissions. Indeed, the growth in travel to more peripheral destinations for scuba diving suggests that the per trip emissions from scuba diving tourism may potentially be higher than average. It is also appropriate to note that, even using the lower figure for emissions from scuba diving, tourism provides a higher figure than that of the combined emissions of several of the small island states which promote scuba diving tourism (United Nations Framework Convention on Climate Change (UNFCCC) 2005).

Ocean Frontiers in the Cayman Islands, one of the first scuba diving companies to offer carbon offsets for scuba holidays, states the amount of carbon emitted by a couple on a round-trip flight from London (UK) to Grand Cayman was 5.76 tons of $CO_2$, while 14 dives during a one-week-trip generate an additional 0.26 tons of $CO_2$ (Sustainable Travel International 2007). Such trips would more than double the amount of greenhouse gas generated on an average domestic or international tourist trip. The figures are even greater than the annual per capita emissions of the average world resident (Scott *et al.* 2012). Scuba diving tourism in locations remote from source markets has higher emission levels because of greater reliance on aviation and/or shipping for access (Hall 2010b). For example, in the case of the Antarctic, which is an emerging scuba diving destination, Amelung and Lamers (2007) found that the average per capita emissions from travelling to the gateway ports of Ushuaia/Punta Arenas (Argentina/Chile) and Christchurch (New Zealand) by Antarctic-bound tourists were 8.58 and 8.48 tonnes per capita, respectively. Average ship-based $CO_2$ emissions per capita was 6.16 tonnes per passenger. However, the contribution varied widely depending on the ship, ranging from 2.09 tonnes per passenger for the *Alexander Humboldt* to 22.63 tonnes per passenger for the *Spirit of Enderby*. The per capita emissions of land-based tourism in Antarctica were estimated as being just under 50 tonnes per tourist, including transport between gateway cities and Antarctica. From their research Amelung and Lamers (2007) estimate that, on a per capita basis, the 14.97 tonnes of greenhouse gases produced during the typical two week travels of the Antarctic tourist is equal to the total emissions produced by an average European in 17 months (Scott *et al.* 2012).

## Habitat loss and species extinction

Nature-based tourism activities, including scuba diving, are a major economic justification for the conservation of species and habitat (Buckley 2009; Frost and

Hall 2009), especially in marine protected areas (Terk and Knowlton 2010). Nevertheless, scuba diving tourism directly affects habitat loss as a result of the construction and development of tourism infrastructure (Steinitz *et al.* 2005), as well as the direct impacts of scuba diving itself (such as damage to reefs [Miller *et al.* 2004]) and indirect effects (such as acting as vectors of disease or invasive species, contribution to climate change). Hall (2010c) found a positive relationship between tourism and the number of endangered species in Pacific and Caribbean island states. Tourism urbanisation processes are spatially and geographically distinct, often being related to high natural amenity areas such as the coastal zone, where ecosystems are subject to urbanisation, land clearance and the draining and clearance of wetlands (Gössling and Hall 2006a). This may lead to situations in which, while tourism has provided the justification for conservation of specific coastal or marine habitats, other areas nearby may still suffer habitat loss because of tourism infrastructure development.

One difficulty in assessing the effects of tourism (including that related to scuba diving) on habitat and species loss is the time lag between the initial tourism stimulus and recognition that change has occurred. Change is quickly visible with respect to the development of tourism infrastructure or coral damage, but the impacts of exotic flora or climate change may take some time before they are recognised (Mozumder *et al.* 2006; Hall 2010b). Given the relationship observed by Ehrlich (1994) between energy and emissions as well as energy use and biodiversity loss, Hall (2010a) conservatively estimated that tourism overall is responsible for approximately 3.5–5.5 per cent of species loss, with a higher figure being likely in future if climate change scenarios are considered. This situation may be even worse when the role of tourism in biological invasion is considered, particularly in peripheral island environments where tourism is of major economic importance.

## Biotic exchange

Tourism is recognised as a major mechanism for biological invasion because of the capacity of tourists and associated infrastructure to act as vectors for disease and exotic species (Mozumder *et al.* 2006). There tends to be a positive relationship between the number of visitors to natural areas and the number of alien species (Lonsdale 1999; Vilà and Pujadas 2001) although the exact contribution of tourism is difficult to determine (Hall 2011a).

Approximately 480,000 species have been accidentally or deliberately introduced by humans beyond the natural limits of their geographic range (Pimentel *et al.* 2001). Invasive alien species have contributed to nearly 40 per cent of all animal extinctions for which the cause is known (Secretariat of the Convention on Biological Diversity [SCBD] 2006). Although the impacts of biological invasions are economically significant for nature-based industries such as fisheries, they can also affect environmental services that support tourism as a result of environmental or species change (Ressurreição *et al.* 2011). This may be particularly important for marine and national parks or other areas with high scenic conservation values, although the effects on tourism are likely to be higher when charismatic species are lost or go into decline compared with aesthetic changes to the environment (Hall *et al.* 2011). In the case of more experienced or special interest scuba divers, the loss of key target species or dive environments can be a significant factor in the relative attractiveness of a dive destination (Flugman *et al.* 2011; Ressurreição *et al.* 2011). The long-term impacts of biological invasion are therefore an extremely important dimension in the calculation of the overall costs and benefits of nature-based tourism, although such issues are usually not included in assessments (e.g. Buckley 2009).

Although the contribution of tourism to the spread of invasive species is frequently noted in the biological invasion literature, there is a relative lack of acknowledgement in the tourism literature of the direct contribution of tourism and recreation to biological invasion and the corresponding loss of species (Hall 2011a). Nevertheless, scuba diving tourism can act as a vector for species invasion in several ways:

- transport to scuba diving destinations;
- divers' clothes and luggage;
- scuba diving equipment.

Air and ship transport is a major contributor to the spread of disease and biological invasion (Tatem *et al.* 2006; Tatem and Hay 2007; Hulme 2009; Tatem 2009; Hall *et al.* 2010). Hull fouling (Drake and Lodge 2007) and ballast water (Endresen *et al.* 2004) are identified as major sources of alien maritime species. Invasive species may also be carried on small boats used for freshwater diving or on scuba diving gear that has not been appropriately cleaned and which is then moved between dive locations. Eurasian water milfoil (Myriophyllum spicatum) is an aquatic invasive weed that has been identified at a number of sites in the western US, including Lake Tahoe, a significant fresh water scuba diving destination on the California–Nevada border. Because Eurasian water milfoil is easily spread by fragments, transport on boats and boating or diving equipment plays a key role in contaminating new water bodies. Unless the weed is controlled, significant alterations of aquatic ecosystems, with subsequent reductions in recreational amenity, can occur (Eiswerth *et al.* 2000).

Another pest species that is being dispersed by recreational boats in Europe and the US is the zebra mussel. This is an extremely invasive bivalve that displaces native species. In a study conducted on Lake St Clair in Michigan, Johnson *et al.* (2001) identified several mechanisms associated with recreational boating that were capable of transporting the larval and adult life stages of the mussel. These included carrying larvae in water in the live wells, bilges, bait buckets and engines of boats, and the direct transport of adult and juvenile mussels on macrophytes entangled on boat trailers and anchors.

Nature-based tourism has also long been implicated in disease spread because of the travel of individuals to often remote locations where they are exposed to new pathogens and where they may, in turn, introduce pathogens to both human

and animal populations (Wilson 1995; Rudkin and Hall 1996). Visitors to peripheral destinations are at increased risk for infection with local diseases for several
reasons: (1) lack of immunologic experience with the pathogens present in the
new location, (2) increased susceptibility due to genetic differences compared
with the local population, and (3) lack of knowledge about the disease risks,
leading to riskier behaviour as compared with the local population (Wilson 1995).
The USDA, APHIS, VS, CEAH, Center for Emerging Issues (2001) identified
five factors associated with disease emergence and ecotourism/nature-based
tourism:

1   movement of people into an undeveloped rural environment;
2   environmental change (e.g. deforestation, road/infrastructure building);
3   increased contact of humans with wildlife;
4   increased contact of humans with arthropod disease vectors (e.g. mosquitos,
    ticks);
5   increased risk of infection with local diseases for people visiting a new area.

According to the USDA, APHIS, VS, CEAH, Center for Emerging Issues (2001:7):
'Tropical areas, which are popular destinations for nature travel and ecotourists,
are particularly likely places for the emergence of new animal and zoonotic
diseases because of the increased biological diversity in tropical regions relative to
temperate regions'. The mobility of scuba divers and other nature-based tourists to
peripheral destinations therefore provides a great challenge for sustainability. On
the one hand, such tourism is clearly implicit in the transfer of pathogens and
disease to both human and animal populations. On the other, nature-based marine
tourism, and especially scuba diving, provides an essential economic justification
for conserving marine environments and species.

## Implications of environmental change for scuba diving tourism: the case of coral reefs

Although not the only dive environment affected by environmental change, coral
reefs are one of the most important marine ecosystems for scuba diving tourism
and are also considered one of the most vulnerable to climate change and other
anthropogenic environmental change (Hughes *et al.* 2010). Reefs are vulnerable
to several climate change-related impacts: ocean acidification, coral bleaching
and, for inshore coral reefs, greater land runoff as a result of increased storm
events (Scott *et al.* 2012).

Ocean acidification reduces the availability of carbonate in seawater. Data-
based estimates indicate that, globally, the oceans have accumulated about 29 per
cent of the total anthropocentric $CO_2$ emissions within the past 250 years (SCBD
2009). Between 1751 and 1994, surface ocean pH is estimated to have decreased
from approximately 8.25 to 8.14 (Jacobson 2005). The observed annual uptake of
anthropogenic $CO_2$ of 2.2 ($\pm$ 0.4) Pg C per year by the oceans for 1990–1999 led
to an estimate that the ocean sink accounted for 24 per cent of total anthropogenic

emissions during 2000–2006 (SCBD 2009). It is predicted that by 2050, ocean acidity could increase by 150 per cent, severely affecting levels of calcium carbonate, which forms the shells and skeletons of many sea creatures, and also disrupts reproductive and physiological activity. Reefs in acidified waters are predicted to decline in the following sequence (SCBD 2009: 53):

• loss of coralline algae causing decreased reef consolidation;
• loss of carbonate production by corals resulting in loss of habitat;
• loss of biodiversity with extinctions.

Such effects will only be amplified by the interaction of the effects of ocean acidification with other dimensions of climate change, including storms, sea level rise, increasing water temperatures and erosion, as well as further anthropogenic change in the form of pollution and over-fishing (Hall 2010d; Scott *et al.* 2012).

Significantly, the effects of acidification are widespread and are not just isolated to tropical waters. Given current carbon emission rates, it is predicted that the surface waters of the Arctic Ocean will become under-saturated with respect to essential carbonate minerals by 2032, and the Southern Ocean by 2050, with disruptions to large components of the marine food web (SCBD 2009). It is predicted that by 2100, 70 per cent of cold-water corals will be exposed to corrosive waters (Turley *et al.* 2007).

Coral bleaching – the whitening of corals due to stress-induced expulsion or death of their symbiotic protozoa, or to loss of pigmentation within the protozoa – can occur for multiple reasons, but temperature change is the primary cause, and changes in water chemistry (acidification) can be a strong contributor. Mass coral bleaching transforms large reef areas from a mosaic of colour (if healthy) to a stark white. With very high confidence, the IPCC (Schneider *et al.* 2007) concluded that a warming of 2°C above 1990 levels would result in mass mortality of coral reefs globally. Hoegh-Guldberg *et al.*'s (2007:1742) review of the future of coral reefs under warmer ocean temperatures and ocean acidification found that, even under low-range IPCC scenarios, 'serious if not devastating ramifications for coral reefs [would occur]'. However, the vulnerability of reefs to the impacts of climate change will vary spatially and temporally, with shallow reefs, reefs with species closest to their thermal maximum threshold, and those closest to sources of pollution or other human impacts the most vulnerable and where impacts will be visible to tourists the soonest. Nevertheless, even moderate further warming will consequently affect the attractiveness of coral reefs to tourists in some destinations. Furthermore, coral reefs provide other important ecosystem services to the tourism sector, including as a fishery resource and coastal protection against storms. For destinations where reefs are the key attraction for tourists, the long-term damage arising from bleaching incidents will have important implications for the quality of dive tourist experiences, and, therefore, for the sustainability of tourism operations (Flugman *et al.* 2011).

The impact of climate change-related reef degradation and loss on dive tourism and tourism destinations remains uncertain (Gössling *et al.* 2007) but, because reef health is thought to be important to the experience and satisfaction of dive tourists (Fenton *et al.* 1998; Roman *et al.* 2007), it has been suggested that the impacts of coral reef bleaching on dive tourism could be highly significant (Scott *et al.* 2012). However, previous bleaching events suggest that the effects may be variable among different markets (Scott *et al.* 2012).

In El Nido in the Philippines, severe coral bleaching in 1998 led to 30–50 per cent coral mortality, and a typhoon that same year caused further damage to local reefs. However, general awareness of coral bleaching among tourists was limited (44 per cent) (Cesar 2000). The bleaching event did not affect budget tourist arrivals, but fewer budget tourists went diving during their stay (Cesar 2000). Studies in Zanzibar, Tanzania and Mombasa, Kenya, in 1999 also found that awareness of bleaching among tourists was relatively low in Zanzibar (28 per cent) and Mombasa (45 per cent) (Westmacott *et al.* 2000). Of those who were aware of the bleaching, 80 per cent stated that knowledge of bleaching in the area would affect their decision to visit the region or to dive there.

In the Caribbean, 76 per cent of tourists at the diving destination of Bonaire (where 99 per cent of respondents took at least one dive during their trip) indicated they would be unwilling to return for the same holiday price in the event that corals suffered 'severe bleaching and mortality' (Uyarra *et al.* 2005). Andersson's (2007) study of tourism perceptions at the African islands of Zanzibar and Mafia found that serious divers who visit Mafia were more aware of bleaching than the recreational divers who visit Zanzibar (62 per cent versus 29 per cent). When asked if they would be willing to dive on a bleached reef, 40 per cent of respondents at Zanzibar and 33 per cent at Mafia indicated that they would. Such results highlight how different scuba diving market segments will be differentially affected by the impacts of climate and other forms of environmental change, depending on motivations, prior experiences and budgets (Gössling *et al.* 2012b; Scott *et al.* 2012). In addition, they also highlight how scuba diving tourism is likely to have a future even in an increasingly acidic and warming sea.

Indeed, in their study of Mauritius, Gössling *et al.* (2007) found that there are significant differences between dive destinations. They found that the state of coral reefs was largely irrelevant to dive tourists and snorkellers, as long as a threshold level was not exceeded. This level was defined by visibility, abundance and variety of species, and the occurrence of algae or physically damaged corals. Gössling *et al*'s (2007) results are consistent with the findings of Main and Dearden (2007) that 85 per cent of recreational divers failed to perceive any damage to reefs in Phuket, Thailand, after the 2004 Indian Ocean tsunami. Dearden and Manopawitr (2011) even question whether future generations of divers will perceive environmental changes, such as bleaching and degraded reef conditions, in the same way as contemporary divers if they have no frame of reference of previous more pristine conditions. Generational cohorts may therefore perceive environmental change in different ways with corresponding influences on behaviours, expectations and travel (Scott *et al.* 2012).

## Conclusions and future

Scuba diving tourism has long been portrayed as being a major contributor to the conservation of marine biodiversity. In many ways it is; however, this chapter has sought to emphasise that any understanding of the relationships between scuba diving tourism and environmental change needs to be understood within the entire tourism system (Hall 2007). Any consideration of the environmental effects of scuba diving tourism needs to weigh up its contribution to habitat and species conservation against its role in environmental change. The difficulty in doing this is that it requires a greater appreciation of the role of time in assessing tourism's impacts than the usual approach (Hall 2011b). Nevertheless, this chapter has indicated that the perceived environmental benefits of scuba diving tourism, especially in peripheral locations that are distant from their main markets, may need a fundamental reassessment. However, although assessments of the consequences of environmental change for scuba diving tourism need to consider the perception of ongoing and expected environmental change (Hvenegaard 2002; Gössling 2007), these perceptions are likely to be complex, translating into non-linear changes in behaviour (Gössling and Hall 2006b; Gössling *et al.* 2012b). This means that change in one or several environmental parameters does not necessarily result in an equivalent change in scuba tourist behaviour.

Most scuba diving tourism research has occurred in specific environments or at a destination scale. Because of this, there is a lack of appreciation of the potential wider impacts of scuba diving tourism, especially in destinations that are distant from their main markets. For example, in the case of long-distance tourism, more than 90 per cent of a typical journey's contribution to climate change usually comes from the transport component and particularly aviation (Gössling 2000; Scott *et al.* 2012) in getting to and from the destination or the study site in which tourists are intercepted by researchers (Hall 2007). As Gössling (2002:200) argued, 'even ecotourism projects often seem to ignore the global environmental aspects of travel. Ecotourism may thus be sustainable on the local level (in the sense that it puts a minimum threat to local ecosystems through the conversion of lands, trampling, collection of species, etc.) but it may in most cases not be sustainable from a global point of view'. The chapter therefore raises the obvious issue as to whether scuba diving tourism can actually be sustainable (Hall 2011b)? The answer is a qualified yes, and lies in the development of more sustainable forms of travel, and a notion of development that is grounded in ecological economics, whereby travel is contextualised within the entire consumptive patterns of individuals and households and within the bio-physical boundaries of environmental services. In order to achieve such a goal, travel needs to be significantly decarbonised as well as localised. As Gössling *et al.* (2002: 2009) concluded, 'in order to become more sustainable, destinations should seek to attract clients from close source markets'. Nevertheless, as Hall (2007) noted, such a conclusion, while environmentally appropriate, presents a major challenge for many scuba diving tourism operations. Unfortunately, some of the locations that most depend on the contribution of scuba diving tourism to local community and economic development are also the most peripheral and therefore distant with respect to source markets. In such situations, difficult or different development decisions may need to be made.

This chapter has also emphasised that, in order to ascertain the full impacts of scuba diving tourism and therefore judge its actual contribution to the environment, a much broader analysis in time and space needs to be conducted. However, to do so may lead not only to results that many tourism stakeholders will not want to acknowledge but also to unwelcome proposed solutions. Therefore, the challenge facing scuba diving tourism is part of the broader challenge facing tourism, in that medium to long-distance travel is not environmentally friendly or sustainable. The scuba-diving polluter, whether labelled an ecotourist or not, needs to pay.

## References

Amelung, B. and Lamers, M. (2007) 'Estimating the Greenhouse Gas Emissions from Antarctic Tourism', *Tourism in Marine Environments*, 4(2/3):121–133.

Andersson, J. (2007) 'The Recreational Costs of Coral Bleaching – a Stated and Revealed Preference Study of International Tourists', *Ecological Economics*, 62:704–715.

Buckley, R. (2009) 'Evaluating the Net Effects of Ecotourism on the Environment: A Framework, First Assessment and Future Research', *Journal of Sustainable Tourism*, 17:643–672.

Cesar, H. (2000) *Impacts of the 1998 Coral Bleaching Event on Tourism in El Nido, Phillippines*, Narragansett: Coastal Resources Center Coral Bleaching Initiative, University of Rhode Island.

Dearden, P. and Manopawitr, P. (2011) 'Climate Change – Coral Reefs and Dive Tourism in South-east Asia', in A. Jones and M. Phillips (eds.) *Disappearing Destinations*, Wallingford, UK: CABI Publishing.

Drake, J. M. and Lodge, D. M. (2007) 'Hull Fouling is a Risk Factor for Intercontinental Species Exchange in Aquatic Ecosystems', *Aquatic Invasions*, 2:121–131.

Ehrlich, P. R. (1994) 'Energy Use and Biodiversity Loss', *Philosophical Transactions: Biological Sciences*, 344(1307):99–104.

Eiswerth, M. E., Donaldson, S. G. and Johnson, W. S. (2000) 'Potential Environmental Impacts and Economic Damages of Eurasian Watermilfoil (*Myriophyllum spicatum*) in Western Nevada and Northeastern California', *Weed Technology*, 14(3):511–518.

Endresen, O., Behrens, H .L., Brynestad, S., Anderson, A. B. and Skjong, R. (2004) 'Challenges in Global Ballast Water Management', *Marine Pollution Bulletin*, 48:615–623.

Fenton, D., Young, M. and Johnson, V. (1998) 'Re-presenting the Great Barrier Reef to Tourists: Implications for Tourist Experience and Evaluation of Coral Reef Environments', *Leisure Sciences*, 20(3):177–192.

Flugman, E., Mozumder, P. and Randhir, T. (2011) 'Facilitating Adaptation to Global Climate Change: Perspectives from Experts and Decision Makers Serving the Florida Keys', *Climatic Change*, DOI: 10.1007/s10584–011-0256–9.

Frost, W. and Hall, C. M. (eds.) (2009) *Tourism and National Parks: International Perspectives on Development, Histories and Change*, London: Routledge.

Gable, F. J. and Aubrey, D. G. (1990) 'Potential Coastal Impacts of Contemporary Changing Climate on South Asian Seas States', *Environmental Management*, 14:33–46.

Gössling, S. (2002) 'Global Environmental Consequences of Tourism', *Global Environmental Change*, 12:283–302.

Gössling, S. (2007) 'Ecotourism and Global Environmental Change', in J. Higham (ed.) *Critical Issues in Ecotourism*, Oxford: Elsevier.

Gössling, S. and Hall, C. M. (eds.) (2006a) *Tourism and Global Environmental Change*, London: Routledge.

Gössling, S. and Hall, C. M. (2006b) 'Uncertainties in Predicting Tourist Flows under Scenarios of Climate Change', *Climatic Change*, 79(3/4):163–173.

Gössling, S., Borgström-Hansson, C., Hörstmeier, O. and Saggel, S. (2002) 'Ecological Footprint Analysis as a Tool to Assess Tourism Sustainability', *Ecological Economics*, 43(2/3):199–211.

Gössling, S., Lindén, O., Helmersson, J., Liljenberg, J. and Quarm, S. (2007) 'Diving and Global Environmental Change: A Mauritius Case Study', in B. Garrod and S. Gössling (eds.) *New Frontiers in Marine Tourism: Diving Experiences, Management and Sustainability*, Amsterdam: Elsevier.

Gössling, S., Ceron, J-P., Dubios, G. and Hall, C. M. (2009) 'Hypermobile Travellers', in S. Gössling and P. Upham (eds.) *Climate Change and Aviation*, London: Earthscan.

Gössling, S., Hall, C. M., Peeters, P. and Scott, D. (2010) 'The Future of Tourism: Can Tourism Growth and Climate Policy be Reconciled? A Climate Change Mitigation Perspective', *Tourism Recreation Research*, 35(2):119–130.

Gössling, S., Peeters, P., Hall, C. M., Ceron, J-P., Dubois, G., Lehmann, L. V. and Scott, D. (2012a) 'Tourism and Water Use: Supply, Demand, and Security. An International Review', *Tourism Management*, 33:1–15.

Gössling, S., Scott, D., Hall, C. M., Ceron, J. P. and Dubois, G. (2012b) 'Consumer Behaviour and Demand Response of Tourists to Climate Change', *Annals of Tourism Research*, 39:36–58.

Hall, C. M. (2001) 'Trends in Coastal and Marine Tourism: The End of the Last Frontier?', *Ocean and Coastal Management*, 44(9/10):601–618.

Hall, C. M. (2005) *Tourism: Rethinking the Social Science of Mobility*, Prentice-Hall, Harlow.

Hall, C. M. (2007) 'Scaling Ecotourism: The Role of Scale in Understanding the Impacts of Ecotourism', in J. Higham (ed.) *Critical Issues in Ecotourism*, Oxford: Elsevier.

Hall, C. M. (2008) 'Tourism and Climate Change: Knowledge Gaps and Issues', *Tourism Recreation Research*, 33:339–50.

Hall, C. M. (2009) 'Degrowing Tourism: Décroissance, Sustainable Consumption and Steady-state Tourism', *Anatolia: An International Journal of Tourism and Hospitality Research*, 20:46–61.

Hall, C. M. (2010a) 'Changing Paradigms and Global Change: From Sustainable to Steady-state Tourism', *Tourism Recreation Research*, 35:131–45.

Hall, C. M. (2010b) 'Tourism and Environmental Change in Polar Regions: Impacts, Climate Change and Biological Invasion', in C. M. Hall and J. Saarinen (eds.) *Tourism and Change in Polar Regions: Climate, Environments and Experiences*, London: Routledge.

Hall, C. M. (2010c) 'An Island Biogeographical Approach to Island Tourism and Biodiversity: An Exploratory Study of the Caribbean and Pacific Islands', *Asia Pacific Journal of Tourism Research*, 15:383–399.

Hall, C. M. (2010d) 'Tourism and Biodiversity: More Significant than Climate Change?', *Journal of Heritage Tourism*, 5(4):253–266.

Hall, C. M. (2011a) 'Biosecurity, Tourism and Mobility: Institutional Arrangements for Managing Biological Invasions', *Journal of Policy Research in Tourism, Leisure and Events*, 3:256–280.

Hall, C. M. (2011b) 'Policy Learning and Policy Failure in Sustainable Tourism Governance: From First and Second to Third Order Change?', *Journal of Sustainable Tourism*, 19:649–671.

Hall, C. M. (2013) 'Ecotourism and Global Environmental Change', in R. Ballantyne and J. Packer (eds.) *The International Handbook of Ecotourism*, Aldershot: Ashgate.

Hall, C. M. and Lew A. (2009) *Understanding and Managing Tourism Impacts: An Integrated Approach*, London: Routledge.

Hall, C. M., James. M. and Wilson, S. (2010) 'Biodiversity, Biosecurity, and Cruising in the Arctic and Sub-Arctic', *Journal of Heritage Tourism*, 5:351–364.

Hall, C. M., James, M. and Baird, T. (2011) 'Forests and Trees as Charismatic Mega-Flora: Implications for Heritage Tourism and Conservation', *Journal of Heritage Tourism*, 6:309–323.

Hawkins, J. P. and Roberts, C. M. (1994) 'The Growth of Coastal Tourism in the Red Sea: Present and Future Effects on Coral Reefs', *Ambio*, 23(8):503–508.

Hawkins, J. P., Roberts, C. M. Hof, T. V., De Meyer, K., Tratalos, J. and Aldam, C. (1999) 'Effects of Recreational Scuba Diving on Caribbean Coral and Fish Communities', *Conservation Biology*, 13:888–897.

Hoegh-Guldberg, O., Mumby, P. J., Hooten, A. J., Steneck, R. S., Greenfield, P., Gomez, E., Harvell, C. D., Sale, P. F., Edwards, A. J., Caldeira, K., Knowlton, N., Eakin, C. M., Iglesias-Prieto, R., Muthiga, N., Bradbury, R. H., Dubi, A. and Hatziolos, M. E. (2007) 'Coral Reefs under Rapid Climate Change and Ocean Acidification', *Science*, 318:1737–1742.

Hughes, T. P., Graham, N. A. J., Jackson, J. B. C., Mumby, P. J. and Steneck, R. S. (2010) 'Rising to the Challenge of Sustaining Coral Reef Resilience', *Trends in Ecology and Evolution*, 25:633–642.

Hulme, P. E. (2009) 'Trade, Transport and Trouble: Managing Invasive Species Pathways in an Era of Globalization'. *Journal of Applied Ecology*, 46:10–18.

Hvenegaard, G. T. (2002) 'Using Tourist Typologies for Ecotourism Research', *Journal of Ecotourism*, 1:7–18.

Jacobson, M. Z. (2005) 'Studying Ocean Acidification with Conservative, Stable Numerical Schemes for Non Equilibrium Air–Ocean Exchange and Ocean Equilibrium Chemistry', *Journal of Geophysical Research Atmospheres*, 110:D07302.1–D07302.17.

Johnson, L. E., Ricciardi, A. and Carlton, J. T. (2001) 'Overland Dispersal of Aquatic Invasive Species: A Risk Assessment of Transient Recreational Boating', *Ecological Applications*, 11:1789–1799.

Lonsdale, W. M. (1999) 'Global Patterns of Plant Invasions and the Concept of Invasibility', *Ecology*, 80:1522–1536.

Main, M. and Dearden, P. (2007) 'Tsunami Impacts on Phuket's Diving Industry: Geographical Implications for Marine Conservation', *Coastal Management*, 35(4):1–15.

Meyer, W. B. and Turner II, B. L. (1995) 'The Earth Transformed: Trends, Trajectories, and Patterns', in R. J. Johnston, P. J. Taylor and M. J. Watts (eds.) *Geographies of Global Change: Remapping the World in the Late Twentieth Century*, Oxford: Blackwells.

Miller, K. J., Mundy, C. N. and Chadderton, W. L. (2004) 'Ecological and Genetic Evidence of the Vulnerability of Shallow-water Populations of the Stylasterid Hydrocoral *Errina novaezelandiae* in New Zealand's Fiords', *Aquatic Conservation: Marine and Freshwater Ecosystems*, 14(1):75–94.

Mozumder, P., Berrens, R. P. and Bohara, A. K. (2006) 'Is There an Environmental Kuznets Curve for the Risk of Biodiversity Loss?', *The Journal of Developing Areas*, 39:175–190.

Musa, G. (2002) 'Sipadan: A Scuba Diving Paradise: An Analysis of Tourism Impact, Diver Satisfaction and Tourism Management', *Tourism Geographies*, 4:195–209.

Pimentel, D., McNair, S., Janecka, J., Wightman, J., Simmonds, C., O'Connell, E. and Tsomondo, T. (2001) 'Economic and Environmental Threats of Alien Plant, Animal, and Microbe Invasions', *Agriculture, Ecosystems and Environment*, 84:1–20.

Ressurreição, A., Gibbons, J., Dentinho, T. P., Kaiser, M., Santos, R. S. and Edwards-Jones, G. (2011) 'Economic Valuation of Species Loss in the Open Sea', *Ecological Economics*, 70:729–739.

Roman, G., Dearden, P. and Rollins, R. (2007) 'Application of Zoning and "Limits of Acceptable Change" to Managing Snorkelling Tourism', *Environmental Management*, 39(6):819–830.

Rouphael, A. B. and Inglis, G. J. (1997) 'Impacts of Recreational Scuba Diving at Sites with Different Reef Topographies', *Biological Conservation*, 82(3):329–336.

Rudkin, B. and Hall, C. M. (1996) 'Off the Beaten Track: The Health Implications of the Development of Special-interest Tourism Services in South-East Asia and the South Pacific', in S. Clift and S. Page (eds.) *Health and the International Tourist*, London: Routledge.

Schafer, A. and Victor, D. G. (1999) 'Global Passenger Travel: Implications for Carbon Dioxide Emissions', *Energy*, 24:657–679.

Schneider, S. H., Semenov, S., Patwardhan, A., Burton, I., Magadza, C. H. D., Oppenheimer, M., Pittock, A. B., Rahman, A., Smith, J. B., Suarez, A. and Yamin, F. (2007) 'Assessing Key Vulnerabilities and the Risk from Climate Change', in M. L. Parry, O. F. Canziani, J. P. Palutikof, P. J. van der Linden and C. E. Hanson (eds.) *Climate Change 2007: Impacts, Adaptation and Vulnerability. Contribution of Working Group II to the Fourth Assessment Report of the Intergovernmental Panel on Climate Change*, Cambridge: Cambridge University Press.

Scott, D., Gössling, S. and Hall, C. M. (2012) *Tourism and Climate Change: Impacts, Adaptation and Mitigation*, London: Routledge.

Secretariat of the Convention on Biological Diversity (2006) *Global Biodiversity Outlook 2*, Montreal: Secretariat of the Convention on Biological Diversity.

Secretariat of the Convention on Biological Diversity (2009) *Scientific Synthesis of the Impacts of Ocean Acidification on Marine Biodiversity*, Technical Series No. 46. Montreal: Secretariat of the Convention on Biological Diversity.

Steinitz, C., Faris, R., Flaxman, M., Karish, K., Mellinger, A. D., Canfield, T. and Sucre, L. (2005) 'A Delicate Balance: Conservation and Development Scenarios for Panama's Coiba National Park', *Environment: Science and Policy for Sustainable Development*, 47(5):24–39.

Sustainable Travel International (2007) 'Scuba Dive Industry Addresses Global Warming and Climate Friendly Diving: World's First Scuba Diving Carbon "Finprint" and Custom Carbon Dive Calculator Developed', Responsible Travel Report, April. Online. Available HTTP: <http://www.responsibletravelreport.com/sti-news/news/2241-scuba-dive-industry-addresses-global-warming-and-climate-friendly-diving> (accessed 1 April 2012).

Tatem, A. J. (2009) 'The Worldwide Airline Network and the Dispersal of Exotic Species: 2007–2010', *Ecography*, 32:94–102.

Tatem, A. J. and Hay, S. J. (2007) 'Climatic Similarity and Biological Exchange in the Worldwide Airline Transportation Network', *Proceedings of the Royal Society B*, 274:1489–1496.

Tatem, A. J., Hay, S. J. and Rogers, D. J. (2006) 'Global Traffic and Disease Vector Dispersal', *Proceedings of the National Academy of Sciences*, 103(16):6242–6247.

Terk, E. and Knowlton, N. (2010) 'The Role of Scuba Diver User Fees as a Source of Sustainable Funding for Coral Reef Marine Protected Areas', *Biodiversity*, 11(1/2):78–84.

Turley, C. M., Roberts, J. M. and Guinotte, J. M. (2007) 'Corals in Deepwater: Will the Unseen Hand of Ocean Acidification Destroy Cold-water Ecosystems?', *Coral Reefs*, 26:445–448.

Turner, B. L., Clark, W. C., Kates, R. W., Richards, J. F., Mathews, J. Y. and Meyer, W. B. (eds.) (1990) *The Earth as Transformed by Human Action*, Cambridge: Cambridge University Press.

United Nations Framework Convention on Climate Change (UNFCCC) (2005) *Climate Change, Small Island Developing States*, Bonn: Climate Change Secretariat (UNFCCC).

United Nations World Tourism Organization (UNWTO) (2007) *From Davos to Bali – A Tourism Contribution to the Challenge of Climate Change*, policy document. Madrid: World Tourism Organization.

United Nations World Tourism Organization (UNWTO), United Nations Environmental Programme (UNEP) and World Meteorological Organization (WMO) (2008) *Climate Change and Tourism: Responding to Global Challenges*, Madrid: United Nations World Tourism Organization, United Nations Environmental Programme, World Meteorological Organization.

US Census Bureau (2009) International Data Base. Online. Available at: <http://www.census.gov/ipc/www/idb/worldpop.html> (accessed 1 April 2012).

US Department of Agriculture Animal and Plant Health Inspection Service, Veterinary Services, Centers for Epidemiology and Animal Health, Center for Emerging Issues (USDA, APHIS, VS, CEAH, Center for Emerging Issues) (2001) Market Watch: Nature Travel and Ecotourism: Animal and Human Health Concerns, October.

Uyarra, M. C., Côté, I. M., Gill, J. A., Tinch, R. R. T., Viner, D. and Watkinson, A. R. (2005) 'Island Specific Preferences of Tourists for Environmental Features: Implications of Climate Change for Tourism-dependent States', *Environmental Conservation*, 32(1):11–19.

Vilà, M. and Pujadas, J. (2001) 'Land-use and Socio-economic Correlates of Plant Invasions in European and North African Countries', *Biological Conservation*, 100:397–401.

Westmacott, S., Cesar, H. and Pet-Soede, L. (2000) *Socioeconomic Assessment of the Impacts of the 1998 Coral Reef Bleaching in the Indian Ocean*, Resource Analysis and Institute for Environmental Science (IVM), Report to the World Bank, African Environmental Division for the CORDIO programme.

Wilson, M. E. (1995), 'Travel and the Emergence of Infectious Diseases', *Emerging Infectious Diseases*, 1:39–46.

Wilson, M. E. (1997) 'Population Movements and Emerging Diseases', *Journal of Travel Medicine*, 4:183–186.

World Health Organization (WHO) (2003) *International Travel and Health*, Geneva: Information Resource Centre Communicable Diseases.

# Review 4: Mabul Island

## The social and environmental impacts on a dive tourism sacrifice area

*Alan A. Lew and Amran Hamzah*

In 2012, one of the major online commercial travel websites, CNN Go, brought together a group of international dive experts with the goal of identifying the top 50 dive sites in the world (Bremner 2012). While several widely recognized contenders made it into the top ten slots, the number one position was granted to Barracuda Point on Sipadan Island in Sabah, Malaysia. Sipadan is famed for its schools of barracuda and bumphead parrot fish, and large numbers and varieties of sharks, turtles and other sea creatures. The island, however, did not receive significant protection until after its disputed ownership was granted to Malaysia by the International Court of Justice in 2002 (ICJ 2002). To protect the unique biodiversity of Sipadan, whose renown had grown steadily since the 1980s, the Malaysian government forced the six resorts on the islands to relocate in 2004, and designated the island as a Marine Protected Area in 2005, limiting divers there to 120 per day (DTW 2012).

Some of the Sipadan dive resorts, which were estimated to have served some 360 divers a day (Musa 2002), migrated to the next nearest island to Sipadan, the island of Mabul. There they joined three existing dive resorts, bringing about the rapid and often questionable development of Mabul. To protect Sipadan's biodiversity, Mabul became a 'sacrifice area'.

Mabul Island is a sandy, low lying, oval shaped island, about 20 hectares in area. About 2,500 people reside on Mabul today in two villages, along with seven larger dive resorts and nine smaller backpacker dive lodges and homestays (about 300 rooms in total). The island's first and largest resort, the Sipadan Mabul Resort, was built in 1992 and covers nearly 20 per cent of the island. However, Mabul's newest resort opens in 2013 with 200 rooms and an oceanarium over a sand and coral area adjacent to the island (Sharma 2008). Only one of Mabul's accommodations, a small homestay, is owned by a local island resident.

The larger of the island's two villages, Kampung Mabul, was first settled in the mid-1970s when the island was a coconut plantation. Today it is mostly comprised of Suluk ('people of the current'), which refers to their origin in the Sulu Archipelago and former Sulu Sultanate (1457–1899) of the Philippines (Tan 2010). The smaller village, Kampung Musu, is mostly made up of Bajau Laut (often referred to as 'sea gypsies') who also have their origin in the Sulu Archipelago, though today they are found throughout the northern portions of insular Southeast Asia

(Langenheim 2010). Although the Suluk were originally nomadic, most on Mabul are now settled there, whereas the Bajau remain a more mobile population which makes them mostly stateless – not recognized as citizens by any country. Most of the Suluk are also not legally recognized as residents by Malaysia.

Both villages have some commercial activities to serve tourists, who can leisurely walk the entire island in under 30 minutes. The Bajau village, with its less permanent stilted houses, is better situated next to the higher-end resorts and has a couple of souvenir shops, as well as a therapeutic massage service and a couple of drink and snack shops. The Suluk village has larger, more permanent houses, about half of which are built on stilts over the water. Backpacker accommodations and homestays are scattered among these, as are restaurants and shops serving both tourists and locals. The Suluk village, in particular, continues to grow as new unregistered immigrants come to the island in search of a better life in Malaysia than they had in the Philippines, where incomes and the standard of living are lower.

The environmental impacts of Mabul's overpopulation are considerable. Environmental awareness is generally low among residents, despite efforts by regional governmental agencies and Non-governmental Organizations (NGOs) that sponsor island cleanup days, along with efforts by dive resorts to keep the waters clear of litter. The government and resorts pay locals residents to dispose of solid waste on a single site, which is then taken by boat to the mainland of Borneo, but that system is not perfect.

Some septic systems exist on Mabul, especially for the larger resorts, but most refuse is disposed of directly into the sea, not too far from the many dive sites on the outer edges of Mabul's coral shelf. In addition, there are no medical services on the island, with residents mostly relying on traditional herbal medicines rather than seeking care in the larger town of Semporna (about 25 minutes away by boat).

The local population is mostly friendly and open to tourists, for whom Mabul's villages provide a colorful backdrop to their dive experiences. Wedding ceremonies, which are public events of music and dancing that last long into the night, are also open for tourists to watch and occasionally participate in, when invited.

Some social tensions between tourists and locals also exist. The local residents are at least nominally Muslim, combined with significant non-Muslim traditions and values, especially among the Bajau. The one mosque on the island is in the Suluk village. Alcohol, which Muslims avoid, is available at the resorts and has made its way into the local population, which has caused concerns. Some residents complain of the improper dress of western tourists and their frequent picture-taking when they come into the villages (Mohamad 2011). Nonetheless, they feel that they have no choice but to welcome them because of their dollars.

The uncertain nationality of the majority of Mabul's population creates many challenges for the island's development. It has marginalized the local community, which has no access to micro credit services to stimulate local entrepreneurship, for which there is also a lack of business acumen and skills. The local community's entrepreneurial activities have been largely restricted to operating sundry shops, food stalls and outlets selling tourist trinkets. At the same time, the rapid increase in the number of tourism accommodations on Mabul Island has resulted in a widespread belief that the community will be relocated to another place so as to turn the whole island into a tourism accommodation zone. Although authorities deny that such plan exists, the fear of displacement makes locals wary of the expanding tourism development on Mabul.

On the other hand, local residents are appreciative that tourism has brought job opportunities with low entry requirement for them to become boatmen, dive tank compressor boys, and front desk and housekeeping staff (Hamzah *et al.* 2012). Most of the operators also conduct inhouse hospitality training suited to the local population. Some traditional dance groups have also been formed to perform for the resorts, but they have not been maintained on a regular basis. However, the general lack of education on the island has restricted locals from securing the higher paying positions, such as being a dive instructor or resort manager. To qualify for the state-sponsored training course to become a dive instructor requires at least a formal secondary school education. Very few of Mabul's young people have opportunities to achieve that.

Of the almost a thousand children under the age of 16 on Mabul, only about 200 have Malaysian identity cards that permit them to attend the government school there. About 70 children attend a non-profit and uncertified evening school (the School of Hope) set up by one of the backpacker dive lodges. The rest of the children do not attend any school. The Bajau Laut children do not attend either of the schools for fear that they will be bullied by the Suluk children, and there is a general attitude in both communities that their children will grow up to be fishermen and boat builders and so there is no real need for them to attend school.

During a visit to the School of Hope in May 2012, a teenager was spotted among the younger children in the class (Hamzah *et al.* 2012). He said that had never received any formal schooling, but had learned to read and write through the classes there. More importantly, his reason for attending the school was to secure the paper qualifications necessary to enroll in a dive instructor training course. Within the limited worldview of the island's children, becoming a dive instructor and dive master is the ultimate and most coveted profession.

Unfortunately, the informal education provided by the School of Hope would probably not be enough for this teenager to achieve his dreams. The school provides almost free basic education for the island's children to give them sufficient reading and counting skills to work at the resorts. However, it has neither a systematic approach nor a structured syllabus and is, in essence, a platform for volunteer tourism. There is one full-time instructor, but often the teaching assignments are created on an *ad hoc* basis, dependent on the availability and interests of volunteers made up of staff and tourists from the resorts and budget lodges. Some tourists extend their stay to help the children, and many more donate books, stationery and even computers.

The current welcoming attitude of Mabul's residents towards tourists will probably remain that way so as long as they can continue to earn a basic livelihood from fishing and entry-level jobs in tourism establishments. However, this situation could change with the island's growing population, the lack of access to career paths that require education, and projected sea level rises that would erode Mabul's small land base that can barely hold its current population.

The relocation of the resorts from Pulau Sipadan in 2004 and subsequent management practices have undoubtedly saved that island from environmental disaster. Those actions, however, have created serious social and environmental challenges on Pulau Mabul. The social and environmental issues affecting Mabul Island are not isolated, but are tied to controversial and sensitive national and international policies relating to international boundaries, nationality and citizenship, environmental conservation, economic development and subsistence livelihood, and human rights and the rights of children to an education.

Mabul is a microcosm of the social, economic and environmental challenges of popular dive destinations in many parts of insular Southeast Asia. Tourism has undoubtedly created jobs and increased the income of the local community, but the lack of opportunity for such a large number of undocumented young people in a time of unprecedented global change is a potential 'time bomb' that could have long-term detrimental implications for the sustainability of dive tourism, both on Mabul and in the region overall.

## References

Bremner, J. (2012) 'Into the Deep: World's 50 Best Dive Sites', *CNN Go*, 6 April. Online. Available HTTP: <http://www.cnngo.com/explorations/escape/outdoor-adventures/worlds-50-best-dive-sites-895793> (accessed 9 September 2012).

Dive The World (DTW) (2012) 'A Brief History of Sipadan Island, Pulau Sipadan'. Online. Available HTTP: <http://www.dive-the-world.com/reefs-and-parks-malaysia-sipadan-history.php> (accessed 9 September 2012).

Hamzah, A., Hilmi, N. and Alias, L. J. (2012) 'Report for Preliminary Socio-cultural Survey at Pulau Mabul', May 2012 Long Term Research Scheme (LRGS) Vote No: 4L801, Ministry of Higher Education Malaysia.

International Court of Justice (ICJ) (2002) 'Sovereignty over Pulau Ligitan and Pulau Sipadan (Indonesia/Malaysia)', press release 2002/39. Online. Available HTTP: <http://www.icj-cij.org/presscom/index.php?pr=343&pt=1&p1=6&p2=1> (accessed 19 September 2012).

Langenheim, J. (2010) 'The Last of the Sea Nomads', *The Guardian*, 17 September. Online. Available HTTP: <http://www.guardian.co.uk/environment/2010/sep/18/last-sea-nomads> (accessed 10 September 2012).

Mohamad, N. H. (2011) 'Residents' Perception of Tourism Development on Mabul Island, Sabah', unpublished MSc, Tourism Planning Dissertation, Universiti Teknologi Malaysia, Skudai.

Musa, G. (2002) 'Sipadan: A SCUBA-diving Paradise: An Analysis of Tourism Impact, Diver Satisfaction and Tourism Management', *Tourism Geographies*, 4(2):195–209.

Sharma, D. S. K. (2008) 'Letter to the Editor: Mabul Oceanarium Development', WWF Malaysia Newsroom, 24 November. Online. Available HTTP: <http://www.wwf.org.my/media_and_information/newsroom_main/?7560> (accessed 10 September 2012).

Tan, S. K. (2010) *The Muslim South and Beyond*, Manila: University of the Philippines Press.

# 12 The future and sustainability of scuba diving tourism

*Ghazali Musa and Kay Dimmock*

## Introduction

Mankind has always been curious about the world. It is part of our nature and we seek to know more about what may lie beyond the little corner in which each of us live. A great poet wrote that 'We shall not cease from exploration' (Eliot 1950: 145). We are all curious about our world. Scuba diving has opened up a new field of exploration. This book deals with important aspects of scuba diving tourism. However many questions remain to be answered concerning the future of the activity.

Among these questions are: Will future generations be able, and wish to continue to, scuba dive? Will marine life with its variety and beauty continue to attract, as it presently does, in the time ahead? What will future advances in technology be able to offer the industry and scuba divers by way of more sophisticated and efficient products and services? Are there likely to be changes in the motivations and behaviour of scuba divers? Will divers be more discerning and discriminating in experience, and look for new features and other forms of satisfaction in scuba diving?

The answers to the above questions are, in their nature, largely speculative. However, some scientific discoveries foreshadow a less favourable future for scuba diving tourism if the human species continues to spoil, exploit and pollute its environment at the current rate. The aim of this concluding chapter is to predict, as far as can be foreseen, the future of scuba diving activity and the future of its efforts to attain sustainable management. The discussion will be guided by the three elements of the Scuba Diving Tourism System (SDTS) which were introduced in Chapter 1. These are 'Environment', 'Divers' and 'Business'. These elements will be examined in the context of sustainable scuba diving tourism.

The sustainability of scuba diving tourism requires the maintenance of a pristine marine environment, the viability of the business and the satisfaction of divers. These major elements are interconnected but can work against one another and threaten the sustainability of the scuba diving industry. The sustainability of the industry is, and will continue to be, a challenge. Scuba diving stakeholders need to strike a judicious balance among these three components to ensure the achievement of the ultimate desired outcome.

## The future 'Environment' of scuba diving tourism

Looking at how climate change is currently handled by the world's superpowers, it may appear that the scuba diving future does not look as good as the industry and divers would wish. Hall (Chapter 11) is encouraging and optimistic as to the activity's sustainability. However, the tasks necessary to achieve this end are daunting and may not be easily accomplished. Not all governments are at the same development stage and have the requisite attitudes. All too often, government policies place heavy emphasis on continuous economic growth and have short term goals which are considered necessary to achieve these.

Global warming according to O'Neill (2011) means that two major dive destinations – the Belize Barrier Reef and the Maldives in the Indian Ocean – will be underwater in the near future. Threats to the Belize Barrier Reef – the world's second longest reef system after the Great Barrier Reef – include coral bleaching from rising sea temperatures, pollution from coastal agriculture, urban development in the form of coastal resorts and increasing visits by cruise ships. At an average elevation of 2.4 meters (8 feet), the 1,190 islands which comprise the Maldives are the world's lowest country, and the most threatened by rising sea levels. When this happens, liveaboards may be necessary to replace island resorts which accommodate and provide services to divers. Other dive destinations at risk are the South Pacific island countries of Nauru and Tuvalu and the Sulu and Sulu-wesi Seas off Malaysia, where Sipadan Island is located (Koerth-Baker 2007; Hughes 2008).

The geography of recreational scuba diving is likely to change as the world's environment changes over the coming century. Coral reefs today may or may not be able to adjust to warming waters and increasing sea levels. Many will die from coral bleaching. Some corals may be able to expand into new areas as they become warmer and inundated with water. Such migrations, however, will take place very slowly, as coral reefs are more likely to die from temperature changes before they can migrate. Temperate waters may become warmer, encouraging more domestic diving in North America and Europe. Cold water dive destinations, including Antarctica, will become more accessible, and will probably be dived more.

Some marine life may disappear, and some forms of marine life (such as jellyfish) may increase dramatically. The Caribbean, Southeast Asia and Africa will come under increasing pressure to protect their coral reefs, and it is to be hoped that their countries will respond in time to do so. More sustainable fishing practices, both by local fishermen and, just as importantly, by the massive industrial fishing boats in the open oceans, can have a huge impact on the diversity and size of fish and coral populations. Addressing climate change impacts, however, requires global cooperation far beyond the powers of any country on its own.

Because of these challenges, low-lying islands are likely to disappear and vast areas of coastal lowlands and cities will be under water, perhaps creating a new diving experience – a form of dark diving tourism. The 71 per cent of the planet that is currently covered by water will increase in the future, forcing human beings to come to terms with their relationship with the oceans. Maybe then we can allow our seas, rivers and lakes to return to their natural states, rich in biological diversity and sustainably supporting the planet's remaining land area. Scuba diving, in its small way, has an important part to play in encouraging greater human understanding and appreciation for our water world.

With the increasingly palpable effect of global warming, the future diversity of marine flora and fauna is eventually likely to diminish. It is possible that, in the future, the underwater world will be lacking in much of the variety and beauty that we are currently taking for granted. By then, landscape diving may become more popular. Divers may develop an appreciation for underwater landscapes such as walls, caves and ledges.

Human beings are inveterate explorers and their desires to experience the unknown will never cease. Divers will soon want to dive deeper. It will only be a matter of time before scientists discover a new technology, either in the form of equipment or air-mixes, that allow divers to venture deeper without the risk of decompression sickness and nitrogen narcosis. The development of Remote Automatic Vehicles will take divers considerably deeper into the abysses of the sea.

Remote Automatic Vehicles are currently available, at a cost, to take divers thousands of metres below the surface. Landscapes and marine life in the deep are a new field for human curiosity and will surely spur future products and services in scuba diving tourism. James Cameron's underwater adventures, particularly the immensely popular film of the *Titanic* tragedy, which included his exploration of the wreck, may have created a similar impact to the publicity and interest created by Jacques Cousteau six decades ago (Than 2012). Cameron's films have been seen by millions of viewers. Even though he expressed intense isolation and loneliness at the depth of 11 kilometres in the Pacific Ocean's Mariana Trench, this very experience may become a powerful motivation to certain people. Before long, this opportunity could be available to the masses.

The future may well witness the development of submarine holidays, some of which will offer luxury services to those who desire the chance to immerse themselves in the mystery of the great deep in safety and comfort.

More dive sites will be discovered and made accessible to divers, especially in the areas of the Coral Triangle and the South Pacific. There are more than 10,000 islands in the Indonesian archipelago and the Philippines. Advanced technology will be used from the surface to scan potential dive sites which are attractive in terms of the richness of marine flora and fauna and attractive underwater landscapes. Accessibility will be facilitated by advances in the design and construction of marine craft which will be bigger, more efficient and more environmentally friendly.

The discovery of new islands – for example in the Coral Triangle – will, unfortunately, intensify environmental, social and cultural impacts when the diving community faces inevitable contacts with different culture, as described by Lew in Review 4 of Mabul Island. In this area, over-population is common, resulting in competition for the same resources in marine flora and fauna. Over-fishing and even illegal dynamite fishing is likely to continue in these areas. Mismanagement of ocean resources will also continue as a consequence of poverty, corruption and lack of policy and enforcement.

## The future 'Divers' of scuba diving tourism

The number of divers will continue to escalate worldwide, especially in Asia. Divers from China and India, both countries increasing in prosperity, will surely grow in number and influence. Greater increase will be seen among tourist divers, who just take up diving as one of the many activities undertaken during their short and frequent holidays. People will have new ways of accessing and experiencing underwater environments without having to take a scuba certification course. As stated in the previous section, new technologies will enable people to go to places that were unthinkable in the past, such as to the site of the sunken *Titanic* (Broad 2011). Such opportunities will not be cheap, though they could become desired bragging rights for adventure tourists.

Kler and Moskwa (refer Chapter 8) provide evidence of how promoting place attachment could be beneficial in preventing unwanted impacts to the environment. The sense of place attachment could be directed to both local people and tourists, as has been seen practised in Mabul Island (Review 4). Beach clean-up by local people instils a sense of place and understanding of the need to look after the environment. Place attachment could also work on divers, by awakening emotional experiences during their dive trips at the destination. The interpretation which relates to natural and cultural history of the place, together with the camaraderie experienced in diving together, can create positive connections among divers with the destination itself. With place attachment firmly assimilated in divers' hearts, any request for environmental protection in the form of responsible behaviour will receive more favourable response. Divers should be ever-willing to contribute to any environmental conservation programme in the area.

Another important aspect in managing experience is identifying and understanding marine flora and fauna. The future will surely see the invention of a portable waterproof device which will give information on the types of fish, corals and other forms of marine life, information which is readily available in book form. This future invention will greatly enhance the interest of divers in what they encounter underwater, and enrich their diving experience. Future divers may also be blessed with the ability to communicate with other divers with their own voices rather than hand signals. The two technologies discussed above, which are yet to be available in the market, will greatly enhance the interactive experience and engagement with the underwater scene. The ability to communicate with other divers will enhance safety and security underwater.

Divers with disability receive growing recognition in the western world, especially in the US and Europe. Khoo and Walsh (Review 2) state that these regions have organizations which not only certify divers with disability but also train diving instructors to provide services to the divers. As the Coral Triangle and the Pacific regions are likely to become more popular in the future (Chapter 3), divers with disability will be seen in greater numbers in these regions. These regions must be ready to provide accessible diving for divers with disability, addressing all accessibility aspects: informational, physical and social needs. The regions must be ready to take advantage of this future trend and not disregard the rights of divers with disability. There should be more awareness and understanding of the needs and the rights of persons with disabilities pertaining to scuba diving.

Lew (Chapter 3) highlights the high percentage of dormant divers who rarely dive beyond the certification dive. Many more will take up scuba diving occasionally when the opportunity arises. This percentage is likely to increase in the future, to include those who splurge on short trips and travel frequently. The challenge for the industry will be to cope with divers' rusty skills and eroded knowledge of environmental protection. Managers need to have efficient services which include effective security and safety measures, firm environmental codes of conduct and, at the same time, ensure that the brief activity provides rewarding and memorable experiences for divers.

Hall (Chapter 11) states the industry must take a wider view of the potential impact of long haul divers travelling to distant destinations. These divers are more environmentally damaging than ordinary tourists. Globally, awareness must be created to encourage slow tourism among divers. There should be specifications for desired limits in the carbon footprint of scuba divers. This information, and the self-discipline required to observe it, should be part of the awareness of individual divers if they are to call themselves responsible divers.

Health issues will always remain and are likely to stay the same. However, as mentioned earlier, the future could see the increase in numbers of certain dangerous species underwater, such as poisonous jelly fish. Perhaps the future technology of decompression treatment could become more portable. Also, the mixture of breathing gases will be more advanced, to reduce the possibility of decompression sickness and nitrogen narcosis.

As elaborated in Chapter 7, the future and sustainability of scuba diving is strongly related to divers' attitudes, knowledge and behaviour, together with the management practices of scuba diving operators. In relation to knowledge, the present curricula of scuba diving certification programmes should include the education of sustainable scuba diving. Among these issues are scuba diving impacts, environmental protection, and the role of divers in the sustainability of the marine environment. Future divers can enhance their commitment to protect the marine environment by getting involved in volunteerism, either for its protection or in research which eventually will contribute to better interpretative experiences and a sense of place attachment.

## The future 'Industry' of scuba diving tourism

There are two global tourism trends which may influence the future of scuba diving. These are the tendency to splurge and the tendency to take up more frequent holidays for a shorter time. The global tendency to spend lavishly on one item during holidays and sacrifice other items may benefit scuba diving tourism. The activity is often a preferred item among backpackers in their spending on their ASEAN trail (Ministry of Tourism Malaysia 2008). The tendency for short frequent travels may see a rise in demand for the most basic scuba diving experience which is Scuba Discovery (see Chapter 5). This activity does not require certification to dive. It involves a short friendly instruction followed by close supervision by diving instructors taking tourists to dive underwater with a complete set of scuba equipment. The challenge will be in providing appealing and seamless instruction without compromising fun, adventurous experience, safety and security.

The most traditional media marketing which is word of mouth, will linger and in fact increase in its power to influence tourists' decision making. Today, this is facilitated by the astronomical growth in social media usage such as Facebook, YouTube and travel blogs. The role of social media will strengthen, with many more specialized social media introduced globally. Marketers must design their promotional messages in an appropriate and attractive form for social media and penetrate deeper into the intended divers' market. The high definition video clip is generally more trusted, and is powerful in influencing divers' decisions. The maintenance of social media sites must be carried out regularly. Communicators' quality must be assured, as any words communicated reflect the image and brand of the organization. Anticipating prospective service failure, a service recovery plan must be instituted efficiently and fairly to further strengthen the organizational image.

With the emergence of the BRIC (Brazil, Russia, India and China) tourism market, all of which are culturally heterogeneous, services provision becomes more challenging. Study of motivation delineates the various needs and wants among them, which can later be translated into product and services provision. Motivation (Chapter 6) is also a factor in responsible behaviour (Chapter 7). The study of satisfaction (Chapter 9) is another research element which will continue to be important. With new markets becoming dominant in scuba diving destinations, the important elements which influence divers' satisfaction will to some extent be different. Promotional messages will have to be redesigned to reflect the uniqueness of a destination in fulfilling divers' satisfaction.

The emergence of new markets (e.g. BRIC) will also present difficulties in human resource management, especially in the provision of multilingual staff, and their open-mindedness to deal with different cultural idiosyncrasies. The different cultures could affect the effectiveness and efficiency of education and training by staff in their relations with tourists. Training and education needs to be carried out in the language understood by divers. Different nationalities may have different service expectations. While fulfilling the needs of a particular group of divers, this very need may not be favoured by other divers. To counter this odd prospect, dive operators are required to clearly communicate the width and depth of their service delivery.

Wreck diving will become more popular, as more ships sink in the years to come. Global warming will diminish varieties of marine life. However, scientists are already using, and will continue to use, biotechnology solutions to plant artificial reefs which will attract marine flora and fauna. Studies have shown that divers derive similar satisfaction when diving artificial reefs and natural reefs (Stolk *et al.* 2007). Divers in Thailand do not recognize difference in the corals before and after the tsunami (Main and Dearden 2007). Divers of the future may be less likely to compare their diving experience with the underwater images illustrated so beautifully in many scuba diving books today. They may simply compare their current with their previous scuba diving experiences. Therefore, divers in the years to come may derive satisfactory experiences despite the prospect of a more restricted variety of marine life.

As stated earlier, liveaboard dives will become more important, especially in areas which will be submerged underwater, such as the Maldives and some parts of the Caribbean. The liveaboard will likely cater to both no frill and luxury markets. The future will see the invention of more effective marine craft which are more environmentally friendly, such as solar powered boats. The water used in these craft could be desalinated by technology powered by solar cells. This in itself is a drawcard for future divers who are likely to regard eco-friendly travel as mandatory in travel decisions, especially when the effect of global warming becomes very apparent to everyone.

Slow tourism will become more fashionable in the future, and this will be beneficial for domestic tourism activities. Complementing this movement will be the consumption of slow food. Scuba diving tourism too will catch the trend, in which divers become more environmentally responsible and ethical, following constant exposure to the need for environmental protection.

Safety and security will become more important, especially as more dive destinations are opening up in exotic locations. To ensure this, more countries will apply international standards to their locations, as has been seen in Egypt and Greece (Review 3). Standards will benefit both tourists and operators by reducing morbidity, with a consequent increase in trust among tourists and a reduction in spending on medical treatment and insurance.

## Concluding remarks

In conclusion, the future sustainability of scuba diving tourism is part of the broader picture of the sustainability of the tourism industry itself. To achieve sustainability, it is proposed that scuba diving tourism be examined and managed from the holistic perspective of STDS. Within the system, there are the three elements of Environment, Divers and Business. Future scholars need to identify the key sustainable indicators for each element of STDS. Researchers, then, need to decide the limit of acceptable change for each indicator that is agreeable to scuba diving tourism stakeholders. As the three elements are liable to work against one another, this is expected to be a highly challenging task. The next step will be designing the measures for responsible scuba diving tourism which must be agreed by all stakeholders. Of the greatest importance is that the responsible authorities take steps to ensure the measures are fully observed.

Human society and the physical world are both undergoing grave changes. These changes affect every aspect of human activity. For survival, it is essential to adapt. The question is whether scuba diving tourism is able to meet the challenges involved. We believe that it must, and it can.

## References

Broad, W. J. (2011) 'Plunging Deep (in Pockets) to See Titanic at 100', *The New York Times*, 4 December. Online. Available HTTP: <http://www.nytimes.com/2011/12/05/science/celebrating-the-titanic-at-100-by-going-to-see-it.html> (accessed 8 April 2012).

Eliot, T. S. (1950) *Collected Poems and Plays*, New York: Harcourt Brace & Company.

Hughes, H. (2008) '11 Places to See before They Disappear', *Frommers*. Online. Available HTTP: <http://www.frommers.com/micro/2008/11-places-to-see-before-they-disappear/index.html> (accessed 7 April 2012).

Koerth-Baker, M. (2007) 'Places to See before They Disappear', *CNN.com/Living/Mental Floss*. Online. Available HTTP: <http://edition.cnn.com/2007/LIVING/wayoflife/11/01/mf.see.b4.die/index.html> (accessed 7 April 2012).

Main, M. and Dearden, P. (2007) 'Tsunami Impacts on Phuket's Diving Industry: Geographical Implications for Marine Conservation', *Coastal Management*, 35(4):467–481.

Ministry of Tourism Malaysia (2008) 'Study on the Potential and Contribution of Backpacker Tourism', Malaysian Tourism Industry (Vote No. 63026).

O'Neill, S. (2011) '10 Natural Wonders to See before They Disappear', *Yahoo! Travel/ Budget Travel*, 26 April 2012. Online. Available HTTP: <http://travel.yahoo.com/ideas/10-natural-wonders-see-disappear-011841843.html> (accessed 7 April 2012).

Stolk, P., Markwell, K. and Jenkins, M. (2007) 'Artificial Reefs as Recreational Scuba Diving Resources: A Critical Review of Research', *Journal of Sustainable Tourism*, 15(4):331–349.

Than, K. (2012) 'James Cameron Completes Record-breaking Mariana Trench Dive', *National Geographic Daily News*, 25 March 2012. Online. Available HTTP: <http://news.nationalgeographic.com.au/news> (accessed 27 October 2012).

# Index